THE ETERNAL
ACT OF
CREATION

NORTHROP FRYE

THE ETERNAL ACT OF CREATION

ESSAYS, 1979 - 1990

edited by
ROBERT D. DENHAM

INDIANA UNIVERSITY PRESS
Bloomington & Indianapolis

The paper used in this publication meets the minimum requirements of American National Standard for Information Sciences—Permanence of Paper for Printed Library Materials, ANZI Z39.48-1984.

Manufactured in the United States of America

Library of Congress Cataloging- in-Publication Data

Frye, Northrop.
   The eternal act of creation: essays, 1979-1990 / Northrop Frye; edited by Robert D. Denham.
    p. cm.
  Includes bibliographic references and index.
  ISBN 0-253-32516-1 (cloth)
   1. Literature– History and criticism. I. Denham, Robert D.
II. Title.
PN45.F73 1992
809–dc20

   1 2 3 4 5 96 95 94 93 92

For Rachel

Contents

Acknowledgments

The provenance of the essays in *The Eternal Act of Creation*:

"Auguries of Experience": an address presented at the 1987 convention of the Modern Language Association. Published in *Visionary Poetics: Essays on Northrop Frye's Criticism*. Ed. Robert D. Denham and Thomas Willard. New York: Peter Lang, 1991. 1-7.

"Literary and Mechanical Models": an address presented at the Conference on Computers and the Humanities, Toronto, 6 June 1989. Previously unpublished.

"Literature as Therapy": an address presented at Mt. Sinai Hospital, Toronto, 23 November 1989. Previously unpublished.

"Repetitions of Jacob's Dream": an address presented at the National Gallery, Ottawa, 13 October 1983. Previously unpublished.

"The Bride for a Strange Land": an address presented at the Holy Blossom Temple, Toronto, 25 May 1985. Published in *Craft and Tradition: Essays in Honour of William Blissett*. Ed. H. B. de Groot and A. Legatt. Calgary: University of Calgary Press, 1990. 1-11.

"Blake's Biblical Illustrations": an address presented at the Art Gallery of Toronto, 4 February 1983. Published in the *Northrop Frye Newsletter* 2 (Summer 1990): 1-12.

"Shakespeare's *The Tempest*": an address presented in Vicenza, Italy, 18 May 1979. Published in the *Northrop Frye Newsletter* 2 (Summer 1990): 19-27.

"Varieties of Eighteenth-Century Sensibility": an address presented at the meeting of the American Society for Eighteenth-Century Studies, Minneapolis, 26 April 1990. Published in *Eighteenth-Century Studies* 24 (Winter 1990-91): 157-72.

"Henry James and the Comedy of the Occult": an address presented at Carleton University, Ottawa, 19 October 1989. Previously unpublished.

"Approaching the Lyric": an address presented at the Conference on Lyric Poetry and the New New Criticism, Victoria College, 14 October 1982.

Published in *Lyric Poetry: Beyond New Criticism*. Ed. Chaviva Hošek and Patricia Parker. Ithaca: Cornell University Press, 1985. 5-17.

"Criticism and Environment": an address presented at the meeting of the Fédération Internationale des Langues et Littératures Modernes, Tempe, Arizona, August 1981. Published in *Adjoining Cultures as Reflected in Literature and Language*. Ed. John X. Evans and Peter Horwath. Tempe: Arizona State University, 1983. 9-21.

"Harold Innis: The Strategy of Culture": an introduction written in 1982 for the collected works of Harold Innis, an aborted project. Previously unpublished.

"Levels of Cultural Identity": an address presented at the Canadian Embassy, Washington, D.C., 14 September 1989. Published in the *Northrop Frye Newsletter* 2 (Winter 1989-90): 2-12.

For permission to reprint four of the essays in this volume, I thank Peter Lang Publishers, the University of Calgary Press, *Eighteenth-Century Studies*, and Arizona State University. I also wish to thank Jane Widdicombe, executrix of the Frye estate, for permission to edit this collection, and my editors at Indiana University Press, Robert J. Sloan and Nancy Ann Miller.

Introduction

*The primary IMAGINATION I hold to
be the living power and prime agent of all
human perception, and as a repetition in
the finite mind of the eternal act of creation in the infinite I AM.* —Coleridge

This is the tenth collection of Northrop Frye's essays. It might be more properly called a collection of "addresses," since all but one were originally heard rather than read. "Addresses" has the advantage of pointing to what was one of Frye's criteria for distinguishing genres—the primary form of their delivery, or what he called the radical of presentation. I have chosen the word *essays*, however, because it conveys the spirit of Frye's discourse. As he reminds us in the first sentence of *Anatomy of Criticism*, essay meant originally "a trial or incomplete attempt." Although Frye speaks with the voice of authority, the occasional pieces brought together here are a part of his long-standing effort to speak, without a sense of closure, in still other words about the mysterious powers of myth and metaphor and the social context of literature and the other arts. Except for one, a lecture on *The Tempest* given in Italy in 1979, all of the essays come from the last decade of his life, and five come from his final year and a half.

The collection begins with "Auguries of Experience," Frye's opening remarks at the first of two sessions devoted to his criticism at the 1987 convention of the Modern Language Association. The talk, published along with the proceedings of these sessions in *Visionary Poetics: Essays on Northrop Frye's Criticism* (New York: Peter Lang, 1991), is reprinted here because it provides an overview of Frye's concerns toward the end of his career. He is disappointed that the critical consensus he had hoped for twenty-five years ago has not emerged and he is vexed by the "infinite variety" in contemporary literary study. Still, he holds firm to his belief that the Bible is central in helping us to understand both the similarities in and the differences between literature and ideology. For Frye, the finiteness of literature, rather than its variety, is what "allows for a progressive increase in understanding," and he still holds out the hope that a consensus in critical understanding may emerge. The first essay concludes with still another variation on one of Frye's central tenets: that what the imagination re-creates is the only thing that can be genuinely real, because it is the only thing that "does not change or changes entirely on its own terms." The infinite variety of the poststructuralist moment works against the idea of consensus, and Frye's disappointment with the directions criticism has recently taken is not too thinly veiled in the opening talk.

In the second essay, "Literary and Mechanical Models," originally an address to a conference on computers and the humanities, disappointment turns into direct critique. Among today's competing schools, "the whole critical enterprise becomes a Tower of Babel, a vast structure largely abandoned, so far as it is a cooperative effort, because its builders have become unintelligible not only to the general public but increasingly to one another." The only saving grace, Frye notes, is that the failure to communicate blunts the often imperialistic tendencies in postmodernism. For Frye, criticism, like literature, has a circumference or containing structure, and we must recognize this structure if we are to make critical progress. The notion of schools carving out their own space and of systems that have "petrified into dogma" does little, he maintains, to achieve a unified vision, one in which different perspectives can interpenetrate with each other. In the second essay he contrasts his own critical vision with the more or less mechanical procedures of the philologists, the *Wissenschaft* school that was prominent until the mid-1930s, and with the critical approaches that followed: the judicial criticism of Leavis, the close readings of Empson and other New Critics, and the deterministic programs of the Marxists, Freudians, and Thomists. Rather than developing still another *ism*, Frye has focused his attention on the structural units of the arts—the conventions and genres and archetypes that lie at their core.

Frye is not a Luddite: he does not oppose the techniques of *Wissenschaft* scholarship, which the computer has made a much more efficient mode of production. What he does resist is *Wissenschaft* becoming an end in itself rather than a means for helping us to reconstruct the past. But the computer, like any form of technology, has its limitations as well as its powers, and it must always be challenged when it moves away from the dynamic of democracy and begins to reinforce current and future power structures. The proper response of the humanist to computer technology is not to resurrect C. P. Snow's "two-culture" polemic but to be alert to the ways it can decrease the drudgery of scholarship and to guard against the ways it can enslave the spirit.

"Literature and Therapy" was an address presented at Mt. Sinai Hospital in November 1989, less than a year before Frye was to undergo chemotherapy himself. Like many of Frye's talks, this one was constructed from notes, and what is printed here is a transcription of the tape recording that Dr. John Roder graciously provided. As Frye's audience is a group of physicians, he develops an extended and witty catalogue of references to the medical profession in literature, illustrating the ways that body and mind were linked together in the Bible and in the works of Chaucer, Shakespeare, Burton, Browne, Molière, Swift, Lesage, and Shaw. A. C. Hamilton has noted that cataloguing is often "a drab (because mechanical) listing of examples, monotonous to compile and boring to read . . . but in Frye, it becomes a joyfully exuberant and creative response to his imaginative, encyclopedic vision of the universe of words" (406). What this creative response leads to in "Literature and Therapy" is a reflection on *catharsis*, which, as Frye understands its implications in tragedy, results in a kind of restorative balance and harmony. This is another of his twists on Aristotle: self-integration rather than detachment is the cathartic reward.

Several decades ago Frye remarked that "the therapeutic power of the arts has been intermittently recognized . . . but the fact that literature is essential to the mental health of society seldom enters our speculations about it. But if I am to take seriously my own principle that works of literature are not so much things to be studied as powers to be possessed, I need to face the implications of that principle" ("Criticism" 84). Frye does draw out the implications of the principle in "Literature and Therapy," noting the restorative power not simply of tragedy but of ironic and comic modes as well. And the conjunction of body and mind in literature leads Frye finally to argue that "the immense recuperative power" of literature is a matter of vision, for literature is a "controlled hallucination, where things are seen with a kind of intensity with which they are not seen in ordinary experience." Literature is therapeutic, in short, because it provides a counterenvironment to the illusions of ideology and the delusions of ordinary experience.

The essays in Part II center on biblical metaphors and myths. The occasion of "Repetitions of Jacob's Dream" was a gallery talk at an Ottawa exhibition entitled "Ladders of Heaven." Here Frye explores the contexts of a particularly central image from the biblical tradition, so central, in fact, that it became the organizing principle of the second half of *Words with Power* (1990), his second volume on the Bible and literature. "Repetitions" illustrates the principle of the first volume, *The Great Code* (1982), that the imagery of the sacred scripture mirrors that of the secular, and so Frye gives us a short history of the ladder image from Genesis to Joyce. But while the essay begins with implications of a particular biblical image, it turns into a study of cosmology and metaphor, and, as in all of Frye's accounts of metaphor, the discussion centers on the principle of identity. Metaphor, he says, is "an effort to extend our own being into the external world, to break down the wall between subject and object and start currents of verbal energy flowing between them." Metaphor thus becomes the path to a "higher existence" and "a more abundant life," and the essay concludes with an oracular testimony about the role played by the eternal act of creation in achieving both.

In *The Great Code* Frye announced that in his second volume on the Bible, already underway when the first was published, he hoped to comment in more detail on stories which "have a particularly obvious literary reference," such as the Book of Ruth (xxii). If Frye originally intended "The Bride from the Strange Land" to be a chapter in *Words with Power*, the chapter got pared down to only a few pages in one of his many revisions of that book. In any event, his commentary on Ruth, presented in 1985 as an address at the Holy Blossom Temple in Toronto, appears in the present volume in its full version. Frye begins by noting three narrative themes about women in the Bible that converge in the Book of Ruth—the themes of the levirate marriage, of the son born to a woman who is past the age of childbearing, and of the bride from the strange land. He then traces the use of the Ruth story in biblical and other literature, discovering that subsequent writers have paid relatively slight attention to Ruth because of "the irrepressible cheerfulness of the story." Still, Frye sees the Book of Ruth as significant because it contains in microcosm the Bible's larger narrative pattern of exile, return, and redemption. He also finds links between Ruth and ancient Near Eastern harvest and fertility themes, though in Ruth the author has displaced the archaic themes into "credible and very warm human relationships." But Ruth is more than simply a serene story for Frye: it expresses the ecological moral "that if human beings give up their murderous and polluting ways, the physical environment will be seen as something identical with the human one, as something to live in rather than to dominate." The third part of the essay, which focuses on themes and images inherited by the author of Ruth, is typical of Frye. Typical too is the essay's final sentence about "the highest vision of human life"; more often than not Frye's conclusions carry us to a third order of experience, one captured only by the power of those radical forms of metaphor that give human form to nature.

In addition to *Fearful Symmetry*, which revolutionized our understanding of Blake's prophecies, Frye wrote at least two dozen articles on Blake. But "Blake's Biblical Illustrations" is the only essay devoted exclusively to Blake's pictorial art. It is, however, less an art of illustration, which Frye associates with fancy and visual commentary, than of illumination or imaginative reconstruction, which means that text and design achieve "a single creative conception." This thesis leads Frye into an account of Blake's mythology, which, with its primary symbolic figures of Urizen, Orc, and Los, turns the traditional Christian and classical cosmology upside down. The essay was originally a talk presented at the Art Gallery of Ontario, and Frye is aware that understanding Blake's mythology is a prerequisite for understanding both his illustrations and his illuminations. The essay, in fact, serves as a kind of primer of Blake's visionary symbolism, especially his understanding of creation and apocalypse. And it serves as a kind of primer of Frye's thought as well.

The essays in Part III focus on specifically literary topics: Shakespeare's *The Tempest*, the primitive forces in eighteenth-century literature, and the occult comedies of Henry James. To these I have added a shorter piece on the lyric, Frye's introductory address to a 1982 conference on Lyric Poetry and the New New Criticism.

The Tempest is arguably Frye's favorite Shakespearean play. He edited the play for *The Pelican Shakespeare* (1959), and in his introduction to that edition he says, taking his cue from Prospero's appeal to the audience in the Epilogue, that "*The Tempest* is a play not simply to be read or seen or even studied, but possessed" (24). We begin to understand what he means by this in his subsequent examinations of the play in *A Natural Perspective*, *The Myth of Deliverance*, and *Northrop Frye on Shakespeare*. Each of these books, in fact, concludes with a commentary on *The Tempest*, and in all three Frye celebrates the power of recognition we experience at the end of the play—an experience that can lift our own lives to a higher level of imaginative intensity. Again, Frye typically ends his essays and books, even chapters within books, by suggesting, often in an oracular voice, that there are recognition scenes in life as well as in literature. And in the present essay he concludes by saying that in *The Tempest* Shakespeare is offering us "seeds to create for ourself new seas and even more enchanted islands." This essay, the most extensive of Frye's several commentaries on the play, was presented as a lecture in Vicenza, Italy, in the spring of 1979.

Given Frye's Romantic temper and his antirealistic predilections, it may seem a bit curious to find him writing on the Age of Sensibility and on Henry James, even though the range of his interests has never been circumscribed. The former paper originated in connection with a special session on "Northrop Frye and Eighteenth-Century Literature" at a 1990 conference of the American Society for Eighteenth-Century Studies. Asked to speak at a plenary session, Frye was actually returning to a topic addressed thirty-four years earlier in "Towards Defining an Age of Sensibility" (1956). The papers in the special session (see Weinbrot) were mostly devoted to a critique of Frye's views on the eighteenth century, especially those outlined in the 1956 essay where he had used a series of oppositions (Aristotelian vs. Longinian, product vs. process, nature vs. history, creation vs. decay, lyric vs. dramatic) to describe the features of eighteenth-century literature. The 1990 address, "Varieties of Eighteenth-Century Sensibility," which casts only a brief glance at the earlier essay, is also schematic but in a much more complicated way. Interpenetration, an idea that occurs frequently in Frye's later work, replaces opposition as the proper term to describe the age, and in the second half of the essay Frye investigates the different contexts in which we might understand the "primitive" models of humanity among the post-Augustans.

Again, one hardly expects to discover a deep interest in James on the part of Frye, and he does confess that he came to James late, even though he had read *The Ivory Tower* and *The Sense of the Past* as an Oxford student. Scattered references to James appear throughout Frye's work (there are seventeen in the *Anatomy*), yet before "Henry James and the Comedy of the Occult" there was little evidence to suggest that Frye had really absorbed James. But in this essay he ranges freely across the entire New York edition ("that extraordinary dinosaur"), his comments on thirty-nine of James's novels and stories illustrating his richly allusive method. It is, of course, not the realism of James that interests Frye. He is clearly attracted to the later James where motifs of the occult, especially in the tales that are unambiguously ghost stories, are explicit. But even in the more representational stories Frye discovers those "ghostlier demarcations" that move us beyond the surface of James's plots. The essay actually hinges on the distinction between the illusions of realistic fiction and the truths of imaginative reality. Or as Frye puts it in the last sentence of the essay, James "turned once again to the ghost story just before he died, because in its fantasy he saw the reality he had sought as an artist, whereas the realism in the social manners of his time had left him with a sense of total illusion."

"Approaching the Lyric" is much less schematic than Frye's catalogue of lyric forms and conventions in the fourth essay of *Anatomy of Criticism*, but the present essay does indicate how Frye can use a simple idea, such as the blocking of normal activity, to provide genuine insights into literary genres. This brief piece does not pretend to offer a comprehensive theory of the lyric, but it does "approach" one. The lyric, as Frye points out, is a discontinuous form, and his own essay may appear to be discontinuous itself. But the free play of Frye's mind always occurs within a structure, the elements of which in this essay will be familiar: what he refers to as *opsis* and *melos* and as charm and riddle in other contexts appears here as well, though the language is different, and the idea that the intensity of poetic experience identifies subject and object runs throughout.

The last group of essays treats things Canadian. In the face of many opportunities to go elsewhere, Frye always remained loyal to his beloved Canada. A year or so before his death he remarked, "The longer I've lived, the more I realize that I belong in a certain context, just as a plant grows in the soil. The more completely I am in a Canadian context, the more acceptable I am to others" ("Ideas" 13). Frye's Canadian writings are less well known than his other work, but they form a substantial body of literary and cultural criticism. Several dozen have been collected in *The Bush Garden* and *Divisions on a Ground*, but on more than ninety occasions Frye has written on specifically Canadian topics. In 1981 Margaret Atwood wrote that it seemed to her "that almost every seminal idea in the newly watered fields of Canlit, including the currently fashionable 'regionalism,' sprang, if not fully formed, at least in some form, from the forehead of Northrop Frye, back in the days when he was dutifully reviewing

Canadian poetry for *The Canadian Forum*" (404). A number of those seminal ideas are recapitulated in "Criticism and Environment," originally a plenary address at a 1981 conference on "Adjoining Cultures," and in "Levels of Cultural Identity," a 1989 speech given at the Canadian Embassy in Washington, D.C. These ideas include the "garrison mentality" in Canadian literature, the inductive sensibility in Canadian culture, and the movement of Canadian literature from its provincial to its mature phase.

In both essays Frye touches on the problems of communication, which has been especially difficult in the vast spaces of the Canadian environment. This leads, in the first case, to an excursus on language—an embryonic form of the opening chapter of both *The Great Code* and *Words with Power*. Investigating the different functions of language, Frye says, "forms probably what is the liveliest area of criticism today," and he urges once again that we develop a synoptic and interconnected view of language. The problems of communication lead, in the second case, to a series of speculations on the various biases toward time and space in the Canadian sensibility, and "Levels of Cultural Identity," drawing on Heidegger's distinction between World and Earth, concludes with still another illustration of Frye's long-standing belief in the social function of art. Our planet can be saved from its self-destructive tendencies, he argues, only by a change in consciousness, and the creative energy of the imagination is the most likely source of such change.

In both "Criticism and Environment" and "Levels of Cultural Identity" Frye draws upon the work of the eminent economic historian Harold Innis, a scholar whose social vision, Frye says, is "of a scope and comprehensiveness unparalleled in Canadian culture." Frye served as general editor of the papers of Innis, but the project never came to fruition for financial and other reasons. The essay on Innis, which outlines the beginning of the project, was written to introduce the first volume, to have been called *Dispersal and Concentration: Historical Aspects of Communication*. I believe the essay worth resurrecting because it is a solid exposition of the powers and limitations of Innis's ideas and of their contemporary relevance. But it also reveals a great deal about Frye, especially his thoughts on social authority. His account of the three social aspects of a *tertium quid* that work to neutralize power conflicts—law, objective knowledge, and art— is particularly astute.

This overview of the volume's contents has only hinted at some of the themes the reader can expect to encounter in the pages that follow. I remain convinced that Frye's legacy will be a long-standing one because his large Blakean vision is perceptually powerful, revealing to us structures we were not able to perceive on our own and often turning our normal modes of thinking upside down. One is always embarrassed in writing about Frye at not being able to imitate his own creative rhetoric, which is another aspect of his legacy. For Coleridge the source of both of these faculties, the perceptive and the creative, lies in the imagination, and Frye's imagination is as large as any in our time. The essays collected here are another chapter in the extraordinary career of a critic all of whose work might well be described as "a repetition in the finite mind of the eternal act of creation in the infinite I AM."

Works Cited

Atwood, Margaret. "Northrop Frye Observed." *Second Words*. Boston: Beacon, 1984. 398-406.

Frye, Northrop. "Criticism, Visible and Invisible." *The Stubborn Structure: Essays on Criticism and Society*. Ithaca: Cornell University Press, 1970. The essay originally appeared in *College English* 26 (1964): 3-12.

_____. *The Great Code: The Bible and Literature*. New York: Harcourt Brace Jovanovich, 1982.

_____. "The Ideas of Northrop Frye." *Northrop Frye Newsletter* 3 (Spring 1991): 5-16.

_____. *The Myth of Deliverance: Reflections on Shakespeare's Problem Comedies*. Toronto: University of Toronto Press, 1983.

_____. *A Natural Perspective: The Development of Shakespearean Comedy and Romance*. New York: Columbia University Press, 1965.

_____. *Northrop Frye on Shakespeare*. New Haven: Yale University Press, 1986.

_____. "Towards Defining an Age of Sensibility." *Fables of Identity: Studies in Poetic Mythology*. New York: Harcourt, Brace & World, 1963. 130-37.

_____, ed. *The Tempest* by William Shakespeare. Rev. ed. New York: Penguin, 1970.

Hamilton, A. C. "Northrop Frye on Myth and Metaphor." *Queen's Quarterly* 98 (Summer 1991): 402-08.

Weinbrot, Howard D., ed. *Northrop Frye and Eighteenth-Century Studies*, a special issue of *Eighteenth-Century Studies* 24 (Winter 1990-91): 159-249.

I

Auguries of Experience

In days so remote that I can barely remember them now, I was reading books on Blake in preparation for writing one myself. In those early times it was an unquestioned axiom that one should read everything available on a subject before trying to write about it, and for Blake in the thirties that was still humanly possible. So I immersed myself in the two or three good books and the hundred and fifty or so bad ones that had been devoted to Blake up to that time. One of the bad ones quoted a couplet from "Auguries of Innocence":

> He who the Ox to wrath has mov'd
> Shall never be by Woman lov'd

and objected that a poet less mentally confused would know that it was quite possible to be both brutal to animals and attractive to women. The critic forgot to look at the word *shall*, and also forgot to take the title of the poem into account. I was still so green that it took me a while to work this out, but when I did I had a new insight into Blake and had acquired the first of my own auguries of experience, that is, the scaled-down expectations acquired from one's own life. Good books may instruct, but bad ones are more likely to inspire. Since then, as the author of criticism which some have found useful and others objectionable, I trust I have done something to inspire as well as instruct.

After finishing my Blake book, I went on to the *Anatomy of Criticism*, which in the innocent fifties, when it was published, was regarded, even by me, as an essay on critical theory. So in a way it was, although my conception of theory has always been different from those generally held. In this age of structural, poststructural, feminist, phenomenological, Marxist, metahistorical, dialogist, and any number of other schools, the word *theory* is essentially pluralistic:

a theory is one of many dialectical formulations that proceed from specific assumptions and conclude with special emphases. My own conception of theory, though in many respects it may look much the same, is closer to the Greek *theoria*, a vision or conspectus of the area of literature, an area distinguishable from, though with a context relating it to, the other arts and the other forms of verbal discourse.

From this point of view there is a very broad consensus among all critical schools, a consensus which the variety of dialectical approaches more or less deliberately conceals. In the *Anatomy of Criticism* I pointed out the existence of this consensus, and even made suggestions for promoting it. Such suggestions look very naive now, and I have no longer any interest in making them. The procedure is rather like proposing the union of the various Christian churches on the ground that they accept most of the same major doctrines, or say they do. It is of course the differentiating dialectics and the special interests of conflicting groups that fill the foreground, and fill it so completely that the area of agreement remains largely unexamined, as no one is interested in it except the charitable.

This is my fortieth year as an MLA member, and so I have just acquired what is called, somewhat ironically, a life membership. Forty years ago literary criticism was dominated by a rather narrow historical approach to criticism which was neither genuinely historical nor genuinely critical. The first MLA meetings I attended resounded with the triumphs of this approach in the seminar rooms and with complaints about it in the corridors. A superstition grew up in graduate schools that only the obscurest aspects of the obscurest poets were still available for thesis material, and that the whole industry was approaching stagnation and exhaustion. When any discipline gets to this point, it blows up and a new conception of it takes its place, as happened in physics around 1900, when Planck and Einstein blew up its nineteenth-century mechanical synthesis. Similarly, it is now taken for granted that not only is the variety of individual works of literature inexhaustible, but the variety of critical treatments of them is equally so.

My own scholarly deficiencies in contemporary critical theory do not imply indifference, much less hostility, to what in itself is a most lively and exhilarating cultural growth. Even if it were not, its development was inevitable if we are to maintain the ideal that everyone on a university staff should be a productive scholar. Whether this ideal is either possible or desirable is not the point; it exists, and it cannot continue to exist without a large number of school badges, so to speak, ensuring one of a seat in front of a cue screen that will suggest some specific critical approach in advance. I have been assigned a badge of sorts myself, usually reading "mythical" or "archetypal," but my view of a latent consensus keeps me in a middle-of-the-road position, cherishing the belief of my age group that in all polarized situations there is much to be said on both sides. The only disadvantage of this position is that so much is *said* on both sides. My Canadian criticism, for example, has led to my being called a formalist critic who ignores or is unaware of the relation between literature and society, and to my being called a thematic critic who exaggerates that relation. I can only feel that as long as the two groups of objectors are approximately equal in numbers, I am still more or less on course, or at least on my course.

No one questions, or is ever likely to question, the right of literary scholars to discuss critical issues indefinitely. What could be questioned is whether the present critical activity exists for its own sake, a type of glass bead game, or whether it is going somewhere in the direction of increased and progressive understanding of both literature and criticism. Despite Enobarbus, nothing is staled by custom more quickly than infinite variety. This would be true even if all the infinite variety were new, but I keep finding also that venerable critical fallacies, whose funerals I thought I had attended many years ago, were not, as I had assumed, buried, but merely stuffed into cryonic refrigerators to await revival in future journals of theory.

Such issues may not matter in themselves, but a crisis may arise when the question of critical debate is confronted by the question of curriculum, of what should be taught to students, or at least undergraduates, over a limited period of time. There is always public concern over what the public is paying for, and the explosive success of some recent books that seem to be largely repeating what many teachers have been saying for half a century indicates one more revival of that concern. I have been listening to such expressions of concern most of my life, and have spent a fair proportion of my own critical energies on trying to do something about them. Another augury of experience I acquired in this process was that all such movements tend to focus on something we shall assuredly never get: a Messianic super-Archimedes who can say: "Give me a place to stand, and I will move the educational bureaucracy." But this time the dissatisfaction does seem to reflect back, however indirectly, on the critical situation I have been discussing. It is as though a psychiatric patient, already hundreds of dollars in arrears, had suddenly realized that his treatment was by definition interminable.

I happen to be one of those who believe that contemporary criticism is going somewhere, although my notion of where it is going antedates most of the activity itself, and has changed very little since. I have spoken of a vision of literature, because I think that there is a literary universe, which, like every other universe, is unbounded and finite. The variety of individual literary works may be infinite; the total body of what can be produced as literature is not. Any given period of criticism, no doubt every period, may have too narrow a view of this total body. The permanent value of, for example, women's studies or black studies is in reminding criticism of the narrowness of its scope of recognition. But there is a totality to what the mythical and imaginative forms of verbal discourse can do: they may be unlimited in depth and complexity, but they are finite in range.

It was this conviction that led me, in the *Anatomy of Criticism*, to consider what I called encyclopedic forms, works of a scope that seemed to suggest a circumference within which the verbal creative imagination operates. Such forms include some epics, some novels, and, above all, sacred books. They also include mythologies, cosmologies, like those incorporated into Dante and Milton, cosmological principles like the chain of being, and ideologies in their primary, or mythical, shape. Such frameworks are always imaginative, and hence literary, in origin, however much science or political theory may be called on to rationalize them. Of the sacred books, the central one for a Western critic was the Bible. The Bible is the only place in our tradition I know where one can get a view of literature that goes beyond literature, and so establishes its relative finiteness, and yet includes all the elements of literature. In this age of posts and metas, I can find nothing in our cultural tradition except the Bible that really illustrates the metaliterary.

It then occurred to me, after finishing the *Anatomy*: suppose one were to reverse the process, starting with the structure of the Bible, and working outwards to literature. No one would attempt a study of Islamic culture without starting with the Koran, or of Hindu culture without starting with the Vedas and Upanishads. I hesitated for many years before attempting to say anything about this, but another augury of experience, this time directly derived from Blake, pushed me toward writing: the axiom not to trust prudence, and to persist in folly. The preliminary study that I produced in 1982, *The*

Great Code, bore the subtitle "The Bible and Literature." The opera-
tive word was *and*: all studies of the Bible as literature that I had read
treated the literary aspect of the Bible as incidental, even as ornamen-
tal.

It seemed obvious to me that while the Bible can hardly be called
a work of literature, every word of it is written in the literary language of myth and metaphor. By myth I mean story or narrative
(*mythos*), and by metaphor a verbal formula of identity. These are
the central elements of literature, but in literature itself they are
hypothetical: in the Bible they are existential, incorporating the
reader with a completeness that literature cannot attempt. So in the
Bible a literary texture forms the content of something else. For this
something else I retained the term *kerygma*, proclamation or revelation, even though that meant opposing the formidable authority of
Rudolf Bultmann, for whom kerygma and myth are mutually exclusive. I am now engaged in disentangling myself from the final
chapter of a sequel to this book.

I can hardly hope to summarize a complex argument in the
minute or two I have left, but a few suggestions about it may interest
you. Literature seems to me to revolve around what I call the primary
concerns of humanity, those that have to do with freedom, love, and
staying alive, along with the ironies of their frustration, as distinct
from the secondary or ideological concerns of politics and religion,
for which the direct verbal expression is expository rather than
literary. Because the content of literature is hypothetical, assumed
rather than asserted, it has always been regarded as a form of verbal
play, and it is only recently that we have come to understand that
play may well be more important than the serious activities promoted
by ideology, such as going to war or exploiting other people or the
other lives in nature. As long as the kerygma or proclamation of the
Bible is opposed to myth, it will be identical with ordinary ideological
rhetoric; when it is made to include myth, it gives us a new perspective on the social function of literature. By squeezing a mythical and
metaphorical proclamation into one book, however long and inexhaustible a book, the Bible provides a kind of experimental model for
what I have called the finiteness of literature. Once again, what I
mean by finiteness is not something that limits or imposes barriers,
but something that allows for a progressive increase of understanding.

Naturally the Bible, being a historical product even though it
transcends history, cannot avoid suggesting specific Jewish and

Christian ideologies, and one has to try to set out its mythical and metaphorical structure as something distinct from them. It should go without saying that this applies even more obviously to all the authoritarian, patriarchal, sexist, racist, and sectarian ideologies that profess to derive from the Bible, as well as from doctrinal and other aspects of what is usually meant by "religion," which is still an ideology expressed in rhetorical or hortatory language.

I was asked recently why I could never write anything without mentioning Shakespeare's *Tempest*. The reason is that I know of no other work of literature that illustrates more clearly the interchange of illusion and reality which is what literature is all about. In drama the illusion on the stage is the reality, and *The Tempest* is a play about the creation of a play through Prospero's magic, where illusion becomes the raw material for a new creation, while the old objective reality turns into illusion in its turn and disappears, leaving not a rack behind. The Bible similarly begins with the creation, the presenting of objective order to a conscious mind, and ends with a new creation. It is written throughout in the language of myth and metaphor because that is the language of illusion. Freud was quite right, however unconsciously, in talking about "the future of an illusion," because nothing can possibly have a future except an illusion. "Reality" can only be what does not change or changes entirely on its own terms: as far as we are concerned, its future has already occurred. But when we wake up from a dream in our bedroom, we are confronted not with "reality" but with a collection of human artifacts. The essential "reality principle," then, consists of what human beings have made, and what human beings have made they can remake. Whether they will or not will depend on the strength of the illusory desires expressed in their dreams.

All this can be taught by literature alone, but literature alone gives us only a relative perspective; every way of turning illusion into reality is equally valid within its orbit. One needs also to try to get outside literature without simply returning to ideology. I am certainly no Moses proposing to lead criticism out of Egypt and a plague of darkness, though I may resemble Moses in not having any very clear notion where the Promised Land really is. On the contrary—and this is my last augury of experience—for many years now I have been addressing myself primarily not to other critics but to students and a nonspecialist public, realizing that whatever new directions can come to my discipline will come from their needs and their intense if unfocused vision.

Literary and Mechanical Models

My qualifications for addressing a conference of this kind are as close to absolute zero as it is possible to get, except for one thing. Nobody can have lived through three-quarters of this century without being aware of the immense number of major revolutions, political, economic, religious, and above all technological, that have taken place during this time. So nowadays I almost invariably begin an address with personal reminiscence. This is not (yet) simple senility, but a means of providing some historical perspective on the contemporary world.

When I was a student at Victoria College, I had as a teacher the scholar Pelham Edgar, who in the early years of the century had gone to Johns Hopkins and done a doctoral thesis on Shelley's imagery. The bulk of the thesis was a catalogue of various images Shelley used and their contexts. Clearly it was of immense benefit to the author of the thesis to steep himself so thoroughly in Shelley's poetic vocabulary, but still most of the thesis could have been done by an appropriately programmed computer in a matter of seconds. From Toronto I went to Oxford, where at that time the greatest prestige and highest status in literary scholarship belonged to editors who were "establishing" the texts of standard authors. I remember hearing one senior scholar, after meeting another on Broad Street and asking him what he was doing these days, getting the answer: "Oh, collating, collating." I remember a preface to another established text in which the editor, in the tone of a triumphant St. George with a very dead dragon, thanked his wife for holding his hand while he fought out his titanic battle with a room full of bulky folios.

These achievements, however useful they were then, are not so highly regarded now. Such editions are routinely described as "monumental," but monuments, from Ozymandias onward, tend to crumble with the years, and the two editions I have referred to are already out of date. It was not the fault of such scholars that there were no computers then, nor am I belittling them in any degree. I am simply calling attention to the amount of difference the computer has made, even in its most elementary activities, to literary scholarship.

A Canadian scholar whose field was early Tudor literature told me that after the first edition of the OED appeared, he found earlier uses of many words in his reading than many that the editors had recorded, and he sent them along to the continuing committee. His contributions were received, he told me, not with expressions of gratitude but with snarls of resentment, presumably because it meant filling up more hand-written slips and sticking them into more pigeonholes. Concordances, again, were partly the work of what Samuel Johnson would call harmless drudges, but were also acts of piety founded on private value judgments. One might devote a large part of one's life to making a concordance to Chaucer or Shakespeare or to the 1611 Bible or a favorite Romantic poet, but hardly to a "minor" writer.

One principle stands out here: the direct mental control of a mechanical operation never guarantees accuracy. One may see that as early as Chaucer's pungent epigram on Adam Scriveyn, who transcribed his manuscripts by hand. The moral seems to be: in some areas of scholarship human intelligence is a crude and primitive form of mechanical intelligence, and anything that can be done better and faster by machinery obviously should be.

Just as societies have to go through a food-gathering stage before they enter a food-cultivating one, so there had to be a stage of gathering information about literature that might be relevant to it, even when there was no clear idea of what literature was or how to arrive at any structural principle that would direct research from the heart of literature itself. This period of literary scholarship, which was dominant until about 1935, is sometimes called the Wissenschaft period, and its great scholars amassed an awesome amount of information. Its imaginative model was the assembly line, to which each scholar "contributed" something, except that the aim was to produce not a finite object, like a motor car, but an indefinitely expanding body of knowledge. There is still, however, a principle of finiteness involved in the methodology. Before the subject of a doctoral thesis would be accepted by a graduate department, there would be a check to see whether the subject "had already been done," and this is still a necessary precaution to take with some types of theses. But the assumption behind it was made on a *Wissenschaft* level.

In those days what general principles of scholarship existed were philological. I remember a classmate interested in pre-Chaucerian literature being told by his supervisor, "Go into Middle English. Don't bother about Old English: the work there has been done." But while it was true that the philological conquest of Old English had been very impressive, it seemed to me that, apart from R. W. Chambers's book on *Beowulf*, hardly a word of anything that I would call genuine literary criticism had yet appeared in that field. As for Middle English, I remember saying to a medieval scholar, a very decent human being but one of the dullest pedants I ever knew, how as a student I had been led to Chaucer through John Livingston Lowes's book on him. My friend said, "Well, I don't know. It's a—a—an inspirational sort of thing, isn't it?"

Whenever there is this conception of doing work, there arises the specter of exhaustion: sooner or later everything essential will be done, and the humanists of the future will have nothing to do. To revert to Lowes, I once remarked to Kathleen Coburn how impressed I had been by the sheer narrative excitement of his account in *The Road to Xanadu* of reading through a thousand pages of (I think) Priestley's *Optics* and finding what he wanted on practically the last page. The great Coleridge scholar said, "Yes. Of course he had the wrong edition."

There are still many scholars who would be frightened by the thought of a computer scanning all the editions on machine time, perhaps leaving them less able to answer the stock idiot's question, "How do you manage to get through so long a summer with nothing to do?" But the fear of exhaustion is totally illusory. Around the year 1900 there was a widespread feeling that physics was in this near-exhaustion state. Physicists had constructed a model of the universe that in its overall design seemed immutable, and only a few details remained to be worked out. A year or so later along came the first work of Planck and Einstein, and there was no more talk of physics being exhausted. The same principle applies to the humanities. As soon as we seem to approach the horizon of what can be done with *Wissenschaft* philological criticism, or any other kind, the horizon vanishes and a new world spreads out.

I have to turn personal for a short time now, because I am coming to a period when, with the *Anatomy of Criticism*, I began to enter the critical scene myself. At that time the limitations of *Wissenschaft* philological criticism were apparent on all sides, and the first efforts to squirm out from under it were beginning. One of these was the judicial criticism of the *Scrutiny* group headed by Leavis. Another was the "ambiguity" or close reading movement fostered by Empson and others. But, as I saw it around 1950, there was still no critical structure that could prevent criticism from being regarded as parasitic on literary practice, or from being sucked into some ideological vortex like Marxism or Freudianism or (then) Thomism.

There was, however, one form of *Wissenschaft* scholarship that seemed to me to open a wider horizon. This was the scholarship applied to ballads and folk tales, where themes and motifs could be identified and indexed. I felt that the difference between this kind of popular literature and the whole of what we ordinarily call literature was a difference in degree of complexity but not a difference in kind. In other words, the conventions, genres, and what I called archetypes or recurring units of literature could form the basis for a new and comprehensive perspective on literature. It would give a shape to the history of literature, which was then only a history of everything in general, plus a catalogue of biographical and publication dates; it would expand the arbitrary division of literature into the different languages to a real interdisciplinary study; it would establish context as the basis of literary meaning.

I also, in my introduction, used the word *scientific*, by which is meant, essentially, progressive. My structural vision of criticism was very generously received, but there was also a revival of the old fears about exhaustion. One critic even asked me if I proposed to lock up all critics in that goddamned jail, where they would do nothing but clean out its cells. Most of this misunderstanding, I now see, came from the word *scientific*, which I used because my view was the opposite of the one assumed by the hostile question. I wanted criticism set free to do something with a direction to it, instead of fighting civil wars on judgmental grounds, or disintegrating a text into ambiguous units, or following the course of a history which had nothing to do with the actual history of literature. Not that I wanted to abolish these activities, but merely to prevent them from becoming dead ends and abolishing themselves.

I have never been impressed by the "hard" and "soft" metaphors applied to science, nor did I care two pins that the conception of science I invoked was as soft as a marshmallow. But such conceptions as "software programming" and "computer modelling" were as yet unknown, and if I were writing such an introduction today I should probably pay a good deal of attention to them and talk less about science. Ballads and folk tales are an obvious area for computer assistance, and an approach to literature through its recurring conventional units might be equally so. Again, I have always suspected that the basis for the prestige of judicial and evaluative criticism was social snobbery: for it, criticism was a gentlemanly, and therefore an unsystematic, occupation. But this was only an intuitive hunch, which the coming of computers has done much to clarify.

Apart from the analogies of ballad and folklore scholarship, I was also influenced by the twentieth-century fluidity of media, in which a story might begin as a magazine serial, then become a book, and then a film. I remember the shock of picking up a copy of *The Brothers Karamazov* and seeing it described as "the book of the film," but I realized that certain verbal cores, of the kind I usually call archetypes, were constants throughout the metamorphoses. The variety of media, in fact, was what made the conventions and genres I was interested in stand out in such bold relief.

It was this that made it impossible for me to go along with McLuhan's "the medium is the message" axiom, despite my general sympathy for what McLuhan was trying to do. McLuhan's formula was essentially an application of the Aristotelian form-content unity. He says, for example, that the form of one medium is the content of a later medium. I could see the identity of form and content: the content of a picture, for example, is the form of that picture, as long as we are talking about it as a picture and not as a representation of something else. I could also see the essential identity of content and message. But McLuhan's aphorism also implied an identity of form and medium, and that I could not buy. A medium is precisely that, a vehicle or means of transmission, and what is transmitted are the real forms. The form of a Mozart quartet is not affected by whether it is heard in the concert hall or over the radio or read in a score, though there would be psychological variants of reacting to it of the kind that McLuhan made so much of. The real forms are not the media but verbal or pictorial structural units that have been there since the Stone Age.

There is today, of course, a large number of critical schools concerned with the humanities. What I have called the *Wissenschaft* or philological school grew up in precomputer days. It would be absurd to regard it as obsolete merely because it has been around for some time, but the necessity of supplementing it with other approaches is fairly obvious. Most of the schools that have appeared since the *Anatomy of Criticism* have their center of gravity in linguistics or semiotics, or else represent some ideological interest, religious or psychological or politically radical or feminist or whatever. I think that as long as all these critical perspectives are thought of as competing schools, the whole critical enterprise becomes a Tower of Babel, a vast structure largely abandoned, so far as it is a cooperative effort, because its builders have become unintelligible not only to the general public but increasingly to one another. It is on the whole fortunate that they have, because most such schools contain a hard core of imperialists anxious to dominate all the others.

I think here of a friend of mine who, about fifty years ago, started an academic career in philosophy. At his first job the department chairman called all the new recruits together and wrote on the blackboard a list of nineteen "isms," which they were required to teach their students. My friend felt that while philosophy might be a genuine subject these "isms" were not, so he did the philosophical thing: resigned and joined an advertising firm. Critical schools, like philosophical ones, are better thought of as programming models. The importance of the computer is in bringing them down to manageable scope, so that their essential assumptions can be worked through in a reasonable time before they modulate into or merge with something else.

The *Anatomy of Criticism* was written just as the Babel clamor was beginning; hence, it has come to be regarded as a document of a "mythological school," and its schematic overview regarded as a "system," which is a schematism petrified into dogma. There is a sentence in the introduction about the schematism being a scaffolding to be knocked away when the building is in better shape. Those who disregard this sentence have totally misunderstood both the book and the spirit in which it was written. The personal reference is not important, but the critical principle is highly relevant to my subject.

II

Humanists are often said to be Luddites or machine-breakers, resisting new technology as much as possible. C. P. Snow even cites Orwell's *1984* as an example of the humanist wish that the future should not exist, though I should think any sane man would wish that *that* future should not exist. But resistance to mechanical developments is a matter of personal habits combined with age: it has nothing to do with whether one is a humanist or not. Humanists can come to terms with technology when it seems feasible. At Oxford I picked up a rumor that Sir James Frazer, author of *The Golden Bough* (twelve volumes), *Totemism and Exogamy* (six volumes), *Folklore in the Old Testament* (three volumes), an edition of Pausanias (two volumes), and a whole shelf of other books, had recently, in his last years, switched to a fountain pen.

I myself have been a touch typist since the age of sixteen, and am also a very laborious and endlessly revising writer, and hence I tend to resist the word processor with its itch to jump around and perform miracles, and stay with my typewriter. But younger people, naturally, have a different attitude. Of course, in so experimental a field some developments are certain to be a bust: one thinks of how badly boards of education got stung on the teaching machines of the fifties, with their inept Pavlovian programming as transmitted by B. F. Skinner and others. The translating machines of the same period, again, have developed their own folklore, of which the most famous story is the rendering of "out of sight, out of mind" as "invisible lunatic."

The Luddite thesis overlooks the fact that three of the most seminal mechanical inventions ever devised, the alphabet, the printing press, and the book, have been in humanist hands for centuries. The prestige of humanists in the past came largely from the fact that they lived in a far more efficient technological world than most of their contemporaries. It is true that today they are sometimes confused about the new possibilities opening up in front of them, though hardly more so than the rest of the human race, and some of them may also be put off by over-enthusiastic forecasting. I often find that, when I read a book about the technology available in the near future, the author's eyes are starry while mine are still glazed. One such book, written around 1970, predicted quite astonishing technical developments for the 1980s, almost none of which occurred. Everything the author predicted may eventually come true, but he did not allow for the normal rate of social metabolism.

At present, in the humanities, computers are doing an immense amount of word-crunching, and could easily do much more. Concordances have multiplied; dictionaries are no longer assembled from hand-written slips; in the study of literature the prospect opens up of having the entire verbal corpus of any given literature placed within easy reach. Those who remember the precomputer age are reminded at every turn of the changes new technologies have made.

A few days ago a good deal of material landed on my desk from a spelling reform enthusiast. My mind went back forty years to the time when supporters of "Anglic" and similar schemes predicted that English would become a world language if its spelling were made as phonetic as Italian. I also thought how quaint this interest looked now, not only when English has become a world language, but when we have computers with entire dictionaries built into them.

When the historian Michel Foucault wrote his book *Les mots et les choses,* he gave it the prophetic subtitle "An Essay on the Archaeology of Knowledge." The word *archaeology* seems to me deeply significant here. Archaeology emerged as an essential basis for historical research, especially for the ancient period, about two centuries ago, and its first efforts were in the general area of treasure hunts, or at least the recovery of startling artifacts. It has now become a patient soil-sifting and strata-separating enterprise, with the aim of reconstructing the continuity of the past: that is, of filling in the gaps in society's record of its own earlier life. Society, like the individual, becomes senile in proportion as it loses its continuous memory. The humanist's preoccupation is concerned with reconstructing that past, not, as in the "two cultures" thesis, with nostalgia for it. The computer can add a fantastic amount of detail to that reconstruction.

My own technological fantasies are very limited. I should hope that within a few years the most mind-numbing of humanist activities, the marking of undergraduate essays, would disappear as the essays were fed into a machine that would not just guess at the mark, would not be affected by prejudice or exasperation, and would not respond to the protests of failed students. It would also, of course, have a complete file of the essays written in the fraud factories, and when it received one would start bellowing over a public address system the name of the student who had bought it. I should also hope to see the end of the conception of "productive scholar," with its nineteenth-century industrial overtones, and "creative scholar" put in its place. In the future, perhaps, someone proposing a doctoral thesis, let us say on the Adonis myth in Milton or metaphors of nature in Wordsworth or color imagery in Tennyson, would look to see whether it had already been done, and discover that there were in existence 9,842 theses on precisely that topic, of which 7,235 were in Japanese. The department would nod its collective head and remark that any thesis that had been written as often as that must be an excellent one. The thesis would add nothing to knowledge, but nobody would read it anyway, and if there were something in it that could conceivably be used it could be made available by other means. So the crazy chain of thesis, thesis rewritten as book, book published, book bought by libraries, book added to an already groaning bibliography, would be broken. The computer would play only a minor role in reducing this academic counterpart of the national deficit, but its role would be crucial.

Such a reverie need not be taken with desperate seriousness, but it contains a genuine point, and the analogy of learning a language may help to explain what the point is. Despite the teaching machines, computers could help a great deal in the learning of language. But no machine will learn the language for us: we have to digest all those idioms and irregular verbs ourselves. In the learning process we are not contributing to any body of knowledge except our own; yet there is normally an advance in fluency and competence. I think of language partly because it is so prolific a source of guilt feelings among humanists: we never know enough languages, and the languages we do know we never know well enough.

Literature itself, especially poetry, is also written in a language of its own, the language of myth and metaphor, which graduate students pick up piecemeal by luck and instinct but are never systematically taught. The kind of thesis I have spoken of would be a pure academic exercise and not, in the *Wissenschaft* formula, "a contribution to knowledge worthy of publication." But it would also be an immersion in the thought and vocabulary of a great poet, which would teach the author the language of poetry in a way analogous to the learning of composition through the study of models. I began this talk with a reference to Edgar's Shelley thesis, which I said could be done now by a computer very quickly, but which undoubtedly represented an experience of great value to Edgar himself. I should like to see most doctoral theses, also, take the form of documents that have educated the author without driving the rest of the scholarly world out of its mind.

III

It is a cliché to say that computers can do only what they have been programmed to do. But a few decades ago biology came up with the DNA molecule and the genetic code, which showed that much the same principle applies to the human organism. For example, there have been experiments in ESP and telepathy which may have established the fact that some human beings possess such powers. They certainly established the fact that the majority of people either do not possess them at all or possess them in an erratic, unreliable, and very largely useless form. Perhaps our remote ancestors possessed them when they had more survival value and they have merely atrophied since; perhaps strenuous efforts of meditation training in yoga or Zen schools could awaken these and other dormant mental abilities.

But the simplest way of looking at this question is to say that human evolutionary history has produced a unique but still limited and finite being, and that there are many theoretically conceivable powers for which our nervous wiring, so to speak, is not well adapted. What we do have is the capacity to construct machinery that can compensate for what is impossible for the human organism, such as the ability to explore the electromagnetic spectrum far beyond the color range or report on what is going on on the planet Neptune. Telepathy and the like, again, may exist in human minds, but it seems to be a poor thing compared to what the technology of telephones and wireless has been providing for a century.

The question of whether computers are or can become conscious or thinking beings is, of course, a pseudoissue. There is a pernicious tendency in the human mind to externalize its own inventions and pervert them into symbols of objective mastery over us by alien forces. The wheel, for example, was perverted into a symbolic wheel of fate or fortune, a remorseless cycle carrying us helplessly around with it. Again, as soon as human beings began to write books and keep records, there arose the nightmare of being confronted after death by a book containing the record of our misdeeds written by a recording angel. The same dreary superstition turns up with computers.

In Samuel Butler's *Erewhon*, written in 1870, the imaginary society he calls Erewhon once had a flourishing technological civilization, but on the urging of a prophet who might fairly be called a Luddite, they destroyed it and refused to allow any more mechanical progress. The argument was that machines were developing so quickly that the human being was certain to become very shortly "an affectionate machine-tickling aphid," a parasite useful only for feeding and grooming machinery. Some writers talk about the computers of the future in very similar terms, predicting the imminent arrival of super-intelligent mechanisms that will—well, I'm not sure what:

you write the book: after fifty years of teaching I feel that I know something about the strength of the human impulse to say "enough is enough." And when a silicon microchip begins to take on the proportions of a world-conquering Messiah, it is perhaps time to say "enough."

What makes human beings unique in the scheme of things is not simple consciousness, but consciousness directed by an autonomous will. Machines extended human capacities in all directions including mental ones, but no machine has yet appeared that has any will of its own to exert its power, that is independent of being plugged in or turned on. In short, there are no perpetual-motion machines. Computers look mysterious and spooky to some people because of the Cartesian fallacy, which survives as an unconscious assumption, that the human being is made up of two separate components, a mind (or soul or whatever) and a physical body which the mind inhabits and which by itself is a mechanism. So a machine that runs faster than our legs, like an automobile, arouses no emotional disturbance, as it belongs to the mechanical body-world, but a machine that can do only what the mind is traditionally supposed to be able to do may seem to threaten our supremacy as lords of the earth. As soon as we put such an assumption into words we can see how absurd it is.

Destruction is the mother of invention, and tyranny its step-father. Technological development has been largely prompted, in every age, by military conflict, and further advance is often frozen by the determination of an ascendant class to preserve its ascendancy. Consciousness is the critic of the directing will, and when the will does not pay attention to its criticisms, human ingenuity is put to very wrong uses. With the coming of the Industrial Revolution a different but related social element entered the scene.

Alluding for the last time to the "two cultures" polemic, I note that many nineteenth-century literary figures, Blake, Dickens, Carlyle, Ruskin, Morris, attacked and ridiculed the material civilization of their time on the ground of its ugliness and filth. But they were not making a mere shudder of refined distaste: they saw in the physical ugliness of their time the sign of a far more sinister spiritual ugliness. Ruskin and Morris in particular denounced the drudgery and misery caused by the division of labor in factories into intolerably monotonous tasks, and they emphasized that bad or mindless design in mass-produced goods was invariably connected with exploitation.

Marx, of course, had a far more comprehensive vision of all this, but the aesthetic criteria were the distinctively humanist ones. And while much of the squalor of working-class nineteenth-century life may have been inevitable, given its coal-based economy, the humanist's opposition to it was in some respects even more deeply prophetic than the Marxist one. Some of it has developed into the "green" political parties of today, which are growing rapidly at a time when Marxism seems to be entering a decline.

The main principle of the humanist case was this: humanity can be genuinely civilized only when it loves and cherishes nature. The exploiting of nature is, in the long run, just as wrong and evil as the exploiting of one's fellowmen. This is not really a Marxist doctrine, as Marxism paid as little attention to environmental factors as laissez-faire capitalism did, so far as the exploiting of nature was concerned. At present, with the apparent weakening of the adversary situation between the two systems, a more centrally conscious attitude is emerging. At least we know that graphite fires and oil spills are major disasters, not minor incidents to be hushed up by whatever authority gets there first.

In the development of computer technology there are two possibly recurring features. It is a relatively clean technology, and it seems to have a curious kind of democratic dynamic built into it. Each advance, so far, seems to have made the mechanism involved simpler, cheaper, and more available to more people. Obviously this can hardly be the whole story, and there could well be Big Brother features in it that would make Orwell's telescreen look very rudimentary as a means of paralyzing all moves toward freedom. But I am concerned here with scholarship in the humanities, which in itself cannot enslave anyone. Besides, whenever a new instrument of production emerges in society, there are both opportunities to be taken advantage of and dangers of reinforcing existing or future power structures. Everybody likes to warn of the dangers; some, including myself, tend to be more attracted to the opportunities. As for how these opportunities may be extended and applied in our own field, I come up against the blank wall of my own technical ignorance once again, and must turn the next chapter over to you.

Literature as Therapy

When I was looking over the connections that came to my mind between literature, more particularly English literature, and the medical profession, I remembered that in the Middle Ages the doctors had a popular reputation for skepticism and that there was a medieval proverb that said that wherever there are three doctors there are at least two atheists. When Chaucer introduces a physician on his Canterbury pilgrimage, he remarks that "His studye was but litel on the Bible," and that was a sort of in-joke, picking up the general assumption. That notion lasted even as late as the seventeenth century, when Sir Thomas Browne, who was a doctor himself, wrote a book called *Religio Medici*, the doctor's religion, which, even at that time, was a catchy title because a doctor's religion would sound like something of a paradox. In fact, Browne speaks in his opening sentence of the general scandal of his profession. Nevertheless, he writes a book on his religion, because it relieves him of the tedium of what he elsewhere calls "the futile portense of uroscopy."

Well, considering how much hysteria there was at that time about the smallest deviation in doctrine, to say nothing of atheism, one wonders why this remained on the level of a relatively harmless joke. One or two things occur to me on that point. There is a very shrewd comment in George Eliot's *Middlemarch* about a doctor who had a reputation for being a skeptic, but, instead of that ruining his reputation in a small Victorian town, his skepticism actually raised his stock very considerably because his patients greatly preferred to deal with somebody who thought entirely in terms of natural causes and natural cures. Then again, the doctors' study of medicine, which at that time was derived very largely from Galen, was intensely materialistic, in the sense of dealing with the body and the mind as a single and indivisible unit. Of course, the practice of medicine then was full of magic, but it was based on the conception of natural sympathies and natural antipathies, a notion which we'll come to later in the context of literature.

A key idea in Chaucer's day was the conception of what we call complexion or temperament. Both words mean mixture, and they referred to the balancing of the four humors or liquids of the body, together with the balancing of the seven planetary influences under which the patient was born. The doctor of Chaucer's time would look first of all to see what complexion or temperament his patient had. His pharmacopia was a much more elaborate one than we would use now. He would use lapidaries, that is, treatises on precious stones, all of which had some use, and herbals, because there was no herb growing in the ground that was not of some use. That is typical of the medieval mind: there is nothing in the world that does not refer directly to human values.

A good deal of what we think of as Chaucer's freshness and insight, his concrete view of people, is actually made up of these observations about humors and planetary temperaments. He says of his Franklin, for example, "of his complexion he was sanguin." That is, of the four humors the blood was the one that dominated in his complexion. That would immediately for Chaucer's readers have summoned up a picture of a ruddy-faced English country squire. The medical principle that came from this was that you were liable to certain diseases because of the temperament or complexion you were born with. If you were tall and dark and sallow, you were probably of a melancholy temperament, probably born under Saturn or the moon, and you would be liable especially to emotional mental disorders or to such diseases as jaundice. If you were short and thick-set and quick-tempered and red-headed, you were choleric and probably born under Mercury. That meant that you would be liable to whatever Chaucer's contemporaries recognized as high blood pressure.

The interesting thing about this knowledge was that it was available to the layman, as well as to the doctor—a fact that sometimes rather disturbed the medical profession. The Wife of Bath, for example, in telling the story of her life, explains her numerous love affairs by the fact that she was born under a conjunction of Mars and Venus, who, as we remember from Greek mythology, carried on in a rather uninhibited way. In *The Nun's Priest's Tale*, which is a story about a cock and a hen, the hen feels that there is something the matter with her husband and, with the greatest confidence, prescribes remedies for him out of the best authorities, having clearly read the fourteenth-century equivalent of *The Reader's Digest*.

In Shakespeare's day this theory of humors and, to a large degree, planetary temperaments was still there, except that of the four humors—the sanguine, the phlegmatic, the choleric, and the melancholic—the melancholic one had assumed the leadership and was the supreme example of the mental/physical disease. You are probably familiar with the wonderful passage in *Macbeth* where Macbeth, in discussing his wife's illness with a doctor, says in a remarkably prophetic passage,

> *Canst thou not minister to a mind diseas'd,*
> *Pluck from a memory a rooted sorrow,*
> *Raze out the written troubles of the brain,*
> *And with some sweet oblivious antidote*
> *Cleanse the stuff'd bosom of that perilous stuff*
> *Which weighs upon the heart?*

All the doctor says is, "Therein the patient must minister to himself," and so Macbeth says, "Throw physic to the dogs. I'll none of it." Well, the reason why the doctor makes this extremely helpless and unenterprising answer is that he sees quite clearly that there is a lot going on in Lady Macbeth's mind that he cannot afford to get mixed up with. Consequently, he simply backs out, and that is what earns him the contemptuous remark of Macbeth.

In the second scene of *Hamlet* we have the court of Denmark all dressed up in their best court finery and Hamlet, just a little withdrawn, dressed in black clothes, allegedly in mourning for the death of his father. The audience of Shakespeare's day would see at once that Hamlet was of a melancholy disposition. They would not be at all surprised at the fact that the scene ends with Hamlet reciting a soliloquy expressing a nauseated vision of the world. But although the physical side of melancholy was left out of *Hamlet*, it was in Shakespeare's day a physical disease, and at the end of the seventeenth century there was a song book published under the title of *Pills to Purge Melancholy*. The conception of the humor lingered on in various forms. Ben Jonson, Shakespeare's younger contemporary, invented a type of comedy in which the humor becomes a kind of obsession, such as miserliness or hypochondria, of which the chief character is either cured or not cured by the end of the action of the play.

A little later than Shakespeare we have Burton's *Anatomy of Melancholy*, a great encyclopedic treatise on this mental and physical disease. The physical reason for it was the excess of what was called "black bile," but it extended over the entire psychiatric area as well. Burton's *Anatomy of Melancholy*—I'm expressing my own opinion here—is one of the supreme masterpieces of English literature. It ranks with Chaucer and the novels of Dickens as a survey of the life contemporary with him, except that it uses books instead of characters. Sir William Osler of McGill paid it a rather chilly and left-handed compliment by saying that it was the greatest book on medicine ever written by a nonmedical person. Burton was an Oxford don and a clergyman. Samuel Johnson paid it a much higher and much more concrete compliment when he said it was the only book that ever got him out of bed to read two hours earlier than he wanted to.

As Burton deals with the disease, melancholy tends to spread over the entire area of human feelings and inadequacies of both body and mind. In the three long volumes of the *Anatomy* there are some amazing digressions. There is, first of all, a "Digression of Spirits," where he talks about devils, demons, fairies, elves, and so forth, and about what hundreds and hundreds of authorities have all said about them and what role they actually play in disease. Here, for example, he is speaking of various books on melancholy of which he does not take a very high view because he does not believe what they say:

> *Many such stories I find amongst pontifical writers, to prove their assertions; let them free their own credits; some few I will recite in this kind out of most approved Physicians. Cornelius Gemma relates of a young maid, called Katherine Gualter, a cooper's daughter, in the year 1571, that had such strange passions and convulsions, three men could not sometimes hold her; she purged a live eel, which he saw, a foot and a half long, and touched himself, but the eel afterwards vanished; she vomited some 24 pounds of fulsome stuff of all colours twice a day for 14 days; and after that she voided great balls of hair, pieces of wood, pigeons' dung, parchment, goose dung, coals; and after them two pounds of pure blood, and then again coals and stones, of which some had inscriptions, bigger than a walnut, some of them pieces of glass, brass, &c., besides paroxysms of laughing, weeping and ecstasies &c. And this (he says), I saw with horror. They could do no good on her by physick, but left her to the Clergy. Marcellus Donatus hath another such story of a country fellow, that had four knives in his belly, indented like a saw, every one a span long, with a wreath of hair like a globe, with*

much baggage of like sort, wonderful to behold. How it should come into his guts, he concludes, could only have been through the artifice and craft of a dæmon. (II, Memb. I, Subs. 2)

Well, it is clear that Burton knows that he is describing a case of hysteria, but what he does not know is whether it was the doctor or the patient who had it. We read about sixty pages of this digression about demons and their power and their shape (because some people say that they are all completely spherical), and we realize that there is probably not an atom of genuine information in the entire passage. It does not follow, of course, that we have wasted our time reading it. On the contrary, what it does is re-create for us the incredible seventeenth century. But all of this had started in the sixteenth century with the heavy dose of magic which Paracelsus reintroduced into medicine and the development of the magus figure. The medical man was very frequently a magician whose cures were magical and, consequently, miraculous. In the seventeenth century the magus figure was giving way to what we would think of more as science, but it gave way very slowly, and in Burton's time almost anything could be true. Magical and scientific explanations could both be given for the same phenomena. Even as late as Sir Isaac Newton, for example, you have a scientist who was just as interested in alchemy and in biblical numerology as he was in the laws of gravitation and motion.

Burton does not say that literature is a therapy for melancholy, except in a wider context of recreation generally. On the other hand, he begins his book by saying that he wrote the book because he was melancholy himself. In other words, it was a form of auto-therapy that inspired him to write it. The other reason for writing it is that *we* are: everybody suffers from melancholy. Consequently, the book itself may have a therapeutic value. It is perhaps worth noting that the longest and most popular section of the book by far is the section on love melancholy, which, of course, coincided with one of the central conventions of literature at that time. If you wanted to write poetry in Shakespeare's day, it was practically obligatory to fall in love and to complain about the cruelty and disdain and neglect with which your mistress treated you. The effect of this was to drive you into a state of melancholy, which, again, was partly physical and partly emotional and self-induced.

In later literature, it seems to me that doctors are rather less of a target than lawyers or the clergy, the chief exception being Molière.

In Molière's last play, *Le malade imaginaire*, the central figure is a hypochondriac. He is waited on by two doctors whose names are Purgon and Diafoirus. (*Diafoirus* is the French word for diarrhea.) Their techniques consist almost exclusively of purging and bleeding. Diafoirus has heard of Harvey's theories of the circulation of the blood, but thinks that that is just a new fad that will very soon wear out and he will then be able to return to his purging and bleeding. The play ends with a magnificent ballet in which a student is admitted to the medical college and is examined by being asked such questions as "Why does opium put people to sleep?" To which he answers, "Opium puts people to sleep because it has a dormant effect." Then there is a dance at the end about the routines of purging and clystering and repurging and reclystering and so forth. A little later, in the eighteenth-century novel *Gil Blas*, the hero is apprenticed to a doctor for a time, who carried out these routines of bleeding and purging so thoroughly that his patients invariably died. For this he took the greatest credit to himself, as a compliment to the thoroughness of his methods.

Another aspect of medical theory was that the digesting of food distilled in the stomach what were called "the vegetative spirits," which were still further distilled and refined into cordial spirits, located in the heart. By a still further distillation, they became the animal spirits—a phrase we still use in a different sense—in the brain or consciousness. This conception or metaphor was of great aid and comfort to Swift in the eighteenth century. It enabled him to explain most of the phenomena of his time of which he disapproved. That is, if the vegetative spirits went up into the brain too suddenly or prematurely, the result was fantasy and illusion. Consequently, you had things like the Nonconformist enthusiasts, of which Swift, who was the dean of St. Patrick's Cathedral, took an extremely dim view. The same view of the spirits led Swift to some extraordinarily penetrating psychological observations on the erotic origin of idealism and ambition and various other things. He says, for example, "The very same principle that influences the bully to break the windows of the whore who has jilted him, naturally stirs up a great prince to raise mighty armies, and dream of nothing but sieges, battles, and victories" [*A Tale of a Tub*].

With later writers, such as Bernard Shaw in *The Doctor's Dilemma*, the interest tends to shift to the doctor as the product of a certain kind of society, as a member of a social establishment and under certain kinds of social pressures. But my central point in trying to trace out this intertwining of literary and medical references is that there was a medical tradition unifying body and mind long before modern psychology. The doctors of the nineteenth century, for example, while they may have lacked a good deal of what we would consider scientific training, may have made up for it partly by their close personal relations with their patients and their familiarity with both the physical and the mental constitution of their patients.

This inseparability of body and mind naturally leads to the question of whether such imaginative constructs as literature and the other arts would have a direct role to play in physical health. The art with the longest record in therapy is, of course, music. Even the most inflexible and uptight Puritan could not deny the possible therapeutic power of music because of the story in the Bible of David's playing a harp in an effort to cure the melancholy of King Saul. Musical theory down to the end of the sixteenth century included a great deal of speculative cosmology, which turned on terms like *harmony* and *rhythm* and assumed a certain correspondence between the balance which made for good health in the body and the balance which kept the world in a state of harmony. Some time ago a book came out called *The Romeo Error*, referring to Romeo's mistake in thinking that Juliet was dead when she was actually suffering from a drug-induced coma. The point of the book, so far as I gathered, was that a person may be clinically dead for a long time without being actually dead. This is a standard device in many of the romances of the time, especially the late plays of Shakespeare. In *Pericles*, for example, the hero, Pericles, goes to sea with his wife, Thaisa. His wife dies. The sailors insist on putting her in a coffin and throwing the coffin overboard, on the grounds that it is bad luck to a ship to have a corpse in it. So her coffin is thrown overboard, but, being made of wood, it drifts to shore. It is picked up there, and her body is brought to the doctor, who says,

> *'Tis known, I ever*
> *Have studied physic, through which secret art,*
> *By turning o'er authorities, I have,*
> *Together with my practice, made familiar*
> *To me and to my aid the blest infusions*
> *That dwells in vegetives, in metals, stones.*

And one of his attendants says, "Your honour has through Ephesus pour'd forth / Your charity, and hundreds call themselves /

Your creatures, who by you have been restor'd." That is, he can bring people back to life again. We are still, of course, within the orbit of the magus, who works in terms of the mysterious virtues of herbs and so on. But my reason for referring to this passage is that what the doctor is most anxious about is getting the music started. He has a kind of private orchestra as a part of his practice. He starts the music going, which is obviously the initiating power in bringing Thaisa back to life. One occasionally sees, even in contemporary newspapers, the suggestion that in thinking of the turmoils of Eastern Europe today one should not overlook the direct influence of American jazz and rock. In any case, there is always a certain amount of mystery about music. We never know quite what is going on in it. Perhaps it is partly to that that it owes its therapeutic reputation.

Literature has never had the prestige of music in that context, partly because, I think, literature is not really defined clearly as a category until about the Romantic period—though, of course, people spoke of the poets. Literary criticism goes back to Aristotle's *Poetics*, which is apparently a set of incomplete lecture notes. At least, what has come down to us is incomplete. Aristotle deals mainly with tragedy. He begins with a definition of tragedy in which he says that it is a form that is complete and of a certain magnitude, varied by different poetic devices, and raising the emotions of pity and fear in order to effect a catharsis of those emotions. Now that is undoubtedly the most celebrated sentence that has ever been written in the history of literary criticism. One wonders why it turns on the word *catharsis*, which is a medical metaphor. The question naturally arises, Would it apply to other genres besides tragedy, such as comedy?

There must be at least fifty theories on the market about the meaning of *catharsis*. I can perhaps save time by giving you the correct one, which by coincidence happens to be mine. I think that by "pity and fear" is meant the moral feelings that draw you either toward or away from certain characters. In such a play as *Othello*, for example, we feel pity for Desdemona, because she is so utterly innocent, and we feel terror for Iago, because he is so unrelieved a villain. But the central figure of the play is Othello, and our feelings about him are very much mixed. If we are watching something in which these emotions of pity and terror predominate, if they are the leading features that we react to, we have something that is usually today called melodrama, rather than tragedy. Melodrama impels us, of course, to hiss villains and applaud heroes. But if these emotions of sympathy and repulsion—pity and terror—are purged through catharsis, as they are in tragedy, then the response to tragedy is a response of emotional balance, a kind of self-integrating process. That is, what we feel when we respond to a tragic action is, well, yes, this kind of thing does happen: it inevitably happens given these circumstances. With Othello, who is the central figure, it does not really matter whether he is a good man or a bad man. He is obviously a mixture of both, or at least a mixture of strength and weakness. In any case, the particular thing called tragedy that happens to a tragic hero does not depend on his moral status. The hero of tragedy may be a very good person or a very bad one. But tragedy itself is the working out of an inevitability which the audience recognizes to be such. There is, according to Aristotle, a kind of excessive action on the part of the tragic hero, which Aristotle calls *hybris*. That is bound to lead to the restoring of balance in the natural order—what he calls *nemesis*. So the action of tragedy is almost physically intelligible, almost as intelligible in terms of a cosmos and the workings of nature as it is in moral or human terms.

Irony is an important genre for us because so much contemporary literature is ironic in its tone. What irony appeals to is a sense of normality on the part of the audience. That is, we recognize a certain action to be grotesque or absurd or evil or futile or whatever, and it is that sense of normality in the audience that enables irony to make its point as irony. Without that sense of the normal, irony would cease to become ironic and become simply a description. That is the trouble that so many writers complain of—that the world itself is so much more ironic a place than any kind of ironic construction they themselves could dream up. In a way, their work has all been done for them.

The appeals and responses of audiences in the tragic and ironic modes have a great deal to do with confrontation. The sense of confrontation is something which writers themselves use within their own fictions, partly to demonstrate how very effective it is. There is a story by the German Romantic writer E. T. A. Hoffmann, for example, about the painter Salvator Rosa, who walks into a situation of a very familiar comic type. There is a young heroine languishing under an old and miserly uncle, who is determined to marry her, and there is a perfectly acceptable hero who wants her instead. The painter gets the old miser out to a theatrical performance in which he acts the part of the miser himself on the stage. This shatters the miser so completely that he loses his miserliness and becomes immediately converted, and the heroine is able to marry the hero. A rather more familiar example would be Shakespeare's *Taming of the Shrew*, where we realize that the story is, to put it mildly, somewhat improbable. Its preposterous sexism, of course, was never taken very seriously even in its own day. Nevertheless, it is tremendously good drama, and it is that partly because it deals with such an admirable dramatic device. Petruchio confronts Katherina with a shrew—with the mirror reflection of her own shrewishness—and so shows her exactly what it looks like when she can see it objectively. It is her recognition of that that casts her shrewishness out of her and converts her. The point is that by putting on a certain dramatic act Petruchio has also performed an act of therapy.

There is also the question of *catharsis* in comedy. Aristotle either did not write a treatise on comedy or we've lost it if he did. In any case, we have to go a little further from Aristotle to discuss comedy. In Greek mythology, there is the earth goddess Demeter who lost her daughter Persephone and went mourning all over the world in search of her. She was in a practically catatonic state. She just sat and stared gloomily in front of her until a servant girl named Iambe made some obscene remarks and an old nurse named Baubo performed an obscene dance, which eventually persuaded her to smile. There is a very similar story, curiously enough, in Japanese mythology. When we look at the earliest of comic writers, Aristophanes, we find that his text is rather startlingly obscene, even for these enlightened days. One wonders how it would have been tolerated in his time—in a culture in which drama, including comic drama, had something of a sacerdotal and ritual side to it. It is obvious that the obscenity is important as a form of psychological release. That kind of release helps to build up the festive atmosphere of comedy, which had at that time a very close connection with certain festival periods of the year.

The Czech writer Milan Kundera has made a very profound remark about comedy. He says that the great comic geniuses are not the ones that keep us laughing, because laughter is simply a reflex: you can laugh for a whole evening and still be bored out of your mind. The great comic geniuses, Kundera says, are those who have discovered or uncovered for their audiences the comic aspects of what those audiences have not previously thought of as comic. If you apply a statement like that to the novels of Dickens, for example, you can see how profoundly true that is. There are many aspects of Victorian civilization which seem so humorless and grim. If you take a look at Engels's *Condition of the Working Class*, you can see how grim the conditions sometimes were. But the comic side of them emerges in Dickens. There is little doubt, I think, of the therapeutic importance of Dickens in his impact on Victorian society. The same thing is true of such figures as Charlie Chaplin or Buster Keaton. Chaplin is an almost unbearably pathetic figure, with his mixture of the dapper and the seedy in his appearance and of the timid and the jaunty in his manner. He seems to dramatize everything that is crushed and neglected and treated with contempt in the world, and yet he uncovers the whole comic side, which, again, restores a balance, in those who watch him, of something that has been repressed. So, of course, does the sick joke, which brings us back very close to Aristotle's *catharsis*, because the sick joke expresses forms of pity and fear which achieve something of a purgation of those emotions. It is very familiar how a certain type of sardonic joke arises among oppressed people or people living under totalitarian governments. This rather subversive humor clearly has a survival value for such people. That is true of the oppressed. It is true also of the other end of the society. One thinks of the role of the fool in *King Lear*, whose function is to tell Lear the exact truth about himself. This makes what he says funny because nothing is funnier than the sudden escape of the exact truth of any situation. That is why Renaissance princes kept fools around them—to remind them of the more human aspects of their own situation and to set out for them a feeling of proportion and balance, which, again, seems to have a great deal to do with both mental and physical health.

I am suggesting that in all this we are really coming back to Galen's principle of magical sympathies and antipathies, except that they are not regarded any longer as forces existing in nature itself. That is, we do not believe in cures by sympathetic magic any more, and we do not, so far as I know, prescribe saffron as a cure for jaundice simply because it is yellow. And so far as I know, Alcoholics Anonymous does not recommend the wearing of amethysts because, being wine-colored, they will keep you sober. The word *amethyst*, in fact, is Greek for "not drunk." The magical sympathies and antipathies that exist now, I think, are rather those that exist between words or pictures and the social environment. That is, literature and painting, particularly, constitute a kind of counterenvironment in which the follies and evils of the environment are partly reflected in the arts but within a context which, again, achieves that type of purgation and, ultimately, of balance which Aristotle is talking about. Such a use of words is rather indirect for many poets, and there is the strong temptation by many writers to become ideologues, to use the same kind of language that political people do, and, to some extent, to turn their backs on their own specific assignment.

Poetic language is very different from rhetorical or ideological language. Rhetorical language appeals to an audience to integrate as a unit and to do certain things or avoid certain other things. Poetic language tends rather to turn its back on the listener and set up something which requires the reader to detach himself. It is the language of rhetoric and the language of ideology that are the spark plugs of history. I have lived through seventy-seven years of the history of this century myself, and the number of changes which have taken place in that three-quarters of a century is, of course, immense. But this has left me with the general feeling that history is a kind of dissolving phantasmagoria, and that all ideologies are sooner or later illusory. To the question of social change there seem to me to be prior questions, such as, Has anything improved in the course of that time? Has anything remained stable? My own view, which my life continually confirms, is that nothing has improved in the twentieth century except science and that nothing has remained stable except the arts.

In the art of literature, particularly, I've never found any better place to start from than the observation of Duke Theseus in *A Midsummer Night's Dream*, where he says in the last act of the play that "the lunatic, the lover, and the poet / Are of imagination all compact." By imagination, Theseus means essentially seeing things that are not there. Lunatics and lovers and poets have a family likeness in that regard. The kernel of truth in Theseus's remark is that in the arts reality and realism are rather different things. Realism is a perfectly legitimate form of literature, but it only takes you so far. Ultimate reality, which includes fantasy and romance and a great many other things as well, is something which is verbal. The structural principles of literature are myth and metaphor, and both of these violate the rules of common sense and logic. A myth, by which I mean the Greek word *mythos*—plot or narrative—is a story which in literature says explicitly, "This is what is happening," and implicitly, "This is what is not happening at all." You have to swallow both statements before you can read a novel. A metaphor says, "This *is* that," or, if you look at Jacob's prophecy in the Book of Genesis, "Joseph is a fruitful bough," "Napthali is a hind let loose," "Issacar is a strong ass," and so forth. The metaphor similarly conveys the explicit statement "A *is* B," and also implicitly the statement "Nobody but a fool would really imagine that A was B."

That is partly what I mean by saying that the arts form a kind of counterenvironment, setting something up which is really antipathetic to the civilization in which it exists. I said that reality is a much more inclusive term in literature than realism is. It seems to me that at a certain point of intensity what literature conveys is the sense of a controlled hallucination. That is, in literature things are not really seen until they become not actual hallucinations, because that would merely substitute a subjective experience for an objective one, but a controlled hallucination, where things are seen with a kind of intensity with which they are not seen in ordinary experience.

I remember my mother telling me of undergoing a very serious illness after the birth of my sister, and in the course of the illness she became delirious. Her father, who was a Methodist clergyman, came along with the twenty-five volumes of Scott's Waverley novels and dropped them on her. By the time she had read her way through them she was all right again. What impressed me about that was her own conviction that the Scott novels were in fact the curative agent. While I suppose any kind of new and absorbing interest might have been equally beneficial, still I've read most of those novels myself and would not be at all surprised if the plots of Scott's novels did not form a kind of counter-delirium which had to do with her own recovery.

Certainly one can find in the whole therapeutic area of the arts many ways that the best words in the best order, which is somebody's definition of poetry, can act in a physical way. Many years ago, when I found myself teaching Milton's *Paradise Lost* with considerable intensity, I discovered that his tremendous lines tended to detach themselves from their context and become individual beings chasing themselves around inside my head. On one occasion when I was very tired and still could not get to sleep, I examined the contents of my brain, so far as I could, and I found there the line from Book X describing the building of the bridge over Chaos to Hell: "Disparted Chaos overbuilt exclaimed." I thought to myself, well, nobody can sleep with a line like that chewing away in the back of his skull, so I concentrated on the line about the planets from Book VIII, "With inoffensive pace that spinning sleeps," and was asleep in no time.

I am not suggesting, or at least not yet suggesting, that literature ought to be read under medical supervision. What I am suggesting is that we should not overlook the immense recuperative power that literature, along with the other arts, could provide in a world as crazy as ours. Poets themselves often do not realize their own potentiality in this regard. I think filmmakers, of all the producers of art, have perhaps the clearest and most consistent notion of it. But in an age when there is such a vogue for forms of meditation and psychosynthesis and the like, it is just barely possible that literature might be what all the great poets have invariably said that it was, that is, a means of concentrating and intensifying the mind and of bringing it into a state of energy, which is the basis of all health.

II

Repetitions of Jacob's Dream

What immediately attracted me about this impressive exhibition [at the National Gallery, Ottawa] was its inspired choice of title, "Ladders to Heaven," and I thought that that would be an appropriate subject for me. As a literary critic, I have a particular interest in images and symbols that are found all over the world from ancient times to the present day, and the ladder, with its various relatives, is one of those images. The primary reference in this particular use of "ladders to heaven" is to Jacob's dream in the Book of Genesis. This story tells us that Jacob came to a place called Luz and lay down to sleep there with his head resting on a stone. (If we are to believe tradition, the stone still lies under the throne at Westminster.) In his sleep he had a vision of a ladder, as it is called in the Authorized Version, stretching from earth to heaven, with angels ascending and descending on it. When he awoke in the morning, he said, according to the same translation, "How dreadful is this place!" He meant, of course, how holy is this place, as the idea of the holy originates in a sense of awe or dread. Jacob called the place of his dream the house of God and the gate of heaven, and he vowed to build an altar there. But he also changed its name from Luz to Bethel, meaning house of God.

Several things about this story strike us at once. First, the antecedents of such a story would most naturally relate to a pre-Israelite sacred site, featuring either a sacred stone or a group of stones. In this earlier version the stone would probably have been much larger, perhaps part of a megalithic monument of a type still found in that part of the world and elsewhere. Second, the ladder that Jacob saw in his dream was a ladder *from* heaven rather than to it: it was not a human construction at all. Third, if the angels were going both up and down on it, it was clearly more of a staircase than a ladder. Finally, although Jacob calls the place the house of God, he does not build a temple there, merely an altar. The ladder is a symbol of a connection between earth and heaven, but the story emphasizes that the real connection is made only by God, and the human response to it is a correspondingly modest one.

So the story, as it reaches us, is the acceptable version, as the Bible sees it, of an image found in all the ancient religions of the Near East. In Mesopotamian cities the temple to the god of the city would normally be in the center and be the highest building: it would therefore be, symbolically, the connecting link between the earth we live on and the world of the gods, which is almost invariably assumed to be "up there," metaphorically, at least, in the sky. In Mesopotamia such temples took the form of what is known as a ziggurat, a building of several stories, usually seven, with each story recessed from the one below it. The different stories were also connected by stairs, usually winding stairs, so that the ascent was in a spiral. There were winding stairs in Solomon's temple, even though it was only three stories high. Herodotus tells us of more elaborate temples in Persia, where there were also seven stories and seven flights of steps, colored differently to symbolize the seven known planets, including the sun and moon. At the top was the chamber in which the bride of the god was laid, awaiting his descent. The story of Danae, shut up in a tower but impregnated all the same by Zeus in the form of a shower of gold, seems connected with the same pattern.

In Egypt the step pyramids had a similar symbolic reference, and in the Pyramid Texts the ascent of a stairway was a crucial stage in the Pharaoh's journey after death to the realm of the gods. In mounting a ladder it is, of course, the last step which is the supremely important one, and we are reminded of this by the Greek word for ladder, *klimax*, which has become our word *climax*. The judge of the dead in Egypt was the god Osiris, and one of the earliest epithets for him was "the god at the top of the staircase." In these so-called "heathen" countries, we notice, the emphasis is on the human construct: man builds the temple, or tower, in the form of something that points to heaven and suggests a final entry into it. This is the emphasis that is ridiculed in another story in the Book of Genesis, the story of the Tower of Babel, whose builders thought to reach heaven but had to abandon their project when their speech was broken into different languages. The Book of Genesis derives the word *Babel* from *balal*, confusion, but Babel actually means what Jacob called the place of his vision, the gate of God.

Neither Babel nor the stairway seen at Bethel are explicitly said to be spiral, but that is how they appear in Brueghel's painting of Babel and Blake's of Jacob's dream. So here we have a cluster of images, ladders, towers, winding or spiral stairs, all with the general symbolic sense of reaching a higher state of existence than the ordinary one. The earth we live on has always been thought of mythologically as "middle earth," with a world above it and another below it. Sometimes the building or tower becomes a mountain, and sometimes it is a tree, the world tree which is also the *axis mundi*, the vertical connection of the three worlds around which the universe revolves.

It seems obvious that the very widespread, almost universal, images of ladders and stairs and mountains and trees owe their existence to the fact that man cannot fly and cannot think of any way to raise himself, physically or metaphorically, in space except by climbing. Some people tell us that the ancient Near East preserved a race memory of visitors from other planets who could blast off in rocket ships: if so, it seems a rather lame conclusion to come down to so homely an image as climbing a tree or ladder, or even a mountain. However, if Herodotus is right, and towers in Persia were equipped with winding stairs painted in different colors to represent the planets, then the planets themselves could be symbolically a stairway to heaven. This seems to have been an important element in the symbolism of Mithraism, the Persian sun-cult that was a rival of early Christianity. In Mithraism there were seven degrees of ascent after death associated with the planets. This association, we are told, was so deeply rooted that Mithraism, if it had won out over Christianity, would have found it difficult to survive the Copernican revolution in astronomy. In Dante the same symbolic cluster is picked up again. Purgatory is a seven-story mountain, and as the redeemed soul climbs it he finds one of the seven deadly sins disappearing at each turn round the mountain, until he stands at the top in the Garden of Eden, where mankind should have been all along. There Dante meets a maid called Matilda, and there Virgil ceases to be his guide and Beatrice takes over. The female elements in the imagery indicate the symbolic descent of the theme from the bride of the god at the top of the tower.

In Dante there follows a second climb through the planetary spheres in the *Paradiso*. In the last of these spheres, that of Saturn, we see Jacob's ladder again, symbolizing the remainder of Dante's journey from the manifest spheres of the redeemed into the heart of the eternal light. Dante's poem being Christian, Dante's ascent is not directed by his own will, but by the divine grace manifested in Beatrice. In Milton the emphasis on divine initiative is even stronger. In the third book of *Paradise Lost* we encounter the "paradise of fools" on the smooth surface of the *primum mobile*, or circumference of the universe, where those arrive who have tried to take the kingdom of heaven by force or fraud. A reference to the Tower of Babel precedes this description and indicates its archetype. There follows a vision of stairs descending from heaven to earth, which, Milton tells us, were "such as whereon Jacob saw" the angels of his vision. These stairs are let down from heaven and drawn up again at the pleasure of God: Satan, on his journey to Eden, arrives at a "lower" stair, from which he descends to earth by way of the planets.

Dante and Milton are following the religious tradition that starts from Jacob's ladder, where there can be no connection between heaven and earth except through divine power. The cause of the divine action is love, in the sense of *agape*, God's love for man which is reflected in man's love for God and for his neighbor, and which the 1611 Bible calls charity (from the Latin *caritas* which translates *agape* in the Vulgate). The story of Babel, we said, was a parody of the human arrogance that tries to reverse the procedure by building a tower to reach heaven. This story is most unlikely to be a fair presentation of Mesopotamian or Egyptian religious attitudes, but there are widespread folktales that associate the attempt to build a ladder to heaven with futility. One such tale is current among British Columbia Indian tribes, where there is an original war between the Sky People and the Earth People, the latter being apparently animals. One animal or bird, generally the wren, shoots an arrow into the moon; another shoots a second arrow that hits the notch of its predecessor, and so on until there is a complete ladder of arrows from earth to sky. Then the animals climb up, until the grizzly bear breaks the ladder by his weight.

In other versions, however, the ladder remains in good shape: I am simply concerned to show that there are both ideal and ironic aspects of the theme. The classical counterpart of the ironic version is the story of the revolt of the Titans, the sons of earth who piled mountains on top of each other to reach their enemy in the sky. One is reminded also of Blake's series of drawings called (in the later version) *The Gates of Paradise*. One of these drawings has the caption "I want! I want!", and shows a young man starting to climb a ladder leaned against the moon. There is a young couple making a gesture toward him, but he ignores them, no doubt in the spirit of Longfellow's mountain-climbing hero, muttering "excelsior" when invited to sleep with an Alpine maiden. There is an ominous bend in the ladder, however, and we are not surprised to find that the next picture, with the caption "Help! Help!", shows him fallen into the sea, like his prototype Icarus.

The starting point of a more secular conception of a ladder from earth to heaven that is at least partly the result of human effort is in Plato's *Symposium*, where we are told how the power of Eros, a human love and energy with its roots in the sexual instinct, raises the lover from the attractiveness of a beautiful body up, step by step, to identification with the Form or Idea of Beauty itself. From Plato there descended a mixed tradition. Some of it was mystical: mystics seem by temperament attracted to ladders and images of climbing by degrees, with or without benefit from Plato. John Hilton's *Ladder of Perfection* is a fifteenth-century English example. The revival of Platonic studies in the Renaissance renewed the emphasis on a secular ladder of love that was planted in human sexuality and took its way to a sublimated but still thoroughly secular goal. In Castiglione's sixteenth-century dialogue *The Courtier*, a panegyric of ladder-climbing love of this kind is pronounced at the end, as a climax to its theme, the education of the ideal courtier, by Cardinal Bembo, to give him his later title.

The imagery seems to have lost nothing of its vitality even in the twentieth century. About fifty years ago the leading writers included T. S. Eliot, W. B. Yeats, Ezra Pound, and James Joyce. In Eliot's early poems there is a curiously urgent emphasis on the highest step of a staircase, where Prufrock and the narrator of "Portrait of a Lady" think of turning back, and where the girl in "La Figlia che Piange," standing "on the highest pavement of the stair," haunts her deserting lover for the rest of his life. In *Ash-Wednesday* Eliot joins the Christian tradition of ladders and follows Dante's *Purgatorio* in placing a winding stair at the center of his poem. In the Quartets there is a great variety of such images, some derived from the Spanish mystic St. John of the Cross, whose *Ascent to Mount Carmel* is one of the best known mystical climbs.

At the time of *Ash-Wednesday*, around 1930, Yeats was publishing books of poetry with such titles as *The Tower* (1928) and *The Winding Stair* (1933) and searching for spirals and gyres in every aspect of experience. In contrast to Eliot, Yeats's imagery is Platonic rather than Christian, at any rate for him, as he says, all ladders are planted in "the foul rag-and-bone shop of the heart." Yeats even went to the length of buying a round tower with a spiral staircase in Ireland, though he did not spend much time living in it. Ezra Pound went directly back to Herodotus and his account of seven planetary staircases in Ecbatana and elsewhere, and he adopted a similar strategy for his own ambitions in *The Cantos*. Even the Pisan Cantos, written out of the terrible experience of being confined in a cage after the war, begin with the still unshaken resolution "To build the city of Dioce whose terraces are the colour of stars." In the fourth Canto he speaks of Danae, the bride of the sky-god placed on the top of the tower, and he follows this immediately with a description of a medieval painting of the Virgin Mary, "the madonna in hortulo" who has a corresponding place in Christian imagery.

James Joyce built his last and most elaborate work on the Irish ballad of Finnegan, the hod-carrier who fell from the top of the ladder, an event Joyce associates with the fall of man on his first page. In the ballad he comes to life at his own wake, demanding a share of the whisky; in Joyce he is persuaded to go back to death by twelve mourners representing the cycle of the Zodiac. His death then modulates into the sleep of his successor HCE, whose cyclical and repetitive dream is human history as we know it. In Joyce we become aware of another aspect of the imagery of ladders and their relatives: it is a vertical movement in direct contrast to images of the turning cycle of nature, where winter is followed by spring and then winter again, darkness by dawn and renewed light, life by death and reborn life.

The Latin word for ladder is *scala*, and that word extends the image of the ladder to the "scale," or measurement by degrees, which is so fundamental in scientific work and in some of the arts as well, notably music. The scale also forms the basis of one of the most persistent conceptions in the history of thought. It is expressed by no one more clearly than by Sir Thomas Browne in *Religio Medici* (1643):

> ... there is in this Universe a Stair, or manifest Scale of creatures, rising not disorderly, or in confusion, but with a comely method and proportion. Between creatures of mere existence, and things of life, there is a large disproportion of nature; between plants, and animals or creatures of sense, a wider difference; between them and Man, a far greater: and if the proportion hold on, between Man and Angels there should be yet greater.

This is the conception of the whole of creation as forming a great chain of being, stretching from God himself at the top to chaos at the bottom. The chain is polarized by the conception of form and matter: God is pure form without matter, and chaos, where the four principles of substance, hot, cold, moist, and dry, keep combining and recombining by chance, is as close as we can get to pure matter without form. Above chaos was the mineral world, which has no life but nonetheless exhibits a hierarchy, with the "noble" metals, gold, silver, mercury, at the top and what we still call the "base metals," tin and lead, directly under them. Above this was the vegetative world, above it the animal world, and above the animals was man, who, being half formal and half material, was exactly in the middle of the chain, the microcosm or epitome of the whole of being. Between man and God was the spiritual world peopled by angels. That curious half-Christian, half-Platonic speculator called the pseudo-Dionysius (he took his name from a convert of Paul mentioned in the New Testament) gave us a table of nine orders of angels, merely for the sake, apparently, of setting up a hierarchy of degrees in an unknown area of being.

This chain or scale or ladder of being was a structure of authority in which all the initiative came down from the top. Without the hierarchy imposed by the ladder, everything would dissolve in chaos. Hence it is necessary for human society to preserve the same kind of scale, or it too will fall into anarchy and savagery. So at least we are solemnly assured in an eloquent speech by Ulysses in Shakespeare's play about the Trojan war, *Troilus and Cressida*, even though Ulysses' motives in making the speech are concerned with the best means of bringing anarchy and savagery to the city of Troy. The cosmic imagery is derived from a social structure. In medieval times the cosmos was reflected in the feudal principle of protection from above and obedience from below, and in Tudor times it was reflected in the authority of the ruler as it filtered down through the courts, legal and secular, to the common people. In the masques of Ben Jonson and others that were acted before King James, we usually move from a vision of a disorderly rabble in the antimasque up through various allegorical levels to the final compliments to the king or queen or whoever was the guest of honor in the audience and the representative of the climax of the ladder. For while ladders and staircases may not appear in the stage scenery of the masque, their invisible presence is everywhere.

Everything in the scale of being has its natural place, or what Chaucer calls its "kindly stead." A heavy object held in the air and released will drop, because it is seeking its natural place in the sphere of earth. Bubbles of air rise in water because they are seeking their own sphere of air, which is above water. Man is an exception: because of the fall of Adam, he is born in a lower state of existence than he was intended to live in, and the order of nature around him, the world of animals and plants, is more alienated from him than it was in the Garden of Eden. Man's primary duty is to regain as much as he can of his original state: the Garden of Eden is gone as a place, but can be regained only as a state of mind. Many things are natural for man that are not natural anywhere else in nature, such as wearing clothes: man belongs in a sphere of nature peculiar to himself, a sphere higher than physical nature. Law, morality, the sacraments of religion, everything that is genuinely educational, will help him rise to his appropriate place in the scene of things. This does not affect his place in human society: it is also natural to man to live in a structured social order, and he can only fulfill his true human destiny of reaching his cosmic natural place by staying in the social place he was born in. To rise above one's station is rebellion; to fall from it is delinquency.

This particular ladder is an expression of authority, as enforced by both church and state, and in many respects it is a most transparent rationalizing of such authority. Because it was an expression of authority, it lasted far longer than it should have done, but even so, by the end of the eighteenth century, with American and French and Industrial revolutions recent or imminent, it was beginning to look like a rather shaky means of ascent to a higher world. From Rousseau on, man is increasingly thought of as a child of nature rather than as a fallen child of God, and more and more emphasis comes to be put on human effort, human rights, human capacities. For Milton, a seventeenth-century revolutionary, liberty is good for man because God wants him to have it: left to himself, man not only cannot achieve liberty, he cannot even desire it. For Byron and Shelley the desire for liberty awakens in the human heart, is justified as a human need and a human right, and will probably involve conflict with the ghosts of old gods who are projections of human tyranny.

If we are looking for a literary work to represent the staircase of being and the human ascent to its proper place in the cosmic order, we shall find it in Dante's *Purgatorio*. The mountain of purgatory has its base on the surface of this earth, though on the other side of what Dante knew to be a sphere. At the top of this mountain is the Garden of Eden, the original home of man, where the soul recovers its original freedom of will and becomes it own pope and emperor. This purgatorial ascent completes the essential pilgrimage of humanity, but even for a saint this pilgrimage needs an extension into an after-death world to be completed.

After the authoritarian construct of the chain of being had collapsed, we should expect another construct of a revolutionary shape, based on human powers and capacities: in short, a successfully completed Tower of Babel. I do not know a work of literature that meets this formidable challenge, but there is one in philosophy, Hegel's *Phenomenology of Spirit*, which, however conservative in itself, has been the basis of revolutionary programs of thought ever since. In this book we begin with ordinary sense experience, trying to connect subject with object, and find that a progressively larger series of structures begins to form, each implying its own negation and expanding beyond its predecessor by swallowing its negation. After the Spirit has eaten all its negations, it becomes absolute knowledge and enters the world of infinite spirit. What is remarkable about this book, from my point of view, is that while the language throughout is strictly philosophical, there is an unconscious (or at any rate unformulated) metaphor of a spiralling stairway that gives narrative shape to the entire argument.

So far we have been taking our ladders and staircases as spatial metaphors, leading to a world above which is thought of as "there," present as though in space. Descending stairways to a lower world are less frequent: Dante's hell is, like his purgatory, a cone that Dante traverses from base to apex, going down toward the center of the earth, but this is an example of the way in which journeys to a lower world have become associated with the demonic. Usually a downward spiralling movement takes the form of a whirlpool, or maelstrom of death. In Shelley's *Prometheus Unbound*, as in other Romantic works, everything that makes for the greater glory of man comes from below, and the heroine Asia descends to the cave of Demogorgon in search of the Titan who eventually moves into the sky and pushes the tyrant sky-god Jupiter off his throne. But we are not told how she gets down there.

In any case, when it becomes too obvious that something does not exist, it begins to lose its appeal even in literature, where its existence ordinarily does not matter. In the nineteenth century Rider

Haggard and others wrote romances about lost cities and kingdoms in the heart of Africa or Asia. Contemporary romancers use the same themes, but in the age of the helicopter they have to put their lost kingdoms somewhere in outer space to make them rhetorically convincing. With a similar loss in credibility in worlds up or down "there," ladders and stairways have to shift from metaphorical space to metaphorical time.

During the centuries when the education of man was thought of as, in Milton's words, an attempt to repair the ruin of our first parents, the ladder of improvement was connected with a paradise lost in the past. In Dante's *Purgatorio* Dante is, among other things, climbing back to his original state of childhood, not his individual childhood, but his generic childhood as a descendant of an unfallen Adam. His climb up the mountain is therefore in one sense a moving backward in time, as he loses one by one the sins which he has accumulated in its forward movement on the other side of the world. Similarly, both the Renaissance and the Reformation were inspired by what is now called a pastoral myth, a belief that there was a state of things in the past which has been lost and must be climbed back to. With the Renaissance this was the Augustan age of first-rate Latin; with the Reformation it was the assumed purity of the early generations of Christianity; but the underlying figure was much the same.

The early twentieth century grew up with the figure implanted in its consciousness of a ladder of time projected into the future. This was suggested, of course, by the biological conception of evolution. Here we learn how the dinosaurs disappeared because they could not meet nature's preference of brains to brawn, after which there was a stairway of humanoids, those on the lower steps shambling and stumbling with their heads bent, those on the higher steps (us) walking erect and clear-eyed and holding their paunches in. The much-slandered Neanderthal man was supposed to be our immediate predecessor on this ascending scale of being. It is obvious that we are not dealing here with evolution or any other scientific conception: this is pure mythology, a product of human concern, where any evidence that does not fit must be squeezed until it does.

In history this mythical analogy of evolution took the form of a doctrine of progress, which has been a most versatile muddler of minds ever since. In my student days it was very generally accepted that socialism, whether of the type envisaged by Marx or by gradualists, represented a higher state of social evolution than capitalism, and that it was the duty of all right-thinking people to help in the general move to the next upward step. However, Communism established itself in largely preindustrial societies, and Communism and capitalism settled down to an adversary relationship. Each "system," as it is called, has improved itself slightly by borrowing from its rival, but of general evolutionary advance there is no sign. That staircase, like Jacob's, is an impressive dream structure, but will not bear any tangible weight.

One of the morals of this talk should have emerged by now: metaphors and diagrams and figures like the ladder underlie all our verbal constructs, those of philosophy and political theory no less than those of literature. And while many metaphorical pictures of reality can be very misleading, still the solid bedrock of metaphor will remain, as something we cannot do without. There *is* a "higher" form of existence, and there *are* ladders and staircases leading to it, however wrong our efforts to locate it in time or space may be. The difficulties begin with *projecting* the metaphor: the first step on the real ladder to a higher existence is the employing of metaphor itself.

In verbal metaphor we usually formulate a phrase of the "this is that" type, asserting that two quite different things are in fact identical. A biblical example would be Jacob's prophecy of the twelve tribes in Genesis 49: "Joseph is a fruitful bough," "Naphtali is a hind let loose," "Issachar is a strong ass," and the like. If we ask what is the point of saying that A is B when A is so obviously not B, the answer is that metaphor is not a matter of asserting identities by over-strained analogies. It is rather an effort to extend our own being into the external world, to break down the wall between subject and object and start currents of verbal energy flowing between them. If we apply this principle of metaphor, which is verbal, to the pictorial arts, we can perhaps see what is involved more clearly. In Paleolithic times the liveliest and most spirited paintings of animals were made in caves under incredibly difficult conditions of position and lighting. Doubtless there was some aesthetic motive at work, some desire to create a work of beauty, but this would be hopelessly inadequate to account for painting in such conditions. We can add such words as "religion" and "magic," but the fact remains that the complexity, urgency, and sheer titanic power of the motivation involved is something we cannot understand now, much less recapture.

The nearest we can come to putting such motivation into words, I think, is to say that the bisons and bears portrayed in those far-off times were a kind of extension of human consciousness and power into the objects of greatest energy and strength they could see in the world around them. This is the real function of what appears in words as metaphor: the assimilating of the energy, the beauty, the elusive glory, latent in nature to the observing mind. I speak of "the mind" as though it were the mind of a separated individual, but of course the community out of which the individual artist emerges guides his hand and controls his speech.

The purest form of metaphor is the god, who is an identity of some kind of personality or consciousness and some aspect of the natural world, as with the sea-god or sky-god or love-goddess. The descent of the god from the animal, recalling a time when man did not think of himself as the lord of creation, but saw in birds and animals powers and abilities he did not himself possess, is clear enough. All the Near Eastern cultures display gods in animal form, and in such myths as Zeus courting Europa in the form of a bull we can see that the same line of descent existed in Greece. Even without any explicit identification with a god, we can see the imaginative assimilation of the animal world in this exhibition, from a powerful early Mesopotamian bull to a delicate mosaic peacock of the Coptic period.

Then again, in the cave drawings we see animal forms with human eyes looking through them, and suspect that we are really seeing a sorcerer or shaman who has identified himself with the animal by putting on its skin. We also see "fish priests" and the like in this exhibition, and in some of the female fetishes, giving great prominence to the sexual organs but having no face, we can see how the primary aim is an identification with power or vitality or fertility rather than a sense of beauty. An aesthetic sense marks a more sophisticated development, because it tends to increase the distance between the object portrayed and the subject regarding it.

Archaeology is a science in which we dig underground, using steps and descending ladders as we go, to find what remains of civilizations that at one time towered high in the air. The theme of underground treasure is one of the most reliable formulas of romance, and in the early days of digging, say with Schliemann at Troy, there was still something of extracting buried treasure about the enterprise. There have been, of course, many dramatic discoveries, like Tutankhamen's tomb or the great man-bull sculptures at Nineveh now in the Louvre. But for archaeologists now the motive of treasure-hunt is a very minor one, yet two levels of their work emerge clearly. So far as they clarify our historical knowledge of the ancient world, they show us competing empires that fought and killed, laid land waste, enslaved whole peoples, and recorded their hideous exploits in paranoid inscriptions. Among these exploits were vainglorious monuments of the type ridiculed in the Babel story, and, much nearer our own time, in Shelley's famous sonnet about Ozymandias, the "king of kings" whose works were the despair of his rivals, but cause no despair now except in those who are trying to find what is left of them. Knowledge of such enterprises extends, without much expanding, our general knowledge of human behavior.

But archaeology also recovers, in the course of its work, objects of great beauty and power, and we realize that above ordinary history there has been a continuous level of craftsmanship, skill, and creative insight. The artifacts of a vanished civilization were produced in the normal climate of human cruelty and folly, but they themselves are in an unchanging state of innocence. They are what we still want to see, and we can take pleasure in them while abstracting their social context from them. Here is a real ladder to heaven, or at least to a paradisal world of beauty and keen intelligence, one that can be constructed only by the creative imagination, the one power that has been able to drive humanity beyond the needs of mere survival into a more abundant life.

Returning finally to Jacob's dream, we note that while its origin was in heaven, angels were ascending as well as descending on it. If we take angels to be instruments of communication between the divine and the human, perhaps the implication is that divine and human activities in creation are not so far apart after all, and that even in a contemporary high-rise city we can still see, with the late Victorian poet Francis Thompson, "the traffic of Jacob's ladder / Pitched between Heaven and Charing Cross."

The Bride from the Strange Land

The Book of Ruth, as we all know, is one of the five short books called "rolls" (*megilloth*) among the Writings which have acquired a specific liturgical importance. It is a rather striking fact that, of these five "rolls," three are narratives centered on female figures. The story of the book is familiar, but needs to be summarized again for clarity.

Naomi is the widow of a Bethlehemite named Elimelech, who had moved into Moab during a famine in Judea, much as the family of Israel had moved into Egypt for a similar reason centuries earlier. He and the two sons Naomi had borne to him all died, leaving her with two Moabite daughters-in-law, both childless. In so patriarchal a society Naomi feels that she is under something of a curse, and she returns forlornly from Moab to Bethlehem to live out the rest of her blighted life. Her Moabite daughters-in-law, Ruth and Orpah, accompany her to the border of Moab, where she tries to persuade them to go back to their own land. She tells them that she is too old to produce more male children herself, and that even if she did it would be twenty years before they were marriageable, by which time their prospective brides would be twenty years older also. Orpah finds this argument conclusive and returns to Moab; Ruth, in the most famous scene of the book, states her resolution to proceed with Naomi to Bethlehem. It has been well observed that for a young foreign widow to identify her fortunes with those of an older woman, also a widow with no prospects, in such a society was an act of almost incredible courage and loyalty.

Back in the Bethlehem country, Ruth finds herself, by one of those accidents which are clearly not quite accidents, gleaning in the field of Boaz, a kinsman of her late father-in-law. It is the harvest season, when the destitute were allowed to glean in the fields after the reapers had passed through. Boaz's attention proves very easy to catch, and, following Naomi's advice, Ruth soon puts him in the position of wanting to marry her. They are married, and a son is born to them named Obed, who was the grandfather of King David.

Stories about women in the Bible fall into a very few well-marked categories, and there are, I think, three narrative themes that converge on the story of Ruth and Naomi. The first of these themes is that of levirate marriage, where a surviving brother-in-law or other near kinsman of a childless widow is obliged to do his best to provide her with children, preferably, of course, male children. Deuteronomy 25:5-6 says:

> *When brothers live together and one of them dies without leaving a son, his widow shall not marry outside the family. Her husband's brother shall have intercourse with her; he shall take her in marriage and do his duty by her as her husband's brother. The first son she bears shall perpetuate the dead brother's name.*

The best known story of this type in the Bible is the story of Tamar in Genesis 38. Tamar was the wife of Judah's son Er, and therefore Judah's daughter-in-law. Er was a bad man and the Lord took his life: Tamar was, according to the levirate custom, transferred to his younger brother Onan, who greatly resented and resisted the whole procedure. As God approved of it, he lost his life also. There was a third brother, still a boy, and Judah proposed that Tamar remain in the house until he had grown up. But the third brother was not assigned to Tamar, so Tamar disguised herself as a prostitute and put herself in the way of Judah, who got her pregnant. Hearing that Tamar had been acting like a prostitute, Judah said, with the casual ferocity of the age, "Let her be burnt." But Tamar produced the tokens he had given her, and he acknowledged that she was right, because the third brother had been denied her. Of the twin sons she had by Judah, one, Perez, was in the direct line of ancestry to David.

Ruth is also a childless widow, but no brothers are involved, and any claim on relatives of her late husband can hardly have been a legal claim, in view of her Moabite nationality. But Boaz is too strongly attracted to her for that to be an obstacle, and he is very willing to take on the levirate obligation, except that he feels that as there is one still nearer kinsman, the latter should have first choice. The other kinsman, who is not named, resigns in favor of Boaz, and the way is cleared for Ruth's marriage. Boaz's motive in approaching this kinsman was perhaps to establish Ruth's status as an Israelite widow instead of leaving her simply a destitute foreigner he had taken a fancy to. The relevance of all this to the custom illustrated by the Tamar story is made clear by the elders of Bethlehem, who say when the marriage is decided on: "May your house be like the house of Perez, whom Tamar bore to Judah" (4:12).

The second story-type is that of the son who is born to a woman past the age of childbearing, so that the birth is a direct manifestation of divine favor. The best known story of this type is the birth of Isaac to Sarah at an impossibly late age. Because Sarah laughed at the prospect of bearing another child, the infant was given a name suggesting "laughter" by a slightly miffed deity. There are several other women who bear children after a long period of barrenness, including Rachel and Hannah, the mother of Samuel. When Samuel is born, Hannah sings a triumphant song in praise of a God who can bring down the great people and raise up the small ones at pleasure. The same themes recur in the New Testament. John the Baptist is born to his mother Elizabeth at a late age, his father Zechariah being struck with a temporary dumbness because of his disbelief. The conception of Jesus by Mary is equally miraculous, though not for the same reason, and Mary's song of triumph, known as the Magnificat, is modelled on the song of Hannah and makes the same point about God's power to reverse ordinary social standards.

In the Book of Ruth this theme of late birth is associated not with Ruth, who is still a young woman, but with her mother-in-law Naomi. After the birth of Obed, Naomi becomes the infant's nurse, and the neighbors offer their congratulations in a very abrupt phrase: "Naomi has a son" (4:12). The identities of Ruth and Naomi are curiously confused in the final chapter, perhaps reflecting an earlier version of the story in which Ruth did not appear at all. In any case the story of Ruth is also a story about the filling, emptying, and refilling of the life of Naomi, for whom Ruth acts as a proxy.

The theme of late birth is connected with another frequent theme in the Bible: the passing over of the eldest son, who inherits by primogeniture but does something to forfeit his inheritance. A son born late would be either an only or a younger son. Thus Ishmael is passed over in favor of Isaac, Esau for Jacob, Reuben for Judah and Joseph, Manasseh for Ephraim, and, in a very slight extension of the theme, Saul, the first king of Israel, for David, who becomes Saul's son-in-law and also survives Saul's son and heir Jonathan. The deliberate choice of a younger son symbolizes a divine intervention into the normal pattern of human affairs, and makes appropriate the theme of God creating revolutions in society, bringing down the great and raising the humble, which we find in both Hannah's song and the Magnificat. It was this aspect of the story of Ruth that impressed Josephus, who gives a rather arid summary of it, clearly regarding it as an interruption of his narrative, and then says (V, ix, 4): "I was therefore obliged to relate the history of Ruth, because I had a mind to demonstrate the power of God, who, without difficulty, can raise those that are of ordinary parentage to dignity and splendor, to which he advanced David, though he were born of such mean parents."

We can also see a more tenuous resemblance between the story of Ruth and many folktales and legends scattered over the world, of the type familiar in the story of Cinderella, in which a young woman who seems to have every kind of social handicap nevertheless attracts the attention of a man much higher in rank, and eventually marries him. Cinderella had a fairy godmother: Ruth has what is usually a more effective ally in this world, a cooperative mother-in-law. For thousands of years we have had stories of the type we frequently get in Shakespeare's comedies, where a clever and imaginative heroine, who knows what she wants but is not really unscrupulous about getting it, brings about a comic resolution that includes a successful marriage for herself. In the New Comedies of the Hellenistic period, some of which were adapted by Plautus and Terence, the heroine is a slave or prostitute, though really of more respectable parentage because stolen by pirates in infancy or the like. Ruth also begins operations on Boaz by saying, at least according to one reading, "treat me as one of your slave-girls" (2:13).

When Boaz lies down to sleep on the harvest field, somewhat drunk, and Ruth comes to him and asks him to spread his cloak over his "handmaid," it is clear that with a very slight change of tone we should have a rather cynical seduction story in which Boaz is, as we say, being set up. Needless to say, that is not the tone of the Book of Ruth, nor what happens in it. But the type of story being told is first cousin to seduction and bed trick tales like that of Jacob's first night with Leah. Keats, whom we shall mention again later, remarks in one of his letters that it is always a pleasure to rediscover the fact that Cleopatra was a gypsy, Helen a rogue, and Ruth a "deep one." A reference to Ruth in Joyce's *Finnegans Wake* (257) makes the same point much more broadly and includes an oblique allusion to Shakespeare: "You're well held now, Missy Cheekspear, and your panto's off! Fie, for shame, Ruth Wheatacre, after all the booz said!"

The third story-type to be linked with Ruth is the most controversial and complex one. This is the story of the bride from the strange land, which is illustrated perhaps most clearly in Psalm 45. This psalm seems to be a wedding song celebrating the marriage of a king of Israel and a bride who apparently comes from Tyre in Phoenicia. The bride is adjured to forget her religion and adopt that of her new home, but there is no suggestion that there is anything wrong with the marriage itself. In history, however, the most notable marriage between an Israelite king and a Canaanite princess was that of Ahab and Jezebel, which led to all kinds of disaster. Similarly, the Song of Songs seems to have connections with King Solomon and a Shulamite bride, and there are certainly affinities between Ruth and the black but comely bride who did not keep her own vineyard but went out to seek her beloved. But in the historical narrative we are told that Solomon's wives prompted him to build temples to foreign gods, including the god of Moab, on mountains facing the temple on Mount Moriah.

The return under Ezra and Nehemiah included stringent regulations preventing any Israelite from having any connection with "foreign" or "strange" women, however innocuous or non-existent their religious views. What connections had already been made were to be immediately dissolved. It has often been suggested that the Book of Ruth, along with the Book of Jonah, supports a more flexible and less racist attitude toward foreign women, in making the point that the great King David had a great-grandmother who was a Moabite. Whether the Book of Ruth is specifically aimed against the policy of Ezra and Nehemiah or not would depend on the date we assigned to it, and there is not much of a consensus among scholars about this, though a majority seem to favor a postexilic date. But however early we may consider the book to be, it can hardly be earlier than the commandment in Deuteronomy 23:3: "No Ammonite or Moabite, even down to the tenth generation, shall become a member of the assembly of the Lord." Again, there is a variant of the levirate-marriage story which takes the form of parody in Genesis 19, where Lot's two daughters, finding a shortage of eligible men in the country they had taken refuge in, make their father drunk and have intercourse with him. The two acts of incest produced the Moabites and the Ammonites.

As it is only from the Book of Ruth that we learn that David had a Moabite woman in his ancestry, it is difficult to avoid the conclusion that the book is making something of a political and religious point.

Ruth has no interest whatever in Moabite religion: she doesn't even have any "teraphim," like Rachel. She is therefore welcomed by Boaz in the spirit of the law forbidding the oppressing of strangers or widows (Exodus 22:21-22). Nothing could be more solidly Israelite than Leah and Rachel, yet they, as well as Tamar, are invoked by the witnesses of Ruth's marriage to Boaz: "May the Lord make this woman, who has come to your home, like Rachel and Leah, the two who built up the house of Israel" (4:11). Elsewhere we are told that David, when fleeing from Saul, took refuge in Moab and left his father and mother there (I Samuel 22:4), and that the mother of Rehoboam, Solomon's son and successor, was an Ammonite. Solomon himself, of course, was the son of Bathsheba, originally the wife of Uriah the Hittite, and therefore no doubt a Hittite herself, whatever that may mean in the way of "foreignness." In any case, there was ample precedent for marriage to "foreign" women, even if much of it is later than the period assigned to Ruth.

II

The Book of Ruth is practically ignored in the New Testament, but there is one curious puzzle in the latter which bears not only on the Book of Ruth but on this particular point of foreign marriage. The New Testament begins with Matthew's genealogy of Jesus, starting with Abraham and going down through David, Solomon, Zerubbabel and the rest. Luke has an even longer genealogy, though it differs from Matthew's, and he speaks only of fathers and sons. Matthew, however, seems to feel that women do somehow get involved with the genealogical process, and so includes five women in his list. The first is Tamar, whose relevance to the Ruth story we have mentioned. The third is Ruth herself, the only explicit reference to her or her book in the New Testament. The fourth is Bathsheba, mother of Solomon, and the fifth Mary, the mother of Jesus. It is the second name that is the puzzle: the mother of Boaz, whose name is given as Rahab.

The name of Boaz's mother does not occur anywhere else in the Bible, and where the compiler of Matthew got it remains a mystery. It is, of course, the same name as that of the celebrated harlot of Jericho, who is twice mentioned approvingly in the New Testament, as a pattern of faith in the Epistle to the Hebrews, as a pattern of good works in the Epistle of James. That Matthew could ever have believed this Rahab to be Boaz's mother, as many commentators assume, seems most unlikely. If in fact they were the same, Boaz's somewhat adventurous approach to the married state may have been inherited. It is true that the names of women often appear in the Bible by accident: we know the names of David's sisters, for example, but not that of his mother. But it is just barely conceivable that the name "Rahab" in this context means simply "foreign woman," as the same name is also attached in the Bible to Egypt, with overtones of the hostile or chaotic world outside Israel (cf. Psalm 87:4). So many of the women who are mentioned in the Bible, whether by name or not, were "foreign" in one way or another that they may have some kind of symbolic significance, as representing either the permeation of the outside world by Judaism or the corruption of Judaism, depending on the women and depending also on whether one takes the view of the Book of Ruth or the Book of Nehemiah.

In Blake's *Jerusalem*, Plate 62, there is a list of "foreign" women, including Ruth. In Blake's symbolism all human beings, men and women, are symbolically male, just as they are symbolically female in orthodox symbolism. What is female for Blake is Nature, and Nature has two aspects. As an order of existence controlled and regulated by the creative imagination, she is what Blake calls an "Emanation," Isaiah's "Beulah" or married land; as an objective otherness remaining aloof from humanity, she is what Blake calls a "Female Will." As the latter, she is still a product of the human imagination, but in a perverted and projected form. The foreign women in Blake's list symbolize this "Female Will": the only allusion to Ruth I have found that distorts her story by exaggerating the purely symbolic and typological side of it. Blake would have the same affection for Ruth, as a character in history or credible fiction, that nearly all her readers have, and he shows that in the fine painting of Ruth, Naomi, and Orpah which he included in his one exhibition.

Other literary references to the Book of Ruth are rare and curiously barren, though for all I know there may be hidden riches in the Bulgarian and Latvian poems mentioned in reference books. A devotional treatise called *Introduction au livre de Ruth* was written by a French abbé named Tardif de Moidrey in the nineteenth century, and was reprinted with a long (hundred-page) introduction by the poet Claudel in 1938. But neither the abbé nor Claudel really tells us much about the book. Dante places Ruth at the end of the *Paradiso* among women destined to be redeemed before the coming of Christ, along with Sarah, Rebecca, and others. But he does not mention her by name: he merely calls her the great-grandmother (*bissava*) of David—though David is not mentioned by name either, but is merely referred to as the author of the "Miserere" or Psalm 51, the one that was traditionally written by him after his sin in the matter of Uriah and Bathsheba. Milton adopts a different kind of typological reference, when he assures a "virtuous young lady," in a sonnet addressed to her, that "The better part with Mary and with Ruth / Chosen thou hast." In the house of Lazarus, where Martha was working in the household and her sister Mary was talking with Jesus, Mary was said by Jesus to have chosen "the better part." Later Christian typology identified these two "parts" with the active and the contemplative lives. The traditional Old Testament types of these were Leah and Rachel, who appear in this symbolic frame in Dante's *Purgatorio*. But of course, the more dramatic contrast in choice between Ruth and Orpah would also be available, and so Milton couples Mary with Ruth. I imagine, however, that Milton's real reason for referring to Ruth was that she provided a rhyme with "truth" and "youth." Again, Bunyan, in the second part of *The Pilgrim's Progress*, telling the story of Christian's wife leaving the City of Destruction to journey to the New Jerusalem, mentions the parallel with Ruth, mainly, one feels, because he could hardly have avoided it.

Ruth is a common name, and many literary uses of it, such as Wordsworth's poem "Ruth," do not relate to the biblical book. Neither does Mrs. Gaskell's Victorian novel *Ruth*, which is a straightforward honest story about what we should now call an unmarried mother, written by a clergyman's wife. Margaret Laurence, who is often quite specifically biblical in her allusions, has a Rachel and a Hagar who certainly reflect something of their biblical namesakes. But there seems to be no Ruth, nor do I think that the Naomi of Joy Kagawa's *Obasan* has biblical connections. Similarly even with works of biblical scholarship. The other day I picked up a volume of essays on literary aspects of the Bible, and found five references to Ruth in the index. Three of them, however, turned out to be the first names of contemporary women scholars—perhaps an example of the hazards involved in making an index by computer.

The finest literary treatment of the Ruth story I know is a poem by Victor Hugo called "Booz endormi," one of the *Légendes des siècles*. In an earlier autobiographical poem in *Les contemplations*, Hugo speaks of his affection for biblical stories, and mentions Ruth, Joseph, and the parable of the Good Samaritan in particular. The juxtaposing of Ruth and the Good Samaritan parable is interesting, as both make the same point: that there may be good people even among hostile or hated nations. There is, I understand, a haggadic tradition that Boaz was an old man of eighty when he met Ruth, and Hugo may have picked this up somewhere, as his Boaz is the same age. In Hugo the dream of Boaz is a wistful, lonely reverie that culminates in a prophetic vision of what is more frequently called the tree of Jesse, the ancestral line stretching from David's father to Jesus, which is the basis of a superb stained-glass window design in Chartres Cathedral.

In English literature the best known allusion to Ruth is in Keats's "Ode to a Nightingale," where the poet says that the nightingale's song may have pierced "Through the sad heart of Ruth, when, sick for home, / She stood in tears amid the alien corn." It is a beautiful but curious reference: as we saw, Keats certainly knew the Book of Ruth, but there is no hint in it that Ruth was ever homesick for Moab or that she regarded the corn fields around her as in any sense alien: after all, her late father-in-law still owned some of them. The tendency to sentimentalize the story recurs in a sonnet by Christina Rossetti, called "Autumn Violets," which has as its last line "A grateful Ruth tho' gleaning scanty corn." This is not, it is true, a direct reference to the biblical book, but we may note that actually, thanks to Boaz's patronage, Ruth did fairly well out of her gleaning. I make these somewhat pedantic comments because I suspect that one reason for the comparative neglect of the Book of Ruth by later writers is the irrepressible cheerfulness of the story, which is all about completely normal people fully understanding one another, and leaves the literary imagination with very little to do. That said, we could justify the Keats allusion by observing that Ruth does not give the impression of being merely a mindless puppet of Providence, and may well have had darker and deeper feelings than the narrative presents.

III

The story of Ruth is so brief and unpretentious that many readers, following Goethe, simply mutter something about a "charming pastoral idyll" and pass on. But if we look at it with any attention its simplicity becomes very deceptive. Naomi is forced into exile by famine, brought to misery and sterility there, and finally makes her way back to her homeland and ends her life as a happy grandmother. Her lament, the only shadow on the general happiness of the story, where she remarks that her name should not be Naomi ("sweet") but Mara ("bitter"), recalls, on a small scale, some of the complaints of Job, and she uses also Job's favorite name for God, El Shaddai. The names of her deceased sons, Mahlon and Chilion ("weak" and "wasting"), seem clearly allegorical. The first chapter, again, rings the changes on the word *return* (*shub*), which is one of the central thematic words of the whole Bible. Obviously Naomi is returning to her original home in Judea; obviously Orpah is returning to her original home in Moab. What is Ruth doing? According to 1:22, "Ruth the Moabitess returned with her Naomi from the Moabite country." Ruth, then, has both a physical and a spiritual home, and she voluntarily chooses the latter. Hence, like the Israelites leaving Egypt for the Promised Land, she is returning to her appropriate place.

The sense of something providential taking charge of Ruth's life appears to Boaz's remark: "May the God of Israel, under whose wings you have come to take refuge, give you all you deserve" (2:12). Later, as we saw, when Boaz lies down to sleep on the harvest field, Ruth comes to him and asks him to spread the "skirts" of his cloak over his handmaid. The word translated "wings" and "skirt" is the same (*kanaph*). There are also repeated references to a grace or kindness (*chen, chesed*) coming to Ruth from God through Boaz. Boaz also becomes the *go'el* of Ruth, a most versatile word rendered in the 1611 translation of Job 19:25 as "redeemer." Boaz is the *go'el* (2:20) of Ruth in the sense of being the most likely person to become her levirate husband, and the *go'el* of Naomi in a more general sense (4:14). Words closely related to *go'el* and translated "redeem" in AV, keep echoing all through the business arrangements with the nearer kinsman (4:2 ff.). It is difficult not to see in the story an epitome or microcosm, in small but concentrated compass, of the entire story of exile, return, and redemption that the Bible is telling, of how those that sowed their seed in bitterness may return in joy, bringing their sheaves with them (Psalm 126).

The book ends with a list of David's ancestors back to Perez, which tells us nothing new and is generally assumed to be an editorial addition. The real question is what, if the addition were removed, would be the last verse of the book: was "Obed was the father of Jesse, the father of David" (4:17) part of the original story or not? If it was, it is clearly the climax to which the whole book is leading up: it indicates a motivation on the part of the writer which is not literary. The statement is given as a historical fact, and it is hard to see how the Book of Ruth could ever have got into the biblical canon if the statement had not been there or had not met with general acceptance. Many commentators are fond of saying that the book is purely literary, by which they generally mean that it is "merely" literary. But it is difficult to imagine the sort of cultural ambience out of which a "purely literary" story could arise in either pre- or postexilic Judea. Certainly the literary merits of the book are remarkable, but the skill with which the writer has encapsulated the entire narrative movement of the Bible in four brief chapters is something else again.

A late colleague of mine, Professor W. E. Staples, wrote an article on the Book of Ruth back in 1937, in which he suggested that it was a midrash on a fertility cult centered at Bethlehem. Staples was a student of S. H. Hooke, who in turn was a disciple of Robertson Smith and Frazer. Staples interprets the names in the book as cultic names: Elimelech, for example ("God is king"), becomes a Frazerian divine king. Naomi is a fertility goddess, and Ruth is related to her as Proserpine is to Demeter, another aspect of the same person. It is really Naomi who is "redeemed" by Boaz and bears the son, whose original name would have been something like "son of Naomi" and not Obed. In this suggestion Staples has been followed by others who also think that an earlier story has been adapted to fit into the genealogy of David. Bethlehem was an ancient cult-center, as its name ("house of bread") suggests, and we remember that St. Jerome, the Latin or Vulgate translator of the Bible in the fifth century, remarks that in Bethlehem there was a grove dedicated to Adonis even in his day. Staples's argument is usually mentioned by later scholars only to be dismissed, and it is of course true that such theses do not carry much conviction now. The main reason is that there is so little evidence for them beyond whatever suggestiveness may be inherent in some of the proper names. But I think that this way of reading the story deserves another look, even if we cannot buy the whole Frazer corn-spirit package. Writers of stories, however literary, do not invent their stories even when they think they do: they inherit them. There are always and invariably earlier versions of the general shape of their plots (*mythoi*), and these earlier versions go back to the most ancient myths we have. The Bible is comparatively a rather late product of Near Eastern culture, and we can often see in it adaptations of earlier mythical themes. Some stories, like those of Jacob's ladder-vision or Jephthah's daughter, give us faint glints of prebiblical cults. With others, like the deluge story, we can now compare Sumerian and other more ancient versions that clearly belong on the same genealogical tree, even if they are not in the direct line of ancestry. So I see no improbability of there being earlier versions of the Ruth story, perhaps centered on Bethlehem, that take us back to very primitive customs connected with harvesting and the myths attached to those customs.

It was inevitable that the Book of Ruth should become associated with the Feast of Weeks, because harvest symbolism and imagery saturate the whole story, especially the two middle chapters. There is no reference to the book in the three volumes of Frazer's *Folklore in the Old Testament*, but *The Golden Bough* has an immense collection of harvest customs from all over the world. Among these we find very frequently ritual copulation on the harvest field, to ensure a productive harvest the next year; the treatment of a passing stranger as an incarnation of the spirit of the harvest; and a mythical relationship between an older and a younger goddess or female nature-spirit, representing the seed-corn of the previous year and the harvest of the present one. The author of Ruth has transformed these plot themes into credible and very warm human relationships: Boaz sleeps on the harvest field and Ruth asks him to shelter her; she returns from her gleaning operation carrying a bushel or so of wheat; the barren Naomi gains a son through Ruth. We may compare the way in which ancient fertility themes are transformed in the Song of Songs into a metaphorical identifying of the bride of the marriage with the fertile land.

I think that when people speak of the Book of Ruth as "charming," they are really using a denatured synonym for something more like "serene." It is the unclouded serenity of the story that impresses the reader, a serenity that does for an agricultural and harvest setting what, let us say, the Twenty-third Psalm does for a pastoral one. Like that Psalm, it expresses the feeling that if human beings give up their murderous and polluting ways, the physical environment will be seen as something identical with the human one, as something to live in rather than to dominate. At that point "serenity" becomes inadequate too, and moves into what is called *agape* in the Septuagint and New Testament and *ahabah* in Hebrew (compare the verbal form *aheb* in Ruth 4:15), and expresses the highest vision of human life within the context of the will of God that words can make.

Blake's Biblical Illustrations

It is rare to have an experience that seems to bring one's past life around in a curve, suggesting the closing up of a period of time rather than the usual open continuity. But when I see the name of Blake in letters of such vast size outside the Art Gallery in my own city (I almost said "of my own city," because I am old enough to think of it occasionally as the Art Gallery of Toronto), it does seem to round off an era with a shape to it. I began working on a book on Blake in the thirties of this century, when I was also around the Art Gallery a good deal because my wife was employed there. At that time there was one workable edition of Blake's poetry and prose and a few presentable collections of reproductions, but very little serious criticism of either. My chief aim in my book was to remove the poet Blake from the mystical and occult quarantine that most commentators assigned him and put him in the middle of English literature, which is where he belongs and where he said he belonged.

Since then, Blake scholarship has put increasing emphasis on the pictorial side of Blake, as it naturally would have done, and its progress has been parallel, establishing a social context for Blake as painter, illustrator, and engraver. You may see a very full and authoritative treatment of this in Professor Bindman's catalogue to the present exhibition, and I am assuming some familiarity on your part both with this catalogue and with the exhibition it describes. The literary critic of Blake has continually to stop and remind himself that Blake was almost totally unrecognized as a poet during his lifetime, and did not begin to influence later poets until nearly half a century after his death. But the painting and engraving Blake had real connections with—Flaxman, Fuseli, Linnell, Samuel Palmer, and many others—have a historical dimension that the poet lacks.

Nevertheless, all Blake's pictorial work was closely associated with books: nothing of real importance that he produced is wholly independent of some kind of verbal context. In thinking about his work, therefore, we have to think first of all of the conception of illustration and its place in the pictorial arts. In reading poetry or fiction we internalize the imagery, vividly or vaguely according to temperament: illustration prescribes our visual response in a definite direction. As a rule our own visualizations, however vague, survive all suggested ones, which may be one reason why the elaborately illustrated literary work, a publisher's conception which did so much to help keep Blake alive, has now less of a vogue than it enjoyed in his lifetime. I should imagine that a film version of a favorite novel, or even a performance of a favorite play, seldom permanently displaces the inner vision of it for most people. The chief exception, a significant one in view of the *Songs of Innocence* and Blake's other connections with the genre, is children's books, where, as in the Tenniel illustrations to *Alice in Wonderland*, text and illustration can hardly be separated in our memory.

As is well known, Coleridge makes a distinction between two aspects of creativity, which he called fancy and imagination. What Coleridge meant by this is not our present concern, but in the relation of Blake's pictorial work to literary texts we can see different levels of vision that are roughly parallel. We may call them, tentatively, the levels of illustration and of illumination. Contrary to what we might think at first, Blake is normally respectful of his text: even his most extraordinary flights can be supported by something in it. In illustrating Gray's "Ode on the Death of a Favorite Cat," for example, Blake demurely illustrates not only Gray's cat and fish, but Gray's poetic epithets as well: the fish are called "genii of the stream" and the cat a "nymph," and we accordingly see very unusual fish and a cat in partly human shape. Such illustrations as these, or those of the fairies in the *Midsummer Night's Dream* illustrations, or the lark and sun and moon of the illustrations of *L'Allegro*, are "fanciful" in a fairly restricted sense, but they are so because the poems they illustrate are also fanciful, or at least are usually read that way.

On this general level of vision there is another and perhaps more serious quality of fancy that operates in the area of the grotesque. In some painters, including Blake, the grotesque verges on the occult. Blake had acquired, partly from his study of Swedenborg, the technique of what some psychologists call a hypnagogic vision, the twilight area of perception which is neither objective, like the walls of a room, nor subjective, like a hallucination. Our senses, Blake says, condense what we see into an objective world, and filter out any perception that disturbs this carefully regulated and predictable vision. But, to use an analogy later than Blake, we could have evolved to see the world in very different ways, and some people can see and converse with other possible modes of being that ordinarily never take definite shape or sound. It is to this world that the "Visionary Heads" belong: these include various historical figures and such creatures as the "Ghost of a Flea."

Blake's friend Varley, we are told, took these visions "seriously": that is, he assumed that they were ghostly but objective, perceived by a kind of X-ray eyesight. For Blake they were among the realities of vision, and no further evidence for their reality was needed beyond the drawing itself. Admittedly we get into something of a block here, because our language instinctively seeks out clear distinctions between objective reality and subjective illusion. For Blake there was a far more important distinction between the passive attitude that stares at the world, and the active or creative one that builds something out of it. The former is what Blake calls "reason" and regards as stupid; the latter, its direct opposite, he calls mental, intellectual, or imaginative. Blake could have given many of his drawings the same title that Goya used: "The sleep of reason produces monsters." But for Blake the word *of* would indicate a different kind of genitive. Goya meant: when reason goes to sleep, monsters are produced in the mind. Blake would have meant: when man falls into the state of sleep he calls reason, monsters inhabit his mind, though only a genuinely creative vision can see that they are monsters.

This kind of fancy, to give it that name again, has run through the whole history of painting: we find it in Hieronymus Bosch and Brueghel, in Blake's contemporary Fuseli, in Redon and the later surrealist and dadaist movement, in much of the "magical realism" of our own time. It shows us the infinite variety of what can be seen by a visionary skill that tries to see more than the conventionalizing apparatus of the eye has been conditioned to show us. Such variety of vision, as we saw, may be "fanciful" in the idiom of the innocent make-believes of children, or it may be terrifying, like the nightmares of children. Blake would say that we live in a hell that is shown to be a hell by the wars and plagues and famines and slavery that exist in it, but which we dare not look at steadily in its real form. Those who consistently see it in the forms of these other possibilities are often said to be mad, and may sometimes actually go mad; but this need not affect the quality of their vision if they are artists. Sanity is not a critical but a social judgment, and no society is capable of making such a judgment beyond a very limited degree. What the vision of Blake shows us is the much profounder insanity of the society he lived in. The Reverend Doctor Trusler, for example, after commissioning from Blake a picture illustrating "Malevolence," refused what Blake sent on the ground that he wished to reject all "Fancy" from his work. But as one of his books was called *The Way to Be Rich and Respectable*, it seems clear that neurotic fantasy may disguise itself as its opposite.

Above this pictorial fancy there is the systematic re-creation of the visible world into what Blake would call its spiritual or imaginative form. From the Paleolithic cave drawings of Lascaux and Altamira to our own day, there has always been something of the unborn world about the art of painting. In contrast to sculpture, which is normally linked to biological form, the two-dimensional aspect of painting suggests a re-creation of vision by the mind, an objective world transfigured. Even when the underlying cultural impulse is a so-called "realistic" one, we have this in Vermeer in seventeenth-century Holland, in Renoir in French impressionism, in the later Turner in Victorian England. Another publication of the Art Gallery of Ontario is David Wistow's *Tom Thomson and the Group of Seven*, which deals with a movement in painting utterly remote from Blake in time, place, setting, technique, and objectives. Yet it begins with an epigraph from Emily Carr which would apply with equal accuracy to Blake:

> Oh, these men, this Group of Seven, what have they
>   created?
> —a world stripped of earthiness, shorn of fretting details,
>   purged, purified;
> a naked soul, pure and unashamed; lovely spaces filled with
>   wonderful serenity.

In Blake's greatest pictorial work, even when the text it accompanies is by someone else, we no longer have the feeling of subordination to a text that the word *illustration* normally suggests. We have rather the sense of turning to an independent art related to the text but no longer "following" it or merely assisting the reader to visualize it. The distinction between illustration and this kind of illumination is roughly parallel to the difference between reciting a poem and setting it to music. In recitation the poem is turned from print to sound, and guides the ear as illustration guides the eye. But when a poem is set to music its rhythm and much of its structure are taken over by the music. It is the same poem, but its setting and context are different. In "illumination," similarly, the context is no longer visual commentary, but an act of creative criticism.

According to Giambattista Vico, writing in Italy at the beginning of the eighteenth century, human culture begins in a mythological and poetic stage, after which it becomes aristocratic and allegorical, then demotic, descriptive, and realistic, and finally goes through a *ricorso* or return back to the mythological. It is a corollary of this conception that much the same structural principles of the arts hold throughout each phase, but are easiest to see in the mythological stage, before they have become adapted to class interest or popular demands for likeness or ordinary experience. Literature that is close to the mythological has an affinity with abstract and conventionalized "primitive" painting, because in myths, where the characters are so often gods, things happen of the kind that happen only in stories, just as highly conventionalized painting presents visual relationships and designs, like a saint's halo, that occur only in pictures. According to Vico, classical culture had passed through its three stages and then gone in a *ricorso* back to mythology at the beginning of the Christian era, and another such *ricorso* seemed to be taking shape in Vico's own time.

Blake had not read Vico, but he had developed parallel intuitions from contemporary books: he had read about the ancient Druids and their caste of bards in Stukeley, about the morphology of myth in Jacob Bryant, about biblical typology in Swedenborg, about the legendary history of Britain as transmitted from Geoffrey of Monmouth down to Milton, about the cycles of Norse mythology in translations of the Old and Prose Eddas. He also regarded his own time as one in which a squalid pseudorealism was about to be swept away on a whirlwind of new mythology coming in the wake of political revolution. It is when Blake is faced with a fairly representative poet of his own century, such as Edward Young or Gray, that we can see most clearly what the direction of his illuminating activity is. Gray wrote in a domesticated eighteenth-century idiom, but took a keen interest in his more "primitive" Norse and Celtic poetic ancestors, and Blake is at his best and boldest, in illuminating Gray, when he gives us his great vision of Hyperion the sun-god in "The Progress of Poesy," or the world-serpent Midgard and the wolf Fenri of Norse apocalyptic at the end of "The Descent of Odin."

Young's *Night Thoughts,* in nine nights ending with a Last Judgment, are less erudite but more speculative, and as what the poet speculates about is frequently cosmological, Blake's drawings expand accordingly. Finally, after 537 efforts to reconstruct Young's meditations into myths, Blake abandoned Young for his own much less inhibited dream of nine nights, known as *Vala* or *The Four Zoas.*

In Blake's illustrations of Milton, who sticks so closely to his biblical and mythological sources, illustration becomes much the same thing as illumination, and we may say this also of the Dante series. Blake's dislike of Dante's literal and legalistic biases in the *Inferno* sometimes leads him to take more liberties with Dante's text than he usually does: Paolo and Francesca, for example, appear to have reached an apotheosis in Blake that Dante does not give them. The picture of the Canterbury pilgrims, on the other hand, is relatively realistic by Blake's standards, and the mythological reconstruction of Chaucer is made only verbally through the Descriptive Catalogue, in which we are told, for example, that "The Plowman of Chaucer is Hercules and his supreme eternal state, divested of his spectrous shadow; which is the Miller." Blake's brief comments about the *L'Allegro* and *Il Penseroso* illustrations indicate a similar type of interest in them.

But naturally it is in Blake's own illuminated poems that text and design reach a perfect balance. Only in the early experiment *Tiriel* do we have a text with accompanying illustrations. Everywhere else the text and design interpenetrate in every variety of proportion, ranging from all text, or text with slight marginal decoration, to all picture, or picture surrounding a title or colophon, or design framing a short lyric. With his own work Blake can provide a constant contrapuntal relation between our verbal and our pictorial experience of the poem, so that there is no shift of attention from verbal to pictorial worlds: the two blend together as aspects of a single creative conception.

In his illustrations to the Bible, again, everything in Blake's design can usually be justified by the text. There are dozens of them that are simply biblical illustrations, and call for no further comment. Such a departure from a specific biblical reference as the picture of the Virgin hushing the child John the Baptist is rare, and even this belongs to a very traditional type of departure. There is a collection of Blake's Bible illustrations made by the late Sir Geoffrey Keynes, in which the Job designs are omitted, because, the introduction tells us, apart from being readily available elsewhere, they are less illustrations to the book than an imaginative reconstruction of it. I think this is a false antithesis. Blake is not imposing his own meaning on Job except insofar as he is trying to make imaginative sense of the text as he read it. It may not be the same as the sense we make of it, and it is certainly a Christian and apocalyptic reading of the book, but its relation to the text of Job is quite as consistent as its relation to Blake's mind. I also have to omit the Job series, but for different reasons.

But still the influence of the Bible on Blake is so pervasive that it is difficult to know where it stops. His picture of the temptation of Christ on the mountain top is closely related to his picture of the temptation on the pinnacle of the temple in *Paradise Regained*. In the former Jesus stands on an eminent but quite solid and horizontal rock: in the latter his foot touches the pinnacle in a way that shows that his balance is miraculous. This detail results from a very sharp insight into the implications of Milton's text. But sometimes an illustration of Milton is reinforced by Blake's view of the Bible. Thus Michael's prophecy of the Crucifixion in *Paradise Lost* features the typological serpent of the temptation in Eden and of the brazen serpent on a pole in the Book of Numbers. Blake is illustrating Michael's line "But to the cross he nails thy enemies," but has done so with the image that had been central in his mind for many years, the dying god as a serpent "wreath'd round the accursed tree," which had appeared in *America* (1793) and elsewhere. Again, the illustration of Jesus' offer to redeem man (*Paradise Lost*, Book V) shows Jesus standing in front of God the Father, a grotesque creature with his face concealed by long hair, as in the portrait of the senile Urizen in the frontispiece to *The Book of Ahania*. Blake is illustrating *Paradise Lost*, but he is also illustrating his own view of Milton's Father, besides anticipating the whole of the "God is dead" theology of a few years ago. Similarly, the explicitly sexual embrace of Eve by the serpent that we see in Blake gives a dimension to that episode which is not in Milton, though it is by no means unknown to tradition, and reappears in Dylan Thomas's "tree tailed worm that mounted Eve." At the end of *The Marriage of Heaven and Hell* Blake tells us that, after converting an "Angel" (conservative) into a "Devil" (radical):

> . . .*we often read the Bible together in its infernal or diabolical sense, which the world will have if they behave well.*
>
> *I have also the Bible of Hell, which the world shall have whether they will or no.*

The "Bible of Hell" is probably the series of prophetic books that includes *The Book of Urizen* and *The Book of Ahania*, which read very like the Genesis and Exodus of a revised Old Testament. We shall come back to these in a moment. The Bible in its infernal or diabolical sense needs a more long-range perspective for its explanation.

We spoke of Vico and his conception of a sequence of cultural languages, running from the mythological through the allegorical to the demotic and back again, and remarked that for Vico one such sequence began in the early Christian centuries and was nearing its *ricorso* in his own time. In Vico's day there had been no permanently successful example of a democratic culture, and he had no evidence for any essential change in the nature of his cycle. But Blake, with the American, the French, and the beginning of the Industrial revolutions before him, felt, at least for most of the productive period of his life, that a far-reaching change was taking place in human fortunes, of a kind that the apocalyptic visions in the New Testament finally did seem to be really pointing to.

We have now to invoke a broader principle than anything Vico gives us. No human society lives directly in nature as an animal or insect society might do. Human consciousness invariably creates some kind of transparent envelope out of its own social concerns, and looks at nature through this transparent cultural filter, which in its verbal aspect is a mythology. A cosmology, or systematic view of nature, usually forms part of the more developed mythologies. The culture of Western Europe, at the time of early Christianity, produced such a mythology and cosmology, mainly out of the Bible, later annexing a good deal of classical myth and philosophy to it. The Bible itself, as I see it, does not set forth a mythological universe of this kind, but it provides any number of hints and suggestions for one, and naturally the construct set up in the Middle Ages, however close to the Bible, was mainly a rationalizing of the social authority of church and state.

This construct was on four main levels. On top was Heaven, in the sense of the place of the presence of God. Strictly it was a metaphorical top, as categories of time and space do not apply directly to God, but the metaphors were invariably drawn from "up there," beyond the sky. Below, on the second level, was the model world that God originally created, saw to be good, and intended to be man's home, the paradisal Eden with no sin or death in it. Man fell out of this world into the third level, the "fallen" world he now inhabits, an alien order of nature to which only animals and plants seem relatively well adapted, as they do not sin. The Garden of Eden has disappeared, and only the stars in their courses, with their legendary spherical music, are left to remind us of the perfection of the original creation. Still further below, on a fourth level, is the demonic world.

This structure is a rigid hierarchy, with the initiative for everything that is good for man coming from above in the form of grace. Even the revolutionary Milton never thought of liberty as anything that man wanted or had a right to: it is good only because it is something that God wishes him to have. The main object of man's existence is to recognize that his fallen world presents him with a moral dialectic: he must move upward as close to his proper level (the second) as he can, or else sink down to sin and a death beyond the physical. The second and third levels constitute two aspects of the order of nature: the higher one is specifically the order of human nature, as many things are "natural" to man, such as wearing clothes, being under social discipline, obeying laws and the like, that are not natural to animals.

Because this mythology was a structure of authority, enforced by authority, it lasted far longer than it would ordinarily have done. Blake was the first poet in English literature, and so far as I know the first person in the modern world, to realize that the traditional authoritarian cosmos had had it, that it no longer appealed to the intelligence or the imagination, and would have to be replaced by another model. Blake gave us a complete outline of such a model, but unfortunately nobody knew that he had done so, and one has to read thousands of pages of poetry and philosophy since his time to pick up bits and pieces of his insight. Like its predecessor, Blake's cosmos is based on biblical imagery and myth, but it turns the authoritarian structure upside down and makes it a revolutionary one.

By the Bible in its infernal or diabolical sense, Blake meant, first of all, replacing the original revolutionary impetus in the Bible which had got explained away by an establishment. This revolutionary impetus is primarily, in the Old Testament, the account of the exodus of Israel from Egypt: in the New Testament it is the account of the execution of the prophet and martyr Jesus. Traditionally, the unique importance of Jesus' life has been thought to reside in his "sinlessness," his perfect conformity to established moral standards. For Blake, a conforming Jesus would have accomplished nothing: it was his open defiance of such standards that made him intolerable to society.

As for the Exodus, we have to distinguish two forces at work there, one revolutionary and the other reactionary. The revolutionary impulse, symbolized in Blake as the red and fiery Orc, inspired the Israelites to walk out of the Egyptian oppressive social system into the desert and set up their own society. Orc's "pillar of fire" guided them on their way. But as they went on, they became more and more hypnotized by the sense of predictable natural order, and so eventually congealed into the same kind of authoritarian structure that they had left behind. Opposed to Orc is the white Urizen, whose name echoes the word *horizon* and who belongs to the family of tyrannical old men in the sky that mankind has projected there since the beginning of history. Urizen's "pillar of cloud" eventually won out: the twelve (actually thirteen) tribes of Israel fell into the rhythm of the predictable revolution of the twelve signs of the Zodiac with its captive sun: a law of negative commandments was handed to Moses from the sky, and finally the story of the brazen serpent on the pole (Numbers 21) associates the defeated Orc with the serpent and the sinister tree that we find in the story of the fall of Adam and later in the Crucifixion.

Now, in Blake's day, there comes a revolt of the American colonies against the repressive government of "Albion," and we see them bearing flags with serpents, trees, and stars on them, as well as an alternation of red and white and a preoccupation with the number thirteen. Both tendencies, to freedom and to repression, are present in slave-owning America, and later both tendencies reappeared in France, producing both a revolution and Napoleonic imperialism. In England itself there is a constant conflict going on between creative and imaginative people and those who insist on rationalizing all the cruelty and injustice in the "dark Satanic mills."

The rebellion of Orc against Urizen produced the French and American revolutions, but as Blake saw it such revolutions do not last, because the youthful Orc grows old, in other words turns into Urizen. History, as Blake saw it, breaks down into a series of cycles beginning with the birth of the terrible "Babe," the annunciation of a new era in time, and ending either with the Babe grown old, as in the poem called "The Mental Traveller," or hung on a tree in youth like Absalom, the victim of youth's impotent protest against tyranny, as in *The Book of Ahania*. A much more permanent human resource is the creative faculty in man that begins by controlling and binding the energy of Orc and then proceeds to transform nature into the home of humanity. The arts themselves—poetry, painting, music— are in the forefront of this transformation, and its presiding genius is Los the blacksmith, the worker in iron, iron being regarded in the Old Testament as a new and suspicious substance, not to be used in constructing altars to the sky-god. Los's name is, I should think, taken from the old English word *los* or *loos*, meaning praise or glory, used by Chaucer and not quite extinct, at least as an archaism, in Blake's day.

Thus Blake's mythological universe neatly turns the traditional one on its head. On top is Blake's Satan, the death principle, the mechanical energy which whirls the stars around in their courses and sets up a model of predictability, or natural law, which is what the energies of man are expected to adjust to. Paul calls Satan the prince of the power of the air, implying that the traditional abode of the gods is really a place of alienation. Under Satan is Urizen's world of experience, the "fallen" world of the traditional biblical reading, where morality tries to become as predictable as natural law; and Urizen sits on top of Orc, the revolutionary power latent in human energy.

In childhood man is in the state of innocence: that is, he assumes that the world makes human sense, and that there is a providential order, incarnate in his parents, that takes care of him. As he grows older, he enters Urizen's world of experience, which is a very different world, and his original childhood vision of innocence is driven underground into what we now call the subconscious, a boiling mass of frustrated and largely sexual desire. This conception of the human soul is commonplace enough to us now, but Blake grasped it before anyone else did. Still deeper down in the human spirit than the natural energy of Orc is Los, the creative power. This Los is the true God, the Holy Spirit who works only within human consciousness, and only as its creative potential. Los's home is in Atlantis, the primeval kingdom of human imagination, now submerged under what Blake calls the sea of time and space. It is with ideas like these that Blake attempts to make his pictures of the Bible intelligible to his contemporaries.

Blake's "Bible of Hell" probably began with the two poems called *The Book of Urizen* and *The Book of Los*. Blake was aware that there were two accounts of the creation in Genesis, and he presents his own creation myth as a collision of opposing forces. Urizen is the tendency to stability and uniformity that finally reveals itself to be a tendency to death; Los is the tendency to expanding and growing life which fights against Urizen. The poems contain some striking anticipations of later theories about the evolving of forms of life and of the immense stretches of time that would be required for such growth. *The Book of Ahania* reshapes the Exodus into a story of revolution betrayed, except that Blake makes an Earth Mother or female principle, who is ignored in the Bible, the chief character. It is possible that the four poems on the continents, *America*, *Europe*, and the two parts of *The Song of Los* called "Africa" and "Asia," correspond to the historical books of the Old Testament: in any case the rather pedantic notion of what amounts to a series of parodies of the Bible was soon given up. The most interesting feature, perhaps, is the pictorial aspect of *The Book of Urizen*, where creation is not the work of an aloof deity commanding the world to exist, but the outcome of a battle of suffering titans.

We have already indicated that it is not always easy to say just what a biblical illustration is in Blake. If it is not explicitly a picture referring to a specific text in the Bible, it may still illustrate Blake's infernal or diabolical Bible, and if it seems to illustrate something in Blake's contemporary world, it may still be a fulfillment or application of biblical prophecy. One of Blake's most famous poems tells us that the real form of England, the "green and pleasant land," and the real Israel, the Garden of Eden, are the same place, and the object of Blake's art is to reunite them, to build Jerusalem in England. In his poem *Jerusalem* the tribes of Israel and the counties of England are superimposed on one another in the most laborious detail, and many events in his own time are seen as repetitions of the history of Israel.

The famous picture called "Glad Day" by Gilchrist, because he associated it with a sunrise image in *Romeo and Juliet*, is, according to Blake's own annotation, a portrait of Albion. It represents mankind in general and England in particular in a sacrificial role (Luvah or Orc in Blake's symbolism), identified, as his phrase "at the mill with slaves" shows, with a regenerate or restored Samson. This Samson figure, along with the identification with Albion, comes from a passage in Milton's *Areopagitica*, not the Old Testament, but the picture has its roots in the Bible, as Blake read it, for all that. Again, there is a picture of an infant snatched up by a female in a chariot drawn by blind horses while another female, perhaps the mother, lies exhausted on the ground. The picture is called "Pity" because it is assumed to illustrate the metaphor in *Macbeth* about pity as a naked new-born babe. Doubtless it does, but it also illustrates the infant who heralds a new era of time, and whose threatened and perilous birth comes into the story of Moses in the Old Testament and that of Jesus in the New. Another picture depicting the attempts of good and evil angels to get control of a similar infant is again not directly biblical, but illustrates the two impulses, toward life and toward death, that have existed in every human being since the fall of Adam. This design appears in reverse in *The Marriage of Heaven and Hell* as a pictorial comment on the point the text is making: that morality, being founded on the forbidden knowledge of good and evil, is a perverted form of religion. At the other end of life such angels appear in an episode that Blake also illustrates, the legendary dispute mentioned in the New Testament of Michael with Satan over the body of Moses.

Although Blake illustrates every part of the Bible, a large number of his most impressive pictures cluster around its beginning and its end, the creation and the apocalypse. But, of course, to understand them we must first understand what creation and apocalypse meant to Blake. In the traditional version, God made a perfect world, free of corruption, and a garden in which he put Adam and Eve, who had only to enjoy themselves and not eat the fruit of a tree mysteriously called the "knowledge of good and evil." Naturally they did eat this fruit, and so were flung out of the garden into a lower world, while God retreated to the sky. So we now inhabit a savage and alienating order of nature, and it's all our fault. For Blake it is indeed all our fault, but the origin of the fault lies in believing in a nonhuman creation in the first place. In the picture called "God Judging Adam," the only figure who is really there is Adam himself, being what Blake calls "idolatrous to his own shadow." The God in the chariot has been projected from the stupidest and most primitive part of Adam's brain. This picture was formerly identified with the ascent of Elijah, and it is something of a parody of that scene, where one prophetic power enters the spiritual world and another carries on in time. In another well known picture, "The Elohim Creating Adam," not in this exhibition, Adam lies prostrate with the serpent of morality coiled around him, while the alleged creator appears to be stuffing mud ("dust of the ground") into his head. All of which means that the creation, for Blake, is the world that registers on our closed-up and filtering senses: creation and fall are the same thing. The powerful painting of the wise and foolish virgins contains for Blake an allusion to the five organized senses and their opposites.

What lies around us now is not God's creation but a quite ungodly mess, and it is the primary task of man to re-create it into a proper home for man, with the vision of the creative artists taking the lead. For most of the mess comes from the uncreative side of man, the side that wages war and supports parasitic rulers because it has accepted the knowledge of good and evil. This knowledge, or pseudo-knowledge, has two aspects. One is the belief in morality, which tells us that the "Mercy, Pity, Peace and Love" of the *Songs of Innocence* are virtues we may practice only as long as we are careful to keep on rationalizing the war and cruelty and hatred and exploitation that make them virtues. The other is the belief that sanity consists in sharply dividing the perceiving subject from the perceived object, and in regarding the subject as the source of illusion and the object as the source of reality.

In traditional Christianity God is male and a creator: the human society he redeems, men as well as women, is symbolically female, a "Bride" called Jerusalem, or, as Blake says, "a City, yet a Woman." In Blake all creative human beings are symbolically male: what is symbolically female is not human women but the objective world. Human beings, we saw, either try to help re-create the world or else stare at it passively: Blake calls the former attitude the "Imagination" and the latter one the "Spectre." Similarly there are two aspects of the object: the retreating elusive object and the responding or trans-formed object. Blake calls the former the "Female Will" and the latter the "Emanation," the total body of what one redeems by love. The "Spectre" cannot love; hence his "Emanation" is an object of posses-sive and panic-stricken jealousy. Such a possessed Emanation is illustrated in the frontispiece to *The Book of Ahania* already mentioned and in the poem *Visions of the Daughters of Albion*. The "Female Will" is Robert Graves's white goddess, represented in the painting called "Hecate," the *diva triformis* who is also the elusive moon in the sky and the invisible virgin of the forest. "Hecate" is again a picture drawn from Shakespeare, but its roots are in the biblical abhorrence of all worship of a female embodiment of nature. The female jealous-ly possessed by an old man, and the female who is a disdainful or tantalizing mistress, are, for Blake, symbolic pictures of human con-sciousness, and are therefore more important as literary conventions than as facts of life.

The creation for Blake, then, was the imprisoning of human consciousness into the form in which we see the world, and the stories of the fall of man and of the flood of Noah are variations on the same theme. Blake speaks of the flood, in the poem *Europe*, as the time "when the five senses rush'd / In deluge o'er the earth-born man." The famous picture of the "Ancient of Days," which is the frontispiece to *Europe*, shows the traditional God, Urizen or the old man in the sky, setting his compasses on the face of the deep, in the phrase of the Book of Proverbs. We see the sky as an overarching vault because we are looking at it with eyes underneath an over-arching vault of bone, and Urizen's compasses are tracing the "horizon" both of the sky and of the human head. By contrast, the apocalypse is the recovery by man of his own proper vision, after he has, so to speak, blown his top and sees the world with his open mind and not with his skull. Blake's pictures of the Last Judgment, with the presence of God where the skull formerly was, indicate the kind of perspective that results. Another form of the skull image is the trilithon of Stonehenge and elsewhere that we see in Blake's *Jerusalem*, derived, as the exhibition shows us, from Stukeley's book on what he regarded as "Druid" temples. According to Blake the upright pillars represent two aspects of human creativity, known in the eighteenth century as the sublime and the beautiful, and the horizontal stone on top is the human "reason," or skull-bound view of reality.

The great apocalyptic visions in this exhibition are largely of monsters, because the passive view of the objective world sees it increasingly as monstrous, as more is known about the world of the stars. The huge mechanism held together with gravitation that stares silently at man from the night sky seems like a constant accuser of man, emphasizing his littleness, his unimportance in the scheme of things, and the inevitability of sin, misery, and the frustration of desire in his life. Ezekiel, according to Blake, saw this image as the "Covering Cherub," the angel who keeps us out of Paradise, the Argus full of eyes who is the demonic parody of the vision of God with which Ezekiel's vision opens. Ezekiel identifies his Covering Cherub with the Prince of Tyre, which means with political tyrants of all kinds, and similarly Blake's demonic figures hold the swords and scepters of temporal rule.

Elsewhere in the Bible such visions of consolidated evil, political tyranny embodying an alien cosmos, explicitly take the form of monsters. In the Book of Job there are two such creatures, a land monster called Behemoth and a sea monster called Leviathan, from whose power Job is delivered at the end of the book. Man's limited view of the cosmos is symbolically either subterranean, as in the story of Adam sent back to the red earth he was made from, or submarine, as in the story of Noah. As we saw, the flood for Blake was not the drowning of mankind but the limiting of man's perception, so that for most of us the flood has never receded, but remains as the "Sea of Time and Space" on top of Atlantis. In Revelation 13 these two monsters again rise out of the sea and the earth. In that context they are politically connected with the Rome of Nero and other persecuting Caesars, but symbolically they are also the Pharaoh of Egypt whom Ezekiel identifies with Leviathan and the Nebuchadnezzar of Babylon who turns into Behemoth. This latter figure especially fascinated Blake, and he appears at the end of *The Marriage of Heaven and Hell*, as the final comment on the state of the world at the time of the French Revolution. It is also in the Book of Revelation that the vision of the old man clutching the young woman turns into its apocalyptic form, of a dragon trying to devour the woman crowned with stars who is the mother of the Messiah, or humanity become divine.

There is another type of apocalyptic subject in Blake, where the open vision taught by the seer on Patmos is applied to Blake's own time. For example, his Exhibition of 1809 contained pictures of the spiritual form of Pitt, the leader of Albion on land, guiding Behemoth, and the spiritual form of Nelson, the leader on the sea, guiding Leviathan. There was also a spiritual form of Napoleon, which has disappeared with no information about what beast he was involved with. A figure guiding such monsters would not always be a tyrant: he could be simply a leader doing what he can in a world where such monsters exist. Pitt and Nelson in Blake's pictures are examples not of apotheosis, as Blake's commentary suggests, nor are they really demonic figures: they are states or functions of human action looked at from an apocalyptic perspective. They also, unfortunately, imply more understanding of biblical symbolism than the public of 1809 was likely to possess, or attach to Blake's work if they did possess it.

A similar figure of this type is the picture of Newton, applying Urizen's compasses to a scroll on the ground, the rolled-up part of which forms a disappearing spiral, an image that Blake often employs in sinister contexts. In the more familiar Tate Gallery version, which is the more carefully finished one, Newton looks almost benignant: the version owned by a Lutheran church in America gives him a harder and more fanatical face. For Blake the apocalypse was, among other things, the separating of a world of life from a world of death, and everything in the latter forms a parody or mimicry of the former.

Hence the consolidation of the passive view of existence is a necessary step in visualizing its opposite. So in the poem *Europe*, which describes the intellectual tyranny exerted over Europe between the birth of Christ and the end of the eighteenth century, the trumpet of the Last Judgment is blown by Newton. This Newton, it is hardly necessary to add, is not the Sir Isaac who was Keeper of the Mint under George I, but the mighty angel Blake's picture presents, his spiritual form. Up to Newton's time, the worship of nature was still possible for some people, who might see, for example, a sun-god in a chariot at the rising of the sun, the presence of a being with whom some kind of "I-Thou" dialogue, to use a current phrase, would still be possible. But Newton had turned everything in nature into an "It," a part of a mechanistic force, and by doing so he achieved a negative deliverance of man from nature worship.

The genuinely apocalyptic form of such a Newton figure is the other mighty angel illustrated by Blake and mentioned in Revelation 10:6, who announces that "time should be no longer," a phrase Blake would have taken to mean just what it appears to mean. The apocalypse for Blake is the triumph of revelation and freedom over tyranny and mystery, and one of its central symbols is the ripping of seals from a scroll, the disclosing to the human mind the world that the human mind exists to see.

In *The Marriage of Heaven and Hell* there is a conflict of visions between the narrator and a panic-stricken conservative "angel" about what lies in store for man in the world beyond this life. The angel churns up a horrifying vision of black and white spiders (i.e., egos who are either "good" or "bad"), and of a serpentine or shark-like leviathan coiling and thrashing in the sea. The angel then runs away, and the narrator, a "devil" who is mostly Blake himself, is left sitting on a pleasant river bank listening to a harper who tells him that the dogmatist, the man in the sleep of reason, breeds reptiles of the mind. For Blake the world that God is trying to reveal to man in the Bible, and the world Blake himself is trying to illustrate, is not a world of superstitious fantasy but a world in human shape that makes human sense. This is symbolized as a world where man lives in fire and yet is not burned, in water and yet is not drowned, a world above time where all the images of man's creative and charitable acts in the past move into the present, and his lost heritage turns into his regained home.

III

Shakespeare's *The Tempest*

In Shakespeare's day, if a cultivated person had been asked what a comedy was, he would probably have said that it was a play which depicted people in the middle and lower ranks of society, observed their foibles and follies, and was careful not to diverge too far from what would be recognized as credible, if not necessarily plausible, action. This was Ben Jonson's conception of comedy, supported by many prefaces and manifestos, and is illustrated by the general practice of English comic writers down to our own day. But the earlier Elizabethan dramatists—Peele, Greene, Lyly—wrote in a very different idiom of comedy, one which introduced themes of romance and fantasy, as well as characters from higher social ranks. The first fact about Shakespeare, considered as a writer of comedy, is that he followed the older practice and ignored the Jonsonian type of comedy, even in plays which are later than Jonson's early ones.

One reason for this is not hard to see. Observing men and manners on a certain level of credibility demands a degree of sophistication, whereas the fairy tale plots of Peele's *Old Wives' Tale* and Lyly's *Endymion* appeal to a more childlike desire to see a show and be told a story, without having to think about whether the story is "true to life" or not. The child wants primarily to know what comes next; he may not care so much about the logic of its relation to what it follows. If the adult completely loses this childlike response, he loses something very central to the dramatic experience, and Shakespeare was careful never to lose it as a playwright. Jonson tends to scold his audiences for not being mature enough to appreciate him: Shakespeare says (in the epilogue to *Twelfth Night*), "We'll strive to please you every day," and never fails to include some feature or incident that is incredible, that belongs to magic, fairyland, folktale, or farce rather than to the observation of men and manners. In Jonsonian comedy the play is intended to be a transparent medium for such observation: we learn about life through the comedy. In Shakespearean comedy the play is opaque: it surrounds us and wraps us up, with nothing to do but to see and hear what is passing. This does not mean that an unusual or unfamiliar type of story is wanted: again, the simple and childlike response is to the familiar and conventional, new variants of well-loved stories that have been told many times before. Shakespeare's comedies are all very different from one another, but he understands this response well enough to keep repeating his comic devices.

Further, not only does Shakespeare adhere to the pre-Jonsonian type of comedy, but he moves closer to it as he goes on. The plays are classified by the First Folio as comedies, histories, and tragedies, but criticism has isolated a fourth genre, that of romance, to which Shakespeare devoted his main attention in his last years. We have also come to realize that the romances are not a relaxation or letdown after the strenuous efforts of *King Lear* or *Macbeth*, as often used to be said, but are the genuine culmination of Shakespeare's dramatic achievement. These are the plays in which Shakespeare reaches the bedrock of drama, the musical, poetic, and spectacular panorama of magic and fantasy in which there is no longer tragedy or comedy, but an action passing through tragic and comic moods to a conclusion of serenity and peace.

We notice that the plays that seem most to have influenced Shakespeare in writing the romances were much cruder than those of Peele or Lyly. One of them was *Mucedorus*, a play of the 1590s revived around 1609, which clearly held the affections of the reading public as well as playgoers, as it went through seventeen editions in about eighty years. It is a very simple-minded play about a prince who goes in disguise to another country to woo a princess, and who gains her after baffling a cowardly villain and rescuing her and himself from a wild man in a forest. There is a prologue in which two figures named "Comedy" and "Envy" engage in a sharp dispute about the shape of the forthcoming action, the former promising a happy ending and the latter many pitfalls along the way. In another early play, *The Rare Triumphs of Love and Fortune*, which features a magician and his daughter, like *The Tempest*, we begin with an assembly of gods and a debate between Fortuna and Venus, again over the character of the story that is to follow.

From such unlikely (as it seems to us) sources, Shakespeare drew hints for an expanding stage action that can include not only all social levels from royalty to clowns, but gods and magicians with superhuman powers as well. The romances end happily, or at any rate quietly, but they do not avoid the tragic: *The Winter's Tale* in particular passes through and contains a complete tragic action on its way to a more festive conclusion, and *Cymbeline*, which has at least a token historical theme (Cymbeline was a real king of Britain, and his coins are in the British Museum), is actually classified as a tragedy in the Folio. Such plays are "tragicomedies," a genre that not only Shakespeare but Beaumont and Fletcher were popularizing from about 1607 onward. In the preface to Fletcher's *Faithful Shepherdess* (ca. 1609), it is said that in a tragicomedy a god is "lawful," i.e., superhuman agents can be introduced with decorum.

But to expand into a divine world means reducing the scale of the human one. The jealousy of Leontes and Posthumus is quite as unreasonable as that of Othello, but it is not on the gigantic human scale of Othello's: we see it from a perspective in which it seems petty and ridiculous as well. The form of the romance thus moves closer to the puppet show, which again, as Goethe's *Wilhelm Meister* reminds us, is a form of popular drama with a strong appeal to children, precisely because they can see that the action is being manipulated. The debates of Comedy and Envy in *Mucedorus*, and of Venus and Fortuna in *The Rare Triumphs* introduce us to another approach to the manipulating of action. Here we are told that the play to follow is connected with certain genres, and that characters who personify these genres are taking a hand in the action. The notion of Comedy as a character in the action of a comedy may seem strange at first, but is deeply involved in the structure of Shakespearean comedy. Let us look at a comedy of Shakespeare that many people have found very puzzling, *Measure for Measure*, from this point of view.

In *Measure for Measure*, Vincentio, the Duke of Vienna (which Shakespeare seems to have thought of as an Italian town), announces his departure, leaving his deputy Angelo in charge to tighten up laws against sexual irregularity. Everything goes wrong, and Angelo, who sincerely wants to be an honest and conscientious official, is not only impossibly rigorous, condemning to death young Claudio for a very trifling breach of the law, but is thrown headlong by his first temptation, which is to seduce Claudio's sister Isabella when she comes to plead for his life. The action leads up to the dialogue of the condemned Claudio and his sister in prison. Claudio's nerve breaks down under the horror of approaching death, and he urges Isabella to yield to Angelo. Isabella, totally demoralized by her first glimpse of human evil, and, perhaps, by finding herself more attracted to Angelo and his proposal than she would ever have thought possible, explodes in a termagant fury. She says: "I'll pray a thousand prayers for thy death"—hardly a possible procedure for any Christian, though Isabella wants to be a cloistered nun. Everything is drifting toward a miserable and total impasse, when the disguised Duke steps forward. The rhythm abruptly changes from blank verse to prose, and the Duke proceeds to outline a complicated and very unplausible comic plot, complete with the naive device known as the "bed trick," substituting one woman for another in the dark. It is clear that this point is the "peripety" or reversal of the action, and that the play falls into the form of a diptych, the first half tragic in direction and the second half comic. Vincentio has the longest speaking part of any character in Shakespearean comedy: a sure sign that he has the role of a subdramatist, a deputy producer of the stage action. *Measure for Measure*, then, is not a play about the philosophy of government or sexual morality or the folly of trying to legislate people into virtue. It is a play about the relation of the structure of comedy to these things. The Duke's actions make no kind of realistic sense, but they make structural dramatic sense, and only the structure of comedy, intervening in human life, can bring genuine repentance out of Angelo and genuine forgiveness out of Isabella.

In *The Winter's Tale* the action also forms a diptych, and again we have first a tragic movement proceeding toward chaos and general muddle. This action comprises Leontes' jealousy, the disappearance of his wife Hermione, the death of his son Mamillius, the exposing of the infant Perdita, and the devouring of Antigonus, who exposes her, by a bear. Then a shepherd and his son enter the action: as in *Measure for Measure*, the rhythm immediately changes from blank verse to prose. The shepherd finds the infant and the son sees the death of Antigonus, and the shepherd's remark, "Thou mettest with things dying, I with things new born," emphasizes the separating into two parts of the total action. This separating of the action is referred to later on in a recognition scene, not presented but reported in the conversation of some gentlemen: "all the instruments that aided to expose the child were even then lost when it was found." Such phrases indicate that the real dividing point in the action is the finding of Perdita at the end of the third act, not the sixteen years that are said to elapse before the fourth act begins. In the final scene of the play Paulina, the widow of Antigonus, says to Hermione, who is pretending to be a statue: "our Perdita is found." This is the formula that first draws speech from Hermione. Paulina, though an agent of the comic structure of the second half of the play, is not its generator: that appears to be some power connected with the Delphic oracle, which had previously announced that Leontes would live without an heir "if that which is lost be not found."

In *The Tempest* there is no clearly marked peripety or reversal of action. The reason is that the entire play is a reversal of an action which has taken place before the play begins. This concentration on the second half of a total dramatic action accounts for many features of *The Tempest*. It is quite a short play, which is why Prospero's role has fewer lines than Vincentio's, though he dominates the action even more completely. Again, we are constantly aware of the passing of a brief interval of time, an interval of a few hours, very close to the period of time we spend in watching the play. The dramatic action is generated by Prospero and carried out by Ariel, whose role is parallel to that of Pauline in *The Winter's Tale*. But because only the second or rearranging half of the action is presented, the characters have no chance to mess up their lives in the way that Angelo and Leontes do. The theme of frustrated aggressive action recurs several times: when Ferdinand tries to draw his sword on Prospero, when Antonio and Sebastian attempt to murder Alonso and Gonzalo, and later to attack Ariel, and when Stephano's conspiracy is baffled. Prospero's magic controls everything, and the effect is of an audience being taken inside a play, so that they not only watch the play but, so to speak, see it being put on.

Ordinarily, in our dramatic experience, this sense of a play being created before our eyes is one that we can only get when we are watching an action that seems to be partly improvised on the spot, where we know the general outline of the story but not its particulars. Various devices such as Brecht's "alienating" techniques and the Stanislavski method of acting attempt to create such a feeling in modern audiences. In Shakespeare's day this type of improvising action appeared in the *commedia dell' arte*, which was well known in England, and influenced Shakespeare in all periods of his production. Some of the sketchy plot outlines (*scenari*) of this type of play have been preserved, and we note that they feature magicians, enchanted islands, reunions of families, clown scenes (*lazzi*), and the like. Such *scenari* are probably as close as we shall ever get to finding a general source for *The Tempest*.

Not only does Prospero arrange the action, but we are seldom allowed to forget that it is specifically a dramatic action that is going on. Prospero orders Ariel to disguise himself as a nymph of the sea, while remaining invisible to everyone else. In reading the play, we might wonder what point there is in dressing up so elaborately if he is to remain invisible, but in the theater we realize at once that he will not be invisible to us. Again, an illusory banquet is presented to and snatched away from the Court Party, and Ariel, as a harpy, makes a somber speech condemning the "three men of sin." It is an impressive and oracular speech, but we hardly notice this because Prospero immediately undercuts it, coming forward to commend Ariel on doing a good actor's job. The opposite emphasis comes in the epilogue, when Prospero says:

> *As you from crimes would pardon'd be,*
> *Let your indulgence set me free.*

The epilogue represents only the convention of asking the audience to applaud the play, so we hardly notice how grave the tone is. Yet it is clear that the restructuring of the lives of the characters in the play is being said to be a deeply serious operation, with an application in it for ourselves. We have not merely been watching a fairy tale, we feel, but participating in some kind of mystery. What kind of mystery?

The Tempest is almost a comic parody of a revenge tragedy, in which there is repentance, forgiveness, and reconciliation instead of revenge. The characters are divided into three groups and each is put through ordeals, illusions, and a final awakening to some kind of self-knowledge. There is hardly a character in the play who is not believed by other characters to be dead, and in the final recognition scene there is something very like a sense that everyone is being raised from the dead, as there is with Hermione in the last scene of *The Winter's Tale*. Prospero actually claims the power of raising the dead in his renunciation speech, and he also pretends that Miranda was drowned in the storm he raised.

The Court Party goes through a labyrinth of "forthrights and meanders" with strange shapes appearing and disappearing around them, but nevertheless they finally arrive at a state of self-recognition where Gonzalo is able to say that each has found himself "when [formerly] no man was his own." Gonzalo himself is on the highest moral level of the Court Party: in contrast to Antonio and Sebastian, he finds the island a pleasant place and his garments fresh, and he is excluded from Ariel's condemnation of the "three men of sin." Alonso comes next: his repentance and his gaining of self-awareness seem equally genuine, and he is clearly the focus of Prospero's regenerative efforts. Next is Sebastian, a weak and ineffectual person who does what the stronger characters around him suggest that he do. In the final scene he seems quite cheerful, and we feel that, while nothing very profound has happened to him, he will be as easily persuaded to virtue as to vice. Antonio, who speaks only once in the last scene, in reply to a direct question, is a more doubtful quantity. Stephano, Trinculo, and Caliban go through a kind of parody of the Court Party ordeals and illusions, yet they too reach some level of self-awareness. Stephano is reconciled to losing his imaginary kingdom, and Caliban, who has emerged as much the most intelligent of the three, is apparently ready to be weaned from idolatry, and so to take the first step in self-knowledge himself.

To the extent that people are acquiring self-knowledge, then, they seem to be taking their places in a moral hierarchy. Yet as we look further into it, it seems to be less a moral hierarchy than an imaginative one. They move from illusion to reality as the play presents these categories. What is illusion? Primarily, it is what such people as Antonio consider reality. As soon as Alonso falls asleep, Antonio starts a plot to murder him: this is *Realpolitik*, the way things are done in the real world. Similarly, he takes a very "realistic" view of the island, in contrast to Gonzalo's. But the play itself moves toward a reversal of this view of reality. Antonio's one remark in the last scene is that Caliban is a "plain fish"—one of several indications that living on his level is symbolically living under water. The illusions in the mazy wanderings of the Court Party are more real than Antonio's life without conscience.

What, then, is reality, as the play presents it? That is more difficult, and Prospero seems to agree with T. S. Eliot that whatever reality is, humankind cannot bear very much of it. But just as "reality" for Antonio turns out to be illusion, so perhaps what is illusion on the much higher level of Ferdinand and Miranda might turn out to be closer to reality. The masque put on for their benefit by Prospero is a vision of the highest form of "reality" in our cultural tradition: the vision of what in Christianity is called "unfallen" nature, the original world before the fall, the model divine creation that God observed and saw to be good. The dance of nymphs and August reapers seems to suggest the "perpetual spring" which is a traditional attribute of Paradise, and the three goddesses of earth, sky, and rainbow suggest the newly washed world after Noah's flood, when the curse was lifted from the ground and a regularity of seasons was promised. The vision, however, is one of a renewed power and energy of nature rather than simply a return to a lost Paradise: a sense of a "brave new world" appropriate as a wedding offering to a young and attractive couple. And it seems highly significant that this vision of the reality of nature from which we have fallen away can be attained only through some kind of theatrical illusion.

The action of the play, then, moves from illusion to reality in a paradoxical way. What we think of as reality is illusion: not all of us are realistic in the criminal way that Antonio is, but, as Prospero's great speech at the end of the masque says, in our world everything that we call real is merely an illusion that lasts a little longer than some other illusions. At the other end, what we think of as real can come to us only as a temporary illusion, specifically a dramatic illusion. This is what the wedding masque symbolizes in the play: the masque is presented to Ferdinand and Miranda, but the whole play is being presented to us, and we must be sure that we omit no aspect of it.

The play keeps entirely within the order of nature: there are no gods or oracles, though Alonso expects them, and Prospero's magic operates entirely within the four elements below the moon. Sycorax, like other witches, could draw down the moon, i.e., bring "lunatic" influences to bear on human life, but this is not Prospero's interest, though it may be within his power. In the action that took place before the play began, when Prospero was Duke of Milan, his brother Antonio had become the *persona* or dramatic mask of the absent-minded Prospero, and gradually expanded until he became "absolute Milan," the entire Duke, until Prospero and the infant Miranda vanished into another world in an open boat (for Milan, like Bohemia in *The Winter's Tale*, appears to have a seacoast). On the enchanted island this dramatic action goes into reverse, Prospero expanding into the real Duke of Milan and Antonio shrinking to a kind of discarded shell. Prospero's life in Milan is what passes for real life in our ordinary experience: the action of *The Tempest* presents us with the aspect of nature which is real but, like the dark side of the moon, constantly hidden from us. We note in passing the folktale theme of the struggle of brothers, the rightful heir exiled only to return later in triumph.

The feeling that the play is some kind of mystery or initiation, then, is a quite normal and central response to it. The connection between drama and rites of initiation probably goes back to the Old Stone Age. In classical times there were several mystery religions with dramatic forms of initiation, the most celebrated being those of Eleusis, near Athens, which were held in honor of the earth goddess Demeter, the Roman Ceres who is the central figure in Prospero's masque. In the eighteenth century Bishop Warburton suggested that the sixth book of the *Aeneid*, depicting Aeneas's journey to the lower world, was a disguised form of Eleusinian initiation, and in 1921 Colin Still, in *Shakespeare's Mystery Play*, applied a similar theory to *The Tempest*. He noted that the route of the Court Party, from Tunis in Africa to the coast of Italy, paralleled the route of Aeneas from Carthage, and the otherwise pointless identification of Tunis with Carthage made by Gonzalo in Act II, along with the equally pointless amusement of Antonio and Sebastian, seems to be emphasizing the parallel. I suspect that Colin Still's book was an influence on T. S. Eliot's *Waste Land*, published the next year, though Eliot does not mention Still before his preface to Wilson Knight's *Wheel of Fire* in 1930.

Colin Still, recognizing that Shakespeare could have had no direct knowledge of classical mystery rites, ascribed the symbolic coincidences he found with *The Tempest* to an inner "necessity," to the fact that the imagination must always talk in some such terms when it gets to a sufficient pitch of intensity. I should add only that the "necessity" is specifically a necessity of dramatic structure. We can see this more clearly if we turn to a dramatic form which not only did not influence Shakespeare but was nowhere in his cultural tradition, the No play of Japan. In a No play what usually happens is that two travelers encounter a ghost who was a famous hero in his former life, and who recreates the story of his exploits in this ghostly world, which is also presented as a world of reconciliation and mutual understanding. This type of drama is linked to Buddhist beliefs in a world intervening between death and rebirth, but we do not need such beliefs to make imaginative sense of No plays. We do recognize in them, however, a very powerful and integral dramatic structure. When we enter the world of *The Tempest*, with its curious feeling of being a world withdrawn from both death and birth, we recognize again that that world is being specifically identified with the world of the drama.

As often in Shakespeare, the characters in *The Tempest* are invited to a meeting to be held after the play in which the puzzling features of their experiences will be explained to them. This seems a curious and unnecessary convention, but it is true to the situation of drama, where the audience always knows more about what is going on than the characters do, besides being in a greater state of freedom, because they are able to walk out of the theater. Each character in *The Tempest*, at the beginning of the play, is lost in a private drama of his own. This is true even of Prospero, in the long dialogues he holds with Miranda, Ariel, and Caliban in Act I, mainly for the benefit of the audience. Through the action of the play, a communal dramatic sense gradually consolidates, in which all the characters identify themselves within the same drama, a drama which the audience is finally invited to enter.

The Tempest, like its predecessor *The Winter's Tale*, is both comedy and romance. In the tradition of comedy that Shakespeare inherited from Plautus and Terence, what typically happens is that a young man and a young woman wish to get married, that there is parental opposition, and that this opposition is eventually evaded and the marriage takes place. Comedy thus moves toward the triumph of youth over age, and toward the vision of the renewal and rebirth of nature which such a triumph symbolizes, however little of nature there may be in a Roman comedy. In *The Tempest*, the conventionally comic aspect of the play is represented by the marriage of Ferdinand and Miranda. Prospero puts up a token opposition to this marriage, apparently because it is customary for fathers to do so, and he forces Ferdinand into the role of servant, as part of the token tests and ordeals which traditionally make the suitor worthy of his mistress.

The corresponding comic element in *The Winter's Tale* is centered on the successful marriage of Florizel and Perdita in the teeth of strenuous parental opposition. Florizel temporarily renounces his princely heritage and exchanges garments with the thief Autolycus, just as Ferdinand takes over Caliban's role as a bearer of logs. Here again the renewal of nature is a part of the theme, more explicitly because of the romance element in the play. The great sheep-shearing festival in the fourth act of *The Winter's Tale* is a vision of the power of nature extending through four seasons, that being probably what the dance of the twelve satyrs symbolizes. Nature has it all her own way throughout this scene, and Perdita, the child of nature, announces that she will have nothing to do with "bastard" flowers adulterated by art. Nor will she listen to Polixenes' sophisticated idealism about art as being really nature's way of improving nature. The traditional symbol of the domination of art over nature, Orpheus, whose music could command animals and plants, appears only in parody, in connection with the ballads of Autolycus.

But this triumph of nature and its powers of renewal and rebirth, with its center of gravity in the future, is only the lesser recognition in the play. The main emphasis comes not on the successful wooing of the younger pair, but, as usual in Shakespearean romance, on the reintegrating of the world of their elders. The greater recognition scene takes place in a world of art, Paulina's chapel, where we are told that we are being presented with a work of sculpture and painting, where music is heard, where references to the art of magic are made. In the vision of the triumph of art, the emphasis is not on renewal and rebirth but on resurrection, the transformation from death to life. And just as the vision of nature's renewal and rebirth relates primarily to the future, so the triumph of art and resurrection relates primarily to the past, where the words of the oracle, spoken sixteen years earlier, are brought to life in the present, and where old sins and blunders are healed up. In his essay *The Decay of Lying*, Oscar Wilde says of music that it "creates for one a past of which one has been ignorant, and fills one with a sense of sorrows that have been hidden from one's tears." Perhaps it is the function of all art to "create a past" in this sense of revealing to us the range of experience that our timid senses and reasonings largely screen out. The power of nature gives us a hope that helps us to face the future: the power of art gives us a faith that helps us to face the past.

The Tempest is concerned even more than *The Winter's Tale* with the triumph of art, and much less with the triumph of nature. This is mainly because Prospero is a magus figure: in Elizabethan English "art" meant mostly magic, as it does here. Prospero renounces his magic at the end of the play: this was conventional, for while magic was a great attraction as dramatic entertainment, it was a highly suspicious operation in real life; hence all dramatic magicians were well advised to renounce their powers when the play drew to a close. But there is more to Prospero's renunciation of magic than this. We recall the deep melancholy of his "our revels now are ended" speech at the end of the masque, and his somber comment on Miranda's enthusiasm for her brave new world: "'tis new to thee." In the world of reality that we can reach only through dramatic illusion, the past is the source of faith and the future the source of hope. In the world of illusion that we take for reality, the past is only the no longer and the future only the not yet: one vanishes into nothingness and the other, after proving itself to be much the same, vanishes after it.

As a magus, Prospero is fulfilling the past, reliving and restructuring his former life as Duke of Milan. To do so, he must take an obsessive interest in time: "the very minute bids thee ope thine ear," he says to Miranda, referring to astrology, and he later tells her that the fortunes of all the rest of his life depend on his seizing the present moment. Antonio's urging the same plea on Sebastian later is a direct parody of this. Prospero's anxiety about time interpenetrates very curiously with his anxieties as a theatrical producer, making sure that Ariel comes in on cue and that his audience is properly attentive and impressed. Such strain and such anxiety cannot go on for long, and all through the play Prospero, no less than Ariel, is longing for the end of it.

Prospero's magic summons up the romantic enthusiasm for magic with which the sixteenth century had begun, in Agrippa and Paracelsus and Pico della Mirandola and the legendary Faust. It continued for most of the next century, and among contemporary scholars Frances Yates in particular has speculated about its curious relation to Shakespeare's romances. But this vision of a power and wisdom beyond human scope seems to be passing away when Ariel is released and melts into the thin air from whence he came. Whether magic was a reality or a dream, in either case it could only end as dreams do. In Shakespeare's day magic and science were very imperfectly separated, and today, in a postscientific age when they seem to be coming together again, the magus figure has revived in contemporary fiction, with much the same dreams attached to it. Such a return may make *The Tempest* more "relevant" to us today, but if so, the weariness and disillusionment of Prospero are equally "relevant."

Just as the mere past, the vanishing age, seems to be summed up in the figure of Ariel, so the mere future, the yet-to-vanish new age, seems to be summed up in the figure of Caliban. Caliban's name seems to echo the "cannibals" of Montaigne's famous essay, a passage from which forms the basis for Gonzalo's reverie about an ideal commonwealth in Act II. Around the figure of Caliban, again, there are many phrases indicating Shakespeare's reading in contemporary pamphlets dealing with the first English efforts to settle on the American coast. Every editor of *The Tempest* has to record this fact, while pointing out that Prospero's island is in the Mediterranean, not the Atlantic, and has nothing to do with the New World. Still, the historical situation of *The Tempest*, coming at the end of an age of speculative magic and at the beginning of an age of colonization in the New World, seems to give Caliban a peculiar and poignant resonance. Caliban is the shape of things to come in the future "real" world, not a brave new world of hope, but, for the most part, a mean and cruel world, full of slavery and greed, of which many Calibans will be the victims.

Of course, we had rather have the past of faith and the future of hope than the past of dream and the future of nightmare, but what choice have we? This is perhaps another way of asking what *The Tempest*, as a dramatic illusion, has to give us in the way of reality. When Shakespeare touches on such subjects he is apt to bury what he says in unlikely places, passages of dialogue that the eye and ear could easily pass over as mere "filler." We find such a passage in the inane babble of Antonio and Sebastian at the beginning of the second act. Sebastian's response to a narrow escape from drowning is a kind of giggling hysteria, and Antonio falls in with this mood and encourages it, because he knows what he wants to do with Sebastian later on. In the course of the dialogue Gonzalo, who is speaking with a wisdom and insight not his own, assures the others that "Tunis was Carthage." We pick up the implication that *The Tempest*, as explained, is repeating the experience of Aeneas voyaging from Carthage to Italy to build a new Troy, and presenting an imaginative moment, at once retrospective and prospective, in the history of the third Troy, as England was conventionally supposed to be. The dialogue goes on:

> *Ant. What impossible matter will he make easy next?*
> *Seb. I think he will carry this island home in his*
> *   pocket, and give it his son for an apple.*
> *Ant. And, sowing the kernels of it in the sea, bring*
> *   forth more islands.*

Gonzalo never claims to make impossible matters easy, but Prospero can do so, and by implication Shakespeare himself can. And it is Shakespeare who gives us, as members of his audience, his island, as one would give a child an apple, but with the further hope that we will not stop with eating the apple, but will use its seeds to create for ourselves new seas and even more enchanted islands.

Varieties of Eighteenth-Century Sensibility

It seems clear that my present assignment is not to produce a scholarly paper, but something in the convention of Denham's famous seventeenth-century poem *Cooper's Hill*, where the poet climbs a height to survey the available landscape and is led from his sight of the Thames River to prophesy an age of smooth and unstoppable couplets:

> *Though deep, yet clear: though gentle, yet not dull;*
> *Strong without rage, without o'erflowing full.*

Such an attempt is bound to be, in its present stage of development at least, a very sketchy, perhaps even a tacky essay. Before you start walking out, however, I should add two qualifications. One is that an audience that knows far more about the eighteenth century than I do can fill in some of my gaps from their superior knowledge, assuming that there is anything between the gaps. The other is that certain critical initiatives I derived from my early study of Blake and the reading around his period that I did fifty years ago may still be of interest to you. The reading affected much more than my Blake study: for example, I took the word "archetype" not from Jung, as is so often said, but from a footnote in Beattie's *Minstrel*.

Again, the *Anatomy of Criticism* owes its title to my special affection for the prose genre that I have tried to identify by that name, the genre that includes the Menippean satire but for me also includes other fiction that expresses itself through information and ideas rather than through study of plot. The eighteenth century is the greatest period in English literature for this genre: eighteenth-century anatomies include not only the main works of Swift and Sterne, but Fielding's *Journey from this World to the Next*, Amory's *John Buncle*, and Blake's *Island of the Moon*, and the genre exerts a strong influence on *Tom Jones*, *Rasselas*, *The Fool of Quality*, and much else besides. What is important about the anatomy is not simply its characteristics, but the fact that it normally approaches its material playfully. We are constantly involved in conflicts of ideas, with all the paradoxes, associated metaphors, and demonstrations of the half-truths of argument that go with such conflicts. The erudition is curious and eccentric for the most part, again bringing out the element of play in collecting information. The period is a refreshing contrast in this respect to the nineteenth century, where, apart from Peacock among the Romantics and Samuel Butler among the Victorians, the soberer virtues of continuity and logical consistency were preferred. As for the contrast with this century of obsessive ideology, the less said the better.

Of course, this is only one strand in the complex weave of an age where no critical issue was discussed more frequently and eagerly than the theory of wit, and its distinction from humor, raillery, ridicule, and half a dozen other terms. The conception of art as play has a solid theoretical basis in Bacon and Sidney, but no previous age was more keenly aware of the difference between reasoning and rationalizing, or of the extent to which argument was propelled by the internal combustion engines of economic or erotic interest. The eighteenth century is often called an age of enlightenment by those who admire it, and an age of prose and reason by those who like it less. It seems to me that the sense of rational paradox is more profoundly enlightened than a belief in reason as such. Certainly a belief in reason alone can make for very humorless writing, and no one would call Godwin's *Political Justice* or his novels playful. The common cliché of the good-natured man, whose instincts are educated, contrasts with the cunning man who plays only for keeps, using his reason to manipulate and—significant word—outwit others. The contrast between Blifil and Tom Jones, or between Joseph and Charles Surface, is closely related.

The age of wit became an age of satire because human beings are what they are, and it became an age of satire by subordinating the vertical perspective of literature, the sense of worlds above and below normal human experience. Poets had been told by Boileau that the revelations of Christianity were too high for poets and the puerilities of classical mythology too low. Eighteenth-century literature in England begins with the final chorus of Dryden's *Secular Masque*:

> *Thy Chase had a Beast in view;*
> *Thy Wars brought nothing about,*
> *Thy Lovers were all untrue.*

These lines are addressed respectively to Diana, Mars, and Venus, and are linked, however obliquely, with a marked decline of interest in mythological language. The Olympian personnel were not totally dismissed, like the false gods in the *Nativity Ode*: the elitism of eighteenth-century culture kept mythology in the poetic vocabulary. But it became increasingly unfunctional: Cowper's reference to Philomela's "mechanick woe" and the fact that Gray's line "And reddening Phoebus lifts his golden fire" was so obviously trade slang for "the sun rises" indicate that we are close to Wordsworth's demythologizing of poetic diction. True, Wordsworth's revolution did not outlive him, but it ends a period when Ovid went, comparatively speaking, out of fashion, and Horace, the incarnation of the man of the world, dividing his time between his rural retreat and the streets of Rome, moved into the foreground.

Dryden and Pope were more interested in religious themes than Boileau would have recommended, but Dryden is concerned with the authority of tradition and the social, even the political, application of religious principles. So far as any enthusiasm for adventuring into the mysteries of revelation is concerned, *Religio Laici* starts with the word *dim* and goes from there. Pope's *Messiah*, though a superb paraphrase of Isaiah and Virgil's Fourth Eclogue, similarly does not express the direct impact of revelation on experience, like the hymns of Watts, Wesley, and Cowper later in the century, and Swift tends to think of Christian dogma and ritual as a kind of leash necessary to restrain a particularly vicious dog.

The aspect of the eighteenth century that we associate with Goldsmith's term *Augustan* is an intensely social aspect: one immediately thinks of the coffee houses and the various literary circles in what was then, at that social level, the small and gossipy town of London. We know how much London, with its full tide of human existence at Charing Cross, meant to Johnson: the contrast with Blake, for whom London was equally essential, but who went about almost totally unrecognized for what he was, is striking enough. Being a trend within a culture, even though a dominant one for much of the period, the Augustan age kept creating, in true Hegelian style, its own opposite, a cultural climate concerned with solitude, melancholy, the pleasures of the imagination, meditations on death, and the like. In an early article I tried to characterize a part of this trend as an "age of sensibility," though the word *age* should not be taken too narrowly. The counter-Augustan trend gradually increases as the century goes on, but, of course, such categories are liquid, not solid. Augustans survive to the end of the century, and poets of sensibility like Anne Finch emerge in Dryden's time.

The eighteenth century has a unique symmetry about it: from the Whig Revolution of 1688 to the French Revolution of 1789, from Locke's *Treatises of Government* of 1690 to Burke's *Reflections on the Revolution in France* of 1790, from the *Secular Masque* in 1700 to the second edition of the *Lyrical Ballads* in 1800, it seems to have some sense of what it means to be a century and to show a proper respect for the decimal system of counting. I think that there is also some symmetry of interpenetration between Augustan and counter-Augustan tendencies, especially in the relation of individual to society and that we can almost see the beginning and end, within the century, of a kind of double-helix movement.

First follow nature, the Augustans said, and not many disputed the axiom. The decline of interest in the evangelical, the marvelous, the mythological, was not felt to be a limitation or sacrifice: the Augustans inherited the framework of Locke's *Essay* and Newton's *Principia*, and they felt a new world of reason and sense experience was opening up to be explored in depth by the poets as well, a world full not merely of interest and beauty but of new kinds of reality. Their enthusiasm for such themes often betrayed them into literary tactlessness: everyone knows the famous lapses, like "Inoculation, heavenly maid, descend!" or Stephen Duck's reaction to the microscope: "Dear Madam, did you ever gaze, / Thro' Optic-glass, on rotten Cheese?" But the stimulus of new discovery was a genuine one, and it extended from the writer to his reader. This was the first age in which the critic moved up to a position of major importance in literature, as the spokesman for a public that looked first and last for entertainment in its literature and demanded to be pleased. Many writers of the time, including notably Addison, tell us that literature in every age must conform to the expectations of its readers, that the taste of the age is the formal cause of poetry. The famous proof-text here is, of course, Johnson's couplet: "The drama's laws the drama's patrons give, / And they that live to please must please to live." Granted that this is perhaps more obviously true of drama than of any other genre, the principle was assumed to apply everywhere. Literature was closely associated with a background of good talk and cultivated conversation, verbal communication preserved in amber. In the second of the *Night Thoughts* Edward Young concludes a panegyric on language in phrases that may sound more ambiguous now than they would have sounded in his time:

'Tis thought's exchange, which, like th' alternate push
Of waves conflicting, breaks the learnéd scum,
And defecates the student's standing pool.

Johnson's essay on Dryden treats him as having accomplished a revolution in literature, in effect parallel to those of Locke in philosophy and Newton in science. His statement that Dryden found English literature brick and left it marble is an epigram derived from Seutonius' statement about Augustus, and one that helped to build up the Augustan stereotype. For us, the revolution accomplished by Dryden in prose was more lasting, and his easy, direct speaking style crept into the subtext of English prose rhythm and has stayed there ever since. Before Dryden in verse there were Denham and Waller, and in prose (even though not published at the time) the letters of Dorothy Osborne, but such things do not affect Dryden's originality. The Locke-Newton framework, we notice, was largely a Whig formation, and the great writers, Dryden, Pope, and Swift, formed a Tory counterenvironment: forming counterenvironments is one of the main activities of literature in all ages.

The trouble with finding a language brick and leaving it marble is that one eventually runs out of marble. We notice at once in reading the *Essay on Dramatic Poesy* that, Dutch fleet or no Dutch fleet, English literature is entering an intensely progressive period, where the crudities of the Elizabethan writers, including Shakespeare, will be out of fashion and a new age of refinement and perfected craftsmanship will succeed. Pope's *Essay on Criticism* and *Peri Bathous* are devoted to this craftsmanship in poetry, the sublime tact that succeeds in definitively expressing meaning instead of merely throwing words in the direction of meaning. Such craftsmanship works in a convention: it is the responsibility of a cultivated public to understand and respond to the subtleties in the convention, to hear all the harsh cluttered consonants in such a line as, "When Ajax strives some rock's vast weight to throw, / (The line too labors, and the words move slow.)"

But whenever literature or any other art is improving, it is moving toward a dead end. What has been done to perfection has been done: the appearance of a "faultless painter" like Browning's Andrea del Sarto means that a convention has exhausted its possibilities, and there is nothing for the next painter to do but start being faulty. This sense of having reached a dead end haunts even Joseph Warton's essay on Pope; however appreciative it may be, *The Lives of the Poets* reflects a similar dilemma. It begins by telling us what was wrong with pre-Augustan poetry, notably Milton's and Cowley's, but the comments on Collins, Gray, and Goldsmith show Johnson's resistance to a dimension of culture in which his standards, flexible as they were, would no longer wholly apply. Johnson's criticism reflects the strengths and weaknesses of all "great tradition" criticism: he is nearly always first-rate on the people with whom he is in sympathy, but he can be insensitive or even perverse about those not quite in his mainstream center.

The feeling of an intensely social view of literature within the Augustan trend has to be qualified by an interpenetration of social and individual factors that was there from the beginning. The base of operations in Locke's *Essay* is the individual human being, not the socially conditioned human being: Locke's hero stands detached from history, collecting sense impressions and clear and distinct ideas. Nobody could be less solipsistic than Locke, but we may notice the overtones in *Spectator* 413, referring to "that great Modern Discovery . . . that Light and Colours . . . are only Ideas in the mind." The author is speaking of Locke on secondary qualities. All Berkeley had to do with this modern discovery was to deny the distinction between primary and secondary qualities to arrive at his purely subjective idealistic position of *esse est percipi*, "to be is to be perceived." If we feel convinced, as Johnson was, that things still have a being apart from our perception of them, that, for Berkeley, is because they are ideas in the mind of God. It is fortunate both for the permanence of the world and for Berkeley's argument that God, according to the Psalmist, neither slumbers nor sleeps. But Berkeley indicates clearly the isolated individual at the center of Augustan society who interpenetrates with that society.

The same sense of interpenetration comes into economic contexts. In the intensely laissez-faire climate of eighteenth-century capitalism there is little emphasis on what the anarchist Kropotkin called mutual aid: even more than the nineteenth century, this was the age of the work ethic, the industrious apprentice, the entrepreneur: the age, in short, of Benjamin Franklin. A laissez-faire economy is essentially an amoral one: this fact is the basis of the satire in Mandeville's *Fable of the Bees*, with its axiom of "Private Vices, Publick Benefits." The howls of outrage that greeted Mandeville's book are a little surprising: it looks as though the age was committed to the ethos of capitalism, but had not realized the intensity of its commitment. The reaction to Mandeville is oddly similar to the reaction to *The Shortest*

Way with the Dissenters, where Defoe's hoax form was the only possible way of showing bigots how brutal their prejudices were.

Of course, much has to be allowed for the polemical and strident tone of Mandeville: later in the century Adam Smith could say that avarice was the spur of industry, and say it to general applause. And, of course, Mandeville may have been raising issues far beyond the amoral nature of the open market. Browning's poem on Mandeville celebrates him as a prophet who penetrated a false antithesis of good and evil to discern that God brings good out of evil. At least I think that is what the poem says, but as it is written in the gabbing doggerel of Browning's later idiom, it is hard to be sure.

The same feeling of the interaction of good and evil in the economic world accounts for the eighteenth-century vogue for picaresque fiction. The heroes and heroines of Defoe may be thieves and whores to begin with, though Defoe carefully explains how they got that way and shows how it was practically impossible that they could have been anything else. They do not like being thieves and whores and fully intend to repent and become respectable as soon as they can afford it. But the implacable ferocity of the will to survive carries them on. It is no good preaching morality unless morality coincides with self-interest, to say nothing of self-preservation. As William the Quaker says in *Captain Singleton*, "I would as soon trust a man whose interest binds him to be just to me as a man whose principle binds himself."

George Borrow, one of the few Victorian writers who felt any affinity with the picaresque, tells us in *Lavengro* of his encounter with an old apple-woman whose Bible is *Moll Flanders* and who would not sell it to him for any money, because "without my book I should mope and pine." I say Bible advisedly, because what she sees in the book is the parable of the prodigal daughter, often wretched and despairing, yet pushing on in the hope of welcome and acceptance at the end. Later in *Lavengro* Borrow meets a Welsh parson who is sure he has committed the unpardonable sin against the Holy Spirit. Borrow picks out of him the perversity of pride that has flattened him into believing that he has done something blacker and more Satanic than any other man, and he points out that sin is a very common, not to say vulgar, condition that no one escapes. He does this by referring to the apple-woman and the heroine he calls "the Blessed Mary of Flanders," whose life repeats the situation of the forgiven harlots in the Gospels.

Not many novels have the driving power of Defoe's best fiction, but the theme he treats so often is not confined to him. *Fanny Hill*, for example, though it is certainly no *Moll Flanders*, also presents us with a young woman unceremoniously dumped in London without resources, so that she has to face the dilemma of whoring or starving. Her decision in favor of life is quite as moral as Moll's, whatever amusement the author or his reader may get from the result. And perhaps the contrast with Pamela is not so great as Richardson would have thought. Pamela is in much the same position as Moll at the beginning of the book, and the energy and resourcefulness with which she gets Mr. B on the bottom line of a marriage contract is by no means free of ruthlessness.

Moll Flanders, Roxana, Pamela, Clarissa, all in very different ways reflect the ethos of an age when women, more particularly working-class women, were especially vulnerable to social injustice, and the will to survive had to be an especially powerful one for females. In many of the novels of the Victorian giants, including George Eliot, female characters are presented mainly in relation to male ones, instead of being representatives of the human race in their own right. The tradition that runs through Defoe and Richardson and spills over into Jane Austen seems to me in this respect a more mature one.

In a novel of Robert Bage two heroines, one conventional and the other pragmatic, are discussing the position of women in a Turkish harem. The conventional one says: "I had rather death a thousand times," and the pragmatic one says: "I had rather a thousand times than death." In Bage's much better known *Hermsprong* the heroine is an insipid idiot of a type common in the minor fiction of the time, with a morbid sense of duty to a father who had no claim to it. But as she is contrasted with a considerably more sensible friend, and as her lover makes a point of the fact that he has not only read but been impressed by Mary Wollstonecraft, it seems clear that deliberate satire is involved. The vogue for horror fiction produces many situations that play a sadistic cat-and-mouse game with its heroines, keeping them surrounded with menace and threats of violation, even though they are often rescued by a divine providence heavily disguised as a public demand on the author. Nevertheless, we occasionally get a glimpse of the frustration and helplessness of an isolated female in a society where she is unable to manipulate any of the social machinery to her advantage, and the glimpse is far more genuinely horrifying than the conventional scary props.

The male picaresque heroes of Defoe and Smollett are obviously related to the ethos of an expanding empire, being adventurers who are often close to being pirates. There is seldom, understandably, the emphasis on violated innocence that we get so often with female protagonists. In Smollett's novels, especially *Ferdinand Count Fathom*, they are not very likable, but then Smollett is a tough satirist and is not out to make you like his characters but to drive home a thesis closely parallel to Mandeville's. Ferdinand, of course, "repents" at the end, but that is only to get his repellent story finished and to satisfy a public like the one assumed to be clamoring for a reprieve at the end of *The Beggar's Opera*.

However, it is only such a time that could have produced the gigantic *Robinson Crusoe*, the story of the solitary individual cast away on an island who proceeds to reconstruct every element of the expanding British imperial power he belongs to. He makes clothes, surrounds a space to make some privacy for himself, opens a journal and ledger, and governs the "native" Friday with the greatest assurance. As long as the British Empire possessed the will to govern, there was never any question of "going native." In his brief reference to *Robinson Crusoe* in *Das Kapital*, Marx underlines the interpenetration of individual and social themes in the book. He also speaks with contempt of Crusoe's amusing himself with religious exercises and the like, though one might have expected Marx, of all people, to understand that preserving one's sanity is mostly a matter of preserving one's social conditioning.

II

First follow nature; but what is nature? For the ethos I have been loosely calling Augustan it embraced two levels: the physical environment, which human beings are in but not of, and an upper level of a specifically human nature. It is natural to man, though not to any other being in the physical world, to wear clothes and engage in rational discourse. Specifically human qualities are all that is left of the paradise that God originally designed for man, and structures of authority, both spiritual and temporal, have to be established because man is no longer capable of living in paradise. Such structures are all that we have as criteria of the humanly natural; hence, the only answer to the question "What is unnatural for man?" is: whatever established authority tells you is unnatural. Even for the revolutionary Milton in *Paradise Lost*, the state of Adam and Eve before the fall was simple but civilized, with angels dropping in for lunch: they do not resemble anything like the noble savages until after their fall.

We saw that Locke, like Descartes before him, based his philosophy on a philosophical man abstracted from his social context, in short a theoretical primitive; also that Robinson Crusoe was an allegory of another abstract primitive, the economic man of capitalist theory, whose outlines are fairly complete already in Adam Smith. These are the individual primitives at the core of Augustan culture. But such primitives have voluntarily entered a social contract and a historical tradition. For this attitude nothing in the area of culture can develop except on the other side of the social contract: literature and the other arts are rooted in a historical context in both time and space.

But there were other cultural traditions that implicitly raised the question: granted that man is not an animal and cannot live like one, can he not find a common ground between the reasonable and the natural in the present physical world? There is no biblical evidence for any such doctrine as the total depravity of nature. And as certainly no one ever denied that human civilization is both corrupt and over-complicated by luxury, perhaps some simplifying and cleansing process might bring us within sight of a genuinely natural society on one level of nature instead of two. Hence the persistence of the pastoral tradition, with its celebration of a simple life in direct contact with the physical world. The pastoral convention was accepted by the Augustans as a complement rather than a contradiction of its prevailingly urban tone: this was, of course, also the role it had in Virgil and Horace. What is particularly significant about the pastoral tradition, from our present point of view, is its conventional assumption that its simple shepherds are also spontaneous poets, untaught but inspired. Here we have the growing point of a conception of different contexts of the primitive and of a different kind of natural society.

Swift at one end of the eighteenth century and Burke at the other are uncompromising defenders of the older two-level view. In the fourth part of *Gulliver's Travels* Gulliver encounters a society of intelligent horses who have formed a natural society on one level of nature. The filthy and degraded Yahoos illustrate what man would be like if he were purely an animal, and although the Houyhnhnms recognize Gulliver to be of the Yahoo species, they also see that he is a very different kind of Yahoo, being rational and capable of discourse. But as Gulliver goes on talking to his Houyhnhnm master about the conditions of eighteenth-century human life, the latter discovers that all discourse in Gulliver's world is shot through and through with "saying the thing that is not," or lying, a vice incomprehensible to the conscious horses. As for reason, Gulliver's master says, the Yahoos of Gulliver's nation merely have some quality that intensifies their natural viciousness, turning a merely animal ferocity into a uniquely hideous malice and sadism. So Gulliver comes, when looking at his reflection in the water, to hate himself more than the Yahoos, precisely because he is a clean and rational Yahoo. But he is stuck with being human on two levels of nature: a natural-rational society on one level of nature is possible only for intelligent animals. So Gulliver returns to his own social context at the end, the same as before, except that his pride in being what his religion calls a fallen creature has been obliterated.

For Burke, especially in his *Appeal from the New to the Old Whigs*, man's social contract is his present social context, the particular continuum of past, present, and future beings into which he happens to have been born. This continuum provides a structure of authority he is bound to submit to, for "natural rights" do not exist, except as duties connected with safeguarding the health and stability of his cultural tradition, for, Burke says, "Art is man's nature." By Burke's time, however, the conception of a natural society on one level of nature had made considerable headway, and in its progress had developed other types of primitive beyond the epistemological primitive of Locke and the acquisitive primitive of Mandeville.

If I have not made it clear what I mean by primitive, I mean an abstract model of a human being, a laboratory specimen, as it were, used as a basis for a study of human behavior in general, without regard to a specific historical period or social setting. The primitives of Locke and Mandeville, however, relate to a functioning society already in existence. The psychological primitive of David Hartley's *Observation on Man*, who works by the association of ideas rather than an inborn moral sense implanted by God, again reflects an age devoted to witty discourse. But he also points in the direction of a much more subjectivized society. For Hartley, what the association of ideas is mainly associated with is pleasure, and pleasure creates a hierarchy of higher and lower pleasures that can take us up Jacob's ladder to God. But when the conception of association enters Hume's discussion of causality, it goes in the direction of an almost

Buddhist disintegration of a continuous ego, a direction that Hume himself thought too paradoxical to follow up.

The discovery of America had brought with it the conception of a society that was also primitive, not in relation to itself, but in relation to a European culture that placed it outside history and regarded it as a natural society to which only the categories of human being and physical environment applied. From Montaigne's essay on the cannibals down to Voltaire's *L'Ingénu*, the vision of this society with its allegedly simpler and radically different lifestyle formed a counter-cultural theme of subdued but distinct significance. *Hermsprong*, which seems to sum up so many later eighteenth-century tendencies, has a hero conventionally educated in Europe, after which he spent some time with an Indian tribe in North America. This sojourn with a primitive society gave, in a curious reversal of normal standards, the final polish to his education. Other related primitive abstractions had already taken shape. They include the emotional primitive or man of feeling, so unforgettably dramatized by Rousseau in his personal life; the brooding melancholy primitive, who follows Ezekiel into the valley of dry bones to meditate on time, death, and immortality; and the evangelical primitive, who comes into the foreground with the Methodist movement and the hymn-writers previously mentioned, who record a direct religious experience detached from earlier centuries of religious tradition.

All these contributed to the process of pushing back the boundaries imposed on poetic experience that were assumed by most of the Augustans. These expanded directions give us three new contexts of particular importance for the primitive: the marvelous, the prophetic, and the cultural. The marvelous provides the vogue for popular romance, the prophetic the renewed sense of the relevance of the Bible to the literary imagination, and the cultural to the fairly new but rapidly growing sense of the social affinity of poetry with the simplest and most untutored states of life.

There are some curious confusions here. A great deal of remarkable historical scholarship accompanied these developments: we have Lowth's very influential lectures on biblical poetry, Hurd's *Letters on Chivalry and Romance*, Thomas Warton's *History of English Poetry*, Mallett's *Northern Antiquities*. The poets responded to this scholarship, and such poems as the *Song to David* and "The Fatal Sisters" could not have been written without it. But it is characteristic of these new breeds of primitive that they have no history, their social context not having yet been born. It is obvious that when we turn from Richardson or Fielding to *The Castle of Otranto* we are in a more primitive world, and this time an unhistorical one: the word *Gothic* to describe such a story means little more than "once upon a time." Ossian, an essential touchstone of sensibility in this period, wanders in an even hazier past; hermetic documents jostle Plato and Aristotle in Berkeley's *Siris*; Percy's *Reliques* may mingle old and new within the same ballad; bards, minstrels, and Druids cover the light of history with clouds of legend.

One by-product of all this primitivism is the rise of the formulaic fiction that has grown so prodigiously since. The forms of the horror story, the detective story (with Mrs. Radcliffe), the Western story (even though the "West" was still very close to the Atlantic coast), were taking shape in this period. One New World story that interests me is Frances Brooke's remarkable epistolary novel *Emily Montague*, written in Quebec soon after the British occupation, which contains much first-hand observation of Indian life. Formulaic fiction includes the "historical" novel developed later by Scott, though, except for sporadic revivals (e.g., Umberto Eco's *Name of the Rose*), this form went out of fashion after the nineteenth century, having perhaps fulfilled most of its cultural functions by providing libretti for nineteenth-century Italian operas. *Waverley* and *Rob Roy*, however, though they belong to the nineteenth century, record one of the great cultural tragedies of the eighteenth, and one very relevant to our present theme: the destruction of the primitive Highland culture by the Hanoverian middle-class establishment in England.

But with all this we have in England and Scotland no visionary of a natural society, on a single level of nature, remotely comparable in scope to Rousseau (or, in a very different way, Diderot) in France, Vico in Italy, or Herder in Germany. The closest approach in English-speaking countries, and he is not very close, is Thomas Jefferson, across the Atlantic. Blake, for example, accepted none of the standard Augustan values, but his distrust of anything called natural was equally great. *The Marriage of Heaven and Hell* does not prophesy a natural society: it ushers in the world of Freud and Marx and Schopenhauer and Nietzsche. Blake comes much closer to an idealized relation of humanity to nature when he speaks of building a new Jerusalem in England's green and pleasant land. Here nature is incorporated into human civilization, which has stopped exploiting, dominating, and polluting nature and has begun to cherish and foster it. This hymn expresses as close an approximation in English poetry as I know to what a book of fifty years ago called the heavenly city of the eighteenth-century philosophers. Otherwise, the natural society remains unborn, not only as a society, but as a conception or model of one. Perhaps, however, it was this unborn society, a classless society where the distinction of elite and popular had disappeared, that Wordsworth was really invoking in his Preface to the *Lyrical Ballads*, as the ideal society for whom he was writing and whose language he was endeavoring to speak.

If Robinson Crusoe, alone on his island and transforming it into a replica of what for him was his real world, is an allegory of one aspect of the eighteenth-century culture, then Tristram Shandy, complacently soaking in amniotic fluid for half of his autobiography, may represent Crusoe's Hegelian antithesis. When I was about sixteen my favorite novel, by all odds, was *Tristram Shandy*, though I did not know why at the time. I know now: *Tristram Shandy* is among other things an allegory of a writer waiting to get born. What really forms Tristram's environment is a world of words, a verbal abstract expressionism represented by the marbled page that Sterne calls his "motley emblem." Walter Shandy lives entirely on words: if irritable, he can be soothed at once if he makes a smart repartee, even to the most inane remark of a servant: he believes in the hidden significance of names like Trismegistus, in meanings concealed in an author's subject—in short, he believes in practically every verbal fallacy there is. Surrounding him is the verbalism of the book itself. If we look at some of the inserted stories—the man who drops a hot chestnut into his open fly; the abbess and novice who try to start a pair of balky mules by shouting obscene words at them (again turning on a linguistic fallacy, that certain words are obscene apart from their context)—we may say that, however exquisitely told, these stories as regards content are simply nothing. Yet we cannot say that they are all style and no substance, because style is itself substantial. We never emerge into a "real world" here, because reality itself has become verbal. Sterne prefigures the cosmos of Mallarmé where the function of everything that exists is to border on (*aboutir*) a book. More immediately, he prefigures the change from eighteenth-century discourse into nineteenth-century language, from wit and Hartleian association into verbal organism, a process completed by Coleridge when he turned against Hartley and began his great treatise on imagination and the Logos, which also remained in embryo.

I began the *Anatomy of Criticism* long ago by remarking that every serious subject, including criticism, seems to go through a kind of inductive metamorphosis, in which what has previously been assumed without discussion turns into a central problem to be discussed. Thus biology assumed that it was a study of the forms of life, but it was only when the forms of life became the study instead of the basis of study that evolution developed and biology became a fully mature science. Years later, when I came to read Michel Foucault's *The Order of Things*, I saw a parallel though greatly expanded thesis in it: that up to the end of the eighteenth century humanity had been assumed to be the basis for studying everything in the human cosmos, and that from the nineteenth century on we have been living in a world in which humanity itself is the study. Therefore, says Foucault, "Before the end of the eighteenth century, *man* did not exist." I confess to being puzzled, even baffled, by this way of putting it: it leaves me very unsure what Pope thought the proper study of mankind was. But if the conception "man" emerged after the eighteenth century, it must have been developing during it, which would be sufficient reason for reexamining it, even as tentatively as I have just tried to do.

Henry James and the Comedy of the Occult

It is a genuine pleasure to be giving a lecture in honor of my old friend Professor Munro Beattie. Our friendship goes back to undergraduate days at Victoria College, when we were fellow-students of Pelham Edgar. Edgar's main scholarly interest was in Henry James, on whom he wrote a pioneering study published in 1927. *Henry James: Man and Author* is a badly organized book, but it is full of the candor and simplicity which was Edgar's great quality as a critic, and is an especially useful quality for such a subject. Munro Beattie shared this interest of Edgar's at once: I took much longer to be attracted to James, much as I respected and even envied my classmate's understanding of him. Whatever understanding of James I may have acquired since, I have at least read him, so I felt that a lecture devoted to him would be an appropriate personal tribute for this occasion.

It was logical enough, I suppose, for a Canadian critic of Edgar's generation, half British and half American in his own cultural background, to be fascinated by Henry James with his North Atlantic preoccupations. James ignores Canada, but then, apart from Boston and New York, he largely ignores the United States as well, at least in his fiction. James thought of the European side of the Atlantic as providing tradition and cultural continuity, and of the American side as having a willingness to experiment and opportunity to expand. A complete human existence, then, would be located in some intermediate Atlantis that never quite comes up for air. One can find similar attitudes in Canadian or pre-Canadian writers from Haliburton to Grove and beyond, sometimes with the suggestion that in default of an Atlantis Canada may have to do instead.

I first became really attracted to James when a student in Oxford, after I picked up, for a shilling apiece, the two novels James had left unfinished at his death, *The Ivory Tower* and *The Sense of the Past*, along with the notes for them that the author had left. *The Ivory Tower*, which I shall return to later, confirmed all the things I felt I disliked about James at that time, but *The Sense of the Past* fascinated me: it was a story of time travel, about a twentieth-century American who walks into the English eighteenth century and exchanges places with an eighteenth-century English namesake equally attracted to the future. By chance a popular version of it, *Berkeley Square*, was running in the movie houses at the time. I could understand James's somewhat possessive interest, in his later years, in H. G. Wells as a writer who could carry on from where he stopped, as Wells seemed to have mastered representational and fantastic themes, including time travel, with equal fluency.

Time travel is one of the major themes developed since by the aspect of science fiction that is really occult fantasy. Another and closely related theme, that of identity in parallel worlds, was also anticipated by James in "The Jolly Corner." These two stories, *The Sense of the Past* particularly, seemed to me central to everything that had preoccupied James from the beginning about the social and psychological culture shocks that the two sides of Atlantic civilization contained for one another. It puzzled me, however, not that *The Sense of the Past* was unfinished, as its theme became almost unmanageably complex even for James as it developed, but that so crucial a story should take the form of what was really a ghost story.

James wrote ghost stories at intervals all through his writing career, and sometimes we tend to ask whether a given story is or is not a ghost story, a question we should never think of asking with, say, Kafka's *Castle* or Beckett's *Molloy*. But the ghost story was a specific English Victorian genre, featured in the Christmas issues of family magazines, and James adhered to its conventions for most of his life: *The Turn of the Screw* is firmly embedded in them. In James's later fiction—in *The Sacred Fount*, *The Beast in the Jungle*, "The Altar of the Dead"—we are well past the ghost story, and yet equally far beyond what is called "realism" too. And even in more representational fictions, such as *The Wings of the Dove* or *The Ambassadors*, we become increasingly aware of what Wallace Stevens calls "ghostlier demarcations, keener sounds," as objective and hidden worlds more and more interpenetrate. The reason for this is not that James came to "believe in" this or that, or that he was beginning to prefer one type of subject matter to another. The reason is purely technical: his work was getting more concentrated, and the imaginative possibilities covered increasingly larger areas than the surface story.

James's stories are mostly ironic versions, or inversions, of conventional comic patterns. In a simple comic action, such as a play of Molière, we have, over and over, the story of how a young couple want to get married but find their way barred by a father with some obsession that makes him want to impose another pattern of life on his offspring. This obsession, called a "humor" by Ben Jonson, acts as a reversing movement, blocking the normal evolution of the action into a state of greater freedom, happiness, sexual fulfillment, and common sense, and dragging us backwards into the tyranny of the obsession. The miser in *L'Avare*, the snob in *Le bourgeois gentilhomme*, the hypochondriac in *Le malade imaginaire*, the pedants in *Les femmes savantes*, stand for a tyrannical past, as the normal action represented by the young people struggles towards a future. The "humors" also represent a partial or mutilated existence, in contrast to the wholeness of experience symbolized by the young lovers, who are, in theory, going to live happily ever after once the humor is won over or outwitted. A contrasting comic type is someone, usually a clever servant (*gracioso*), who is sympathetic to the young couple and helps to forward the comic action.

James occasionally approaches the traditional comic form, as in the brilliant *The Europeans*, where old-world people come to Boston, and where there are at the end three marriages, and a near-miss at a fourth, quite in the manner of a Shakespearean romantic comedy. But the ironic variants predominate, and in ironic actions there can be any degree of complication, from total frustration to a split decision. In James the positive goal of the comic action, which in an ironic story is so often missed or thwarted, is not the sexual fulfillment of young lovers, but an intensity of experience that sexual satisfaction only approximates. The vision of this intensity is what Strether, the central character of *The Ambassadors*, sees at the end of the story, and clings to in spite of his growing isolation from the other characters. Again, no scene in Henry James is more powerful than the scene in *The Wings of the Dove*, where Milly, realizing that she has a terminal illness and has only a short time to live, walks through London streets and parks, feeling the atmosphere around her as something so vibrant as to be almost tangible. Characters in Henry James are going through this intensity all the time: the reader can see this, in the long dialogues and explanations in which the tiniest modulations of tone can have a portentous significance. But the characters themselves realize it only very seldom.

The story *What Maisie Knew*, being about a child, is, as the preface explains, the story of what Maisie knew but didn't altogether know she knew. That, incidentally, is the technical reason for an omniscient narrator, to tell us what his characters know but don't know they know, or feel but don't feel that they feel. In several of James's introductions to his works he mentions how the idea for them had originated in the smallest germ or seed of some anecdote, or even a passing reference, picked up perhaps at a dinner conversation. *What Maisie Knew* is one of these "seed" stories, and of his heroine there James says after a few pages: "it was to be the fate of this patient little girl to see much more than she at first understood, but also even at first to understand much more than any little girl, however patient, had perhaps ever understood before." Quite a statement when one looks at it. The phrase used about Lilly Theale in *The Wings of the Dove*, "the potential heiress of all the ages," fits more quietly into its context, but is startling nonetheless. In *The Ambassadors* Strether sees young Chad open the door of a theater box and the author says that his "perception of the young man's identity had been quite one of the sensations that count in life." In short, there is no such thing as a trivial incident: an immense amount of significance is always present potentially, and there are no limits to that amount.

In a story called "The Birthplace" a man gets a job, a tremendous windfall for him, of guide at Stratford to Shakespeare's house. As he goes on, he gradually loses his belief in the historical authenticity of what he is pointing to, and the quality of his sales talk is noticeably affected. A lot of tourist money is involved, so his bosses threaten him with dismissal, whereupon he pulls up his socks and goes into his spiel harder than ever. The implication is partly that the institution is more important than his views about it, his function being that of a guide, not a scholar. But the ramifications go much further. The story never uses the words *Stratford* or *Shakespeare*: the locale couldn't be more obvious, but their absence suggests another dimension. References to priests and temples are spattered all over the story, so much so that the reader is bound to ask: what kind of story would this be if this man were the guide to the Church of the Nativity at Bethlehem? Shakespeare is referred to throughout as "He" and "Him" with capitals; there's a comment about how the crowds kill him every day, and so on. So what seems on the surface a trivial story expands into, among other things, a vision showing us how every historical religion in the world has got started, by switching from history to mythology. This quasi-allegorical expansion is not typical of James, but it indicates his direction.

In another story, "The Real Thing," a painter who specializes in illustrations of fashionable life is confronted by a lady and a gentleman down on their luck, who propose to earn some money as his models, on the ground that they have practiced being a lady and a gentleman all their lives, and are consequently "the real thing." The experiment is, of course, a failure, and the painter has to go back to his professional model, the lower-middle-class Miss Churm. For James, as for many writers since, realism and reality are very different principles. Realism aims at the "real thing," the objective world; reality, for a writer, is not objective but verbal. Realism gives us a surface that is "like" reality; reality itself is far more complex. Virginia Woolf's polemic "Mr. Bennett and Mrs. Brown" is a simplified version of a thesis that James constantly expounds in his prefaces and other critical statements. William James once remarked that his brother's later novels were made out of "impalpable materials, air and the prismatic interferences of light, ingeniously focussed by mirrors upon empty space." One may reasonably read two things into this remark. First, William is saying that Henry's characters are treated as though they were ghosts, moving through ghostly incidents and settings in a transparent world. Second, that Henry James is doing with words what, say, Turner in his latest period was doing with paint: not representing objects so much as concentrating on the pictorial elements of color and lighting.

The characters in James may be good or bad, but whatever they are they never let the verbal texture down. When they engage in dialogue, they "follow" like professional dancers; they "make out" incredible subtleties through the gaps in what is said; they "keep it up" if there is the slightest chance of their saying anything commonplace; their conversation never dangles a participle or bungles a subordinate clause. James understands very well that there are many areas of the psyche which are linguistically structured, and that everything actually said is a selection from many things that could have been said, and that would lead to quite different outcomes for the story if they had been said. In *The Golden Bowl* the heroine, Maggie Verver, spends hundreds of pages *not* saying to her stepmother: "keep your hands off my husband." What the characters cannot say the author says for them, weaving around them complex patterns of implication, explication, complication, and replication.

The leisure class, which devotes itself to visiting, dining out, seeing and being seen, which does not regard itself as withdrawn from society but feels that it *is* society, constitutes for James a novelist's laboratory, a place where the nuances of human relationship can be studied under controlled conditions. A leisure class means very complex and elaborate conventions, ritual dances around the two maypoles of sex and money which fill up its life. It forms a world in which, when Spectator A sees male B and female C together in a Paris suburb or the National Gallery, an emotional to-do can result that readers a century later have to make a considerable effort of historical imagination to understand. Sociologically, this may be all tinsel and puppet show, but sociological categories, however plausible, have to be handled with great care in literary criticism. For literary critics, what the novels of James give us, especially in the later period, is a shimmering texture of verbal brilliance. The function of a leisure class is to put on a show for the rest of society, and James sees to it that it does, at least verbally, whatever else it may do.

Next to intensity of experience comes intensity of observation, which is, of course, the quality that reproduces James's own work as a novelist. The observer is often a central character in a James story: Maria Gostrey, in *The Ambassadors*, understands so much of what goes on around her that she seems like a sibyl or prophetess, but she expressly says she is nothing of the kind: she simply "sees." Observers may intervene in the action at crucial points, like Fanny Assingham in *The Golden Bowl*, who considers it "great fun" to be an observer, but, like many other observers in James, also has guilt feelings about her responsibility for the action she watches. The unnamed heroine of *In the Cage* is a telegraph operator who decodes a love affair through the messages sent through her office, though she doesn't get it quite right. Such observant characters, who often affect the action in some way, correspond to the clever servants and similar forwarders of the action in traditional comedies. They intervene between the action and the reader, who observes everything but affects nothing.

Naturally this concentration is achieved at a considerable price. James's method is to proceed by indirections, oblique movements that keep avoiding the big dramatic scene which is the stock in trade of so many novelists. One feature of this is the retreat from what James calls "affairs" and E. M. Forster the world of telegrams and anger. In his nearest approach to a detective story, *The Other House*, the theme is the callous murder of a four-year-old child. No police are brought in; the doctor is apparently squared and got to write a certificate for accidental death, and of the murderer it is said, in a phrase of numbing banality, "her doom will be to live." *The Pupil* is a story of a tutor and a boy belonging to an utterly dishonest family who exploit the tutor's fondness for the boy by not paying him, and are absorbed in a social climbing that is too blatant to get them anywhere. At the end they are about to go to smash. It would be interesting to know how such a feckless lot does go to smash, but that would involve the author in "affairs," so he simply cuts off the story by killing the boy. In the notes to the unfinished *Ivory Tower*, where the theme involves the world of business, James speaks of the work it will take to conceal not merely his lack of knowledge of the business world from the reader but his lack of interest in it.

Sometimes there is a big dramatic scene at the beginning of a novel: two notable examples are *The Princess Casamassima* and *The Wings of the Dove*. The first is a powerful scene in which the hero, as a child, is brought by his adopted mother into the prison where his real mother is dying. Nothing is communicated, because the mother speaks only French, a language no one else present can follow. *The Wings of the Dove* starts with a scene between Kate Croy and her no-good father, who then disappears from the story. Such scenes are prologues only: they play no part in the story itself except as background to show us what a prominent character is trying to escape from. There is no mystery about why James should have failed as a dramatist, the drama being a form that can hardly get along without scenes of confrontation. The mystery is why he should have wanted to succeed in such a form. Like Browning, James was a dramatist in reverse: his genius was for considering situations from the point of view of individual characters. In *The Ring and the Book* Browning took a dramatic situation and worked it out through the points of view of all the major characters (and others) in turn. James's corresponding experiment in reversed drama was *The Awkward Age*, and he was apparently trying to repeat the device in *The Ivory Tower*.

Even the novelist, however, has an audience whose attention must be held from page to page. James's habit was to write (or, later, dictate) a long sketch of his novel in which he talked to himself about his plans for it. For unfinished novels, such as *The Ivory Tower* and *The Sense of the Past*, such notes are invaluable; for the finished books they were destroyed, but his attitude toward them is curiously ambivalent. In a story called "Death of a Lion," one of the most pungently written of all his stories, a shy, retiring writer is seized on by a socialite who makes him a victim of her parties. In its own eyes her society is utterly benevolent and appreciative, but the effect on him is more or less that of falling into a school of piranhas. He finally completes a manuscript on the verge of death; naturally someone wants to borrow it, naturally he loses it, and naturally he makes a half-hearted search for it and can't find it (must have left it on a train). The writer dies after instructing his one real friend to rescue the notes and print them instead.

This suggestion that notes in which the author talks to himself about his book are the equivalent of the finished product connects in my mind with that extraordinary dinosaur the Collected Edition, where James seems to be trying to transform his entire oeuvre into one colossal logocentric monument to himself. His unwillingness to let his earlier selves die produces a great number of editorial changes that are usually in the direction of altering direct statements to oblique ones. In the prefaces he sometimes expresses regret that he had not eliminated some lively and attractive character, like Henrietta Stackpole in *Portrait of a Lady*, as though he felt some distaste for getting a casual reader interested in his book. In general, the revisions seem to move in the direction of giving the reader the idiom of the author's notes for the novel instead of the novel itself. One disadvantage of James's approach is that the uniform articulateness of his characters tends to make them sound more or less alike when they speak, and the revising tendency not only increases this, but assimilates their speaking style to James's own. I say this because it seems to me connected with the fact that many of his best realized later stories are occult fantasies which could also be read as existing entirely within the central character's mind.

II

In the traditional comic action in Molière and others the "humor," or obsessed blocking character, is outwitted, usually by some unexpected twist in the plot that (as a rule) enables young love to emerge triumphant. In ironic actions the humor is more likely to retain some ascendancy throughout. But in Henry James we cannot have simple humors with simple obsessions, like Molière's miser. For James all obsessions have a miserly aspect, a clutching and clinging to some substitute for genuine human experience. A recurring theme in James is the fetishism that is absorbed by some substitute symbol of the intensity of experience. The obvious example is *The Spoils of Poynton*, where the central character of the story is a collection of furniture, which gets burned up at the end. An early story, "The Last of the Valerii," features an exhumed Classical statue; there is a wax mannequin in a story called "Rose Agathe," a portrait in "The Special Type," and so on. The symbolic objects of the last works, the golden bowl and the ivory tower, have similar connections. So do various morbid fascinations with the dead in the ghost stories, or with, for example, the *Nachlass* of a dead author. Closer to the traditional miser is the role of money in many of the international stories, where, usually, the Americans have it and the Europeans want it.

In *The Golden Bowl* Adam Verver, who has made millions in America, retires from business and becomes a great collector for a museum of his own, and his son-in-law, the Italian Prince Amerigo, acquires the status of an expensive but uniquely desirable collector's item. This is only one element in his marriage, but it is the element symbolized by the crack or flaw in the golden bowl that gives the book its title. Then again, the pedant is a familiar comic humor, but in James many characters who fail to achieve full experience have a pedantic or over-theoretical quality in them, a retreat from a genuine human life into the pseudologic of obsession. T. S. Eliot made a celebrated remark about James's having a mind so fine that no idea could violate it. As a character in *The Europeans* says: "I don't entertain ideas; ideas entertain me." This means among other things that the reader of Henry James gets nothing from the story except the whole story: there are no extractable things to be got out of it. James made this point in a spoof or parody story, "The Figure in the Carpet," which turns on a pun on the word "in." A novelist writes a story which is believed to contain some ineffable precious secret— the metaphor of a buried treasure, something to be removed from where it is, is employed. There is no secret, but the belief that there is one inspires a whole cult.

At the same time James's stories are full of characters who are victims of positive gang-rapes of ideas, and will go to any lengths to defend and elaborate them. In *The Bostonians*, for example, Olive Chancellor takes a younger woman under her protection to educate her in advanced feminist views, including the superior virtue of celibacy, with little if any awareness that she is rationalizing a considerably over-heated Lesbian crush. Closer to our present theme is an early story, "Diary of a Man of Fifty," featuring a narrator who had walked out on an Italian countess because she received, and eventually married, the man who had killed her husband in a duel (she said her husband was a brute anyway). Twenty-five years later the narrator goes back to Florence and finds her daughter there with a young Englishman whom he feels to be in exactly the same situation he was. He is so convinced that the situations are identical that he imposes on the reader, who is almost ready to believe that the story is a Kafkaesque nightmare. Gradually it dawns on the reader that the narrator is a nut, and fortunately it dawns on the young man too, who marries the daughter and is very happy with her. "I had a complete theory about her," the narrator says plaintively.

A story called *Lady Barberina*, which is about as near to straight farce as James ever came, tells us of a pompous American doctor who marries a stupid English mooncalf, whose one accomplishment is to sit on a horse while it jumps fences. The American says he wants "race" in his marriage, with the result that his highly unadaptable partner regards him to the end as a "foreigner." This marriage, we learn, is suggested, in fact practically arranged, by an American woman with a theory: she is married very well in England and wants to build a "bridge" between the two countries. In *The Wings of the Dove* Maud Lowder, a socialite, takes the brilliant but impoverished Kate Croy under her protection and refuses to allow her to marry anyone who is not a "great man": again a typical comic action with a blocking character acting out an obsessive theory. Mrs. Newsome in *The Ambassadors*, who never enters the action except by proxy, has a theory that her son Chad is living an immoral life in Paris, which he is, from her point of view, and the whole action of the novel turns on this inflexible and provincial parental "humor." In *Portrait of a Lady* Ralph Touchett bestows a large fortune on the heroine Isabel Archer because of a theory that she will do something interesting with it. She does, too: she immediately constructs a theoretical air-castle of her own that leads her to refuse a most attractive proposal and throw herself away on a broken-down slob ("sterile dilettante," the text calls him).

These theoretical humors have a peculiarly close relation to the occult stories, because the occult by definition is unknown, and what we don't know we are impelled to concoct theories about. In a story called "The Marriages" the central figure, a woman named Adela, is bitterly opposed to her father's remarrying because she is fixated on her dead mother's memory. She admits that her father seems happy, "and it is dreadful of him to want to be." So she breaks up the engagement by calling on the prospective stepmother and telling her a slanderous rigmarole about her father and mother. The step-mother-elect backs out, not because of what's told her, but because she can't stand the prospect of living with such a creature as Adela, and Adela's father won't give her up. A relevant detail is that Adela believes that she is in spiritual communication with her mother, but considering what she does the connection seems morally dubious.

In another story, "The Friends of the Friends," which is explicitly a ghost story, a woman breaks off her engagement to her fiancé because she thinks he is more devoted to a dead woman than he is to her. He has seen the dead woman only once, and that was when she came to call on him, apparently after her death. It seems a somewhat strained reason for breaking off an engagement, but the living woman, who is also the narrator, has her theory to safeguard: "Everything in the facts was monstrous, and most of all my lucid perception of them: the only thing allied to nature and truth was my having to act on that perception. . . . When six years later, in solitude and silence, I heard of his death I hailed it as a direct contribution to my theory." One step further takes us to a much more celebrated theoretician, the governess in *The Turn of the Screw*.

The setting of *The Turn of the Screw* is familiar: a governess is hired to supervise two beautiful children, a boy and a girl named Miles and Flora, in a country house. Her employer pays for the set-up but refuses to have anything else to do with it—a convention straight out of folktale. The house is inhabited by a housekeeper and two dead servants, Peter Quint and Miss Jessel, who have, according to the housekeeper, exerted evil influences on the children. The governess sees the ghosts of the servants at various times, and is convinced that the children, for all their beauty and almost preternatural intelligence, are aware of these influences and continue to respond to them. This becomes obsessive with her, and her reaction to apparent evidence that this is true of Flora is merely an exultant: "Thank God! It so justifies me!"

It seems clear that the governess is a mass of sexual neuroses herself, and in general is as batty as a Kentucky cave. One episode will illustrate the point: she sees Miss Jessel looming behind Flora on one occasion; she tries to make the housekeeper see the ghost too; the child is frightened and says "I don't know what you mean. I see nobody. I see nothing. I never *have*. I think you're cruel. I don't like you!" This sounds like what any normal unhaunted child would say in the circumstances: the governess's reaction is to throw herself on the ground and go into hysterical convulsions. At the end of the story she is trying to get Miles to admit that he has been in connection with Peter Quint, whom she sees outside the window. Miles finally answers her question with "Peter Quint—you devil!", where the devil is clearly the governess rather than the evil ghost. The shock of realizing his condition kills him, perhaps: anyway, the story ends with a fully justified governess and a dead child.

If we look at *The Turn of the Screw* from the standpoint of realism, the story can be seen only as the fantasy of a madwoman, bolstered by the gossip of an illiterate housekeeper. One has to think also of the Victorian governess's uncertain hold on the middle class, where servants are always vaguely menacing ghosts, threatening to pull her down to their social level. Much is said about Peter Quint as a "menial," and Flora's outburst is said to be that of "a vulgarly pert little girl in the street." The reading of the story as a straight neurosis was more or less that of Edmund Wilson, who never understood anything in literature except realism, but such a reduction is far too simplistic for James. The governess seems to be telling her own story as a first-person narrator, but her story is actually being read aloud by someone else who knew her, and gives the strongest guarantees of her sanity and responsibility. James himself seems to confirm this in the preface to *The Princess Casamassima*, where he includes her with Maisie and Fleda Vetch in *The Spoils of Poynton*, both impeccable heroines.

No, the governess is rather a Cassandra figure who does see what she thinks she sees, though she may be crazy, as Cassandra was. As Hamlet discovered, it is not always possible to preserve one's mental balance when confronted with ghosts. How far the children are aware of the evil influences around them is another question. Miles may be if Flora isn't: he was, we are told, expelled from his school without explanation, although he keeps teasing to be sent back there. In any case, the governess's efforts to save the children are a violation of them as disastrous as anything the dead servants do. She is, in short, taken over by the evil she tries to fight.

Of the many things *The Turn of the Screw* connects with, one is the total deadlock of conventional standards of "good" and "evil." There is a picture by Blake generally called "Good and Evil Angels Struggling for the Possession of a Child." Judging from the various contexts in which this design appears in Blake, the child might be as badly off under the good as under the evil one. Similar deadlocks appear in various stories about writers and artists, though as a rule without ghosts. In *The Author of Beltraffio* the narrator visits a novelist who lives with a wife and small son. The wife has not read her husband's famous novel *Beltraffio*, but she "knows" it is a bad book, and she bends all her energies to keep control of the boy, to the point of sending away a doctor when he is dangerously ill. The boy dies—James is a prolific killer of children—and the mother repents sufficiently to put *Beltraffio* on her reading list. Conventional people's fears of literature or art that they think disturbs their moral values very quickly turn into a hatred of human intellect and imagination, and the conventional person is soon in the grip of an unseen evil force. James's father was interested in Swedenborg, and Swedenborg suggests that we are constantly surrounded by evil spirits, who are there but invisible, like the stars in daytime, but are unaware of us unless we do something to attract their attention. James himself owed something to Swedenborg—Lewis Lambert Strether, the hero of *The Ambassadors*, is named after a Swedenborgian novel by Balzac.

Again, *The Turn of the Screw* is one of James's puzzle stories that admit of more than one reading, none of which we can say with confidence to be the right one. In a story called *The Sacred Fount*, a character at a weekend house party makes up fantasies about other people there, confides them to a woman, and is told they are nonsense. End of long and remarkably pointless story. Practically everybody reads the book on this level—the realistic level—and wonders why James wrote it. But there are various layers of ambiguity underneath. It is true that what the narrator is doing is a parody of an imaginative process rather than an example of it: no novelist goes to work by making up stories about the people around him. But still the narrator's construct has a reality of sorts: it is subjective reality confronted with objective reality, even if the two fail entirely to coincide. Beneath that is a still more elusive question: why couldn't the narrator's fantasy be a real version of what is going on, told with a different perspective and emphasis? When the woman says impatiently about one of his figures, "there's really nothing in him at all," is she making a factual statement about any conceivable human being? But then we go back to the surface meaning, and realize that that is doubtless truth also, if not *the* truth: James has many observers who get things wrong, and was bound to write a parody of the process sooner or later.

Such a story as *The Sacred Fount* brings the relation of reality and realism into sharp confrontation: either there is some hidden reality that the narrator's fantasies point to, however vaguely and inaccurately, or there is no discernible reason for setting them forth at all. This principle, which runs through all of James's work, gives the occult stories a particular significance. A ghostly world challenges us with the existence of a reality beyond realism which still may not be identifiable as real. *The Wings of the Dove*, for example, is not a ghost story, but it is a story of two attractive young lovers, Kate Croy and Morton Densher, who want to marry but are blocked by poverty and impotence. As in a Molière comedy, they outwit the blocking character Maud Lowder, but they do it by descending on a dying American heiress and extracting her money like vultures battening on a corpse. Morton Densher struggles for some sense of self-respect to the very end of the story, but is powerless in the grip of something quite as sinister as any Quint or Jessel. Nor can we identify this sinister force with Kate Croy: she is more resolute and ruthless than he is, but is quite as trapped in what seems to her an inescapable situation. Lilly Theale, the heiress, dies in Venice, the city of Ben Jonson's play *Volpone*, where the theme of parasitism is set out brutally with nothing of James's ironic niceties or scruples.

It is also Venice that forms the setting of *The Aspern Papers*. Here Juliana, the ex-mistress of the young Romantic American poet, Jeffrey Aspern, dead for many years, lives with her niece Miss Tina in possession of all Aspern's papers. An American scholar, the narrator and one of a breed evidently as rapacious in James's day as now, comes to rent rooms in their palazzo. Juliana is a ferocious old harridan who is determined to extract as much American money from the scholar as she can, but has no intention of giving up a scrap of the papers, unless, perhaps, she can benefit her niece, the only human being now that she cares anything about. So Juliana and the narrator settle down to a watching and waiting game. The narrator remarks that the greatest vice is not knowing where to stop, and he is carried along to the point where he is mentally a thief and burglar and seducer of virgins, though he shrinks from the two physical acts of actually seizing the papers and actually marrying Miss Tina. His self-rationalizings get more desperate as the story proceeds. He is warned at the beginning that he may have to make love to Miss Tina: he says he would, recalls this later, and calls it a "joke without consequences." He breaks into Juliana's room and is caught by her, but maintains that he wasn't really about to steal the papers, just to "test a theory." Finally Juliana dies and Miss Tina destroys the papers, as she doesn't want anything to do with a man who in effect turned her down when she in effect proposed to him.

The Aspern Papers is not a ghost story, except to the degree that the dead poet may be watching the action sardonically from his portrait, as there are indications that he is. Several of James's stories deal with a dead author's reactions to the disposal of his papers. The fact that Aspern and his ex-mistress are Americans (the originals for the story were Shelley and Jane Clairmont), and his period, around 1820, bring the theme very close to *The Sense of the Past*. The story seems in any case as frightening as *The Turn of the Screw*, and more ambiguous in its moral categories. If Quint and Jessel do exist as ghosts, they are identifiably evil. But in *The Aspern Papers* there is once again a total deadlock which the categories of good and evil are quite useless to resolve. Modern morality would be solidly against Julia and for the scholar, because this is an ironic age, which believes that a figure interesting to the public belongs totally to the public and has no right to the smallest shred of privacy. But at the time of *The Aspern Papers*, privacy had its rights too: burning one's papers at death was a normal procedure, and for Julia to keep her lover's letters safe from prying eyes carried its own justification.

I mentioned the Venetian setting of the story, and towards the end the narrator remarks that "the Venetian figures, moving to and fro against the battered scenery of their little houses of comedy, strike you as members of an endless dramatic troupe." There seems to be a reference to the bedrock of all European comedy, the *commedia dell'arte*, with its stock characters, its improvised plots, and its close relation to puppet theater. One is reminded of the ballet-like plots of *What Maisie Knew* and *The Golden Bowl*, with their characters twining and intertwining in symmetrical patterns: a convention that runs all through fiction, especially comic fiction, though perhaps introduced in its modern form by Goethe's *Elective Affinities*, the title of which is a metaphor from chemical reactions. A James novel is "really" a story of forces of demonic evil and angelic innocence sweeping across fully articulate and intelligent beings who are largely unaware of them. It is just as "really" a story of chess pieces moving through an endgame that can result only in checkmate or stalemate. One has to read James with a stereo vision that brings the two realities into focus.

III

Apart from the various "humors," the fetishists and pedants, who fail to achieve any real intensity of experience, is there a general force that acts as a cause, apart from these effects? There are many answers, but one important one is certainly the narcosis of time. We eat and sleep, not when we are hungry or sleepy, but when it is time to eat or sleep, and the habit grows on us of committing experience to time, so that we drift along with its irreversible movement instead of withdrawing from it occasionally to become fully self-aware. The narcosis of time operates with peculiar power in the realm of expectation, where something is to happen in the future, as with the revolutionary programs, feminist in *The Bostonians* and social in *The Princess Casamassima*, that bemuse many of James's characters. There is also a struggle with time peculiar to the writer or artist, where the creator has to learn to relax his will and let things take their own time without drifting into laziness. This theme haunts James from *Roderick Hudson* on: a short story, "The Madonna of the Future," is a more conventional tale of an artist (American in Europe, of course) who keeps dreaming of a supreme masterpiece but never lifts a brush. The archetype for the story, referred to in the text, is Balzac's *Chef d'oeuvre inconnu*, but the man in that story at least worked on his delusion. The theme means a good deal to James because he himself was no infant prodigy; he took a long time to develop, and the feeling of having to die before one has really begun to understand one's art comes into many stories, most poignantly "The Middle Years."

But the transfer of experience to expectation is at its clearest in the terrible story *The Beast in the Jungle*, where John Marcher has been obsessed all his life by the notion that some tremendous experience, exhilarating or disastrous, awaits him at some time or other. Meanwhile he passes up every opportunity to achieve genuine experience, such as loving the sensitive and intelligent woman who loves him. Eventually the beast springs, along with Marcher's awareness that its name is Nothingness, and that he is now only a lost soul.

A gentler irony pervades a shorter tale called "The Bench of Desolation," where an elderly couple are sitting together on a bench beside the sea. The woman (I simplify slightly) has sued the man for breach of promise, and he has beggared himself for a lifetime in attempting to repay her—a theme slightly resembling de Maupassant's famous "Necklace" story. The woman tells him that she has carefully saved every penny he has paid her, because she knew more about money than he did, and she is paying it back with fivefold interest. What she forgot about was the passage of time, and that while she was saving his money he was spending his life. No other story in James has quite the eerie, other-worldly atmosphere of this one, in which, as in a Japanese No play, we seem to be in a world between death and birth, where all regrets have lost their relevance.

The next step takes us into the "international" theme so central in Henry James, where an American goes to Europe in search of deeper and richer experience. The movement is almost always eastward, and the protagonist is more frequently female than male. Again, the theme is a comic one, and the normal happy ending would be, as remarked earlier, not the right marriage necessarily, but the achievement of some kind of initiation into a fuller life. Ironic versions of this comic theme lead to frustrations of various kinds. One common story-type has the general pattern: naive innocent wealthy American girl goes to Europe, marries some very dubious Count de Spoons character, and wrecks her life.

The earliest major treatment of this theme, I think, is a story belonging to James's Paris period, *Madame de Mauves*. Here a romantic American girl named Euphemia, her convent-educated head turned by historical romance, feels that marriage to a Frenchman of a very old aristocratic family would be marriage to a superman. The Baron she marries is not a superman and his eye soon wanders, and Euphemia's life becomes miserable. The Baron's sister gives her a severe lecture: the male de Mauves have been having it on the side since Merovingian times, and who does Euphemia think she is to object to such hoary whoring? The sister actually seems to think that if a vice has a long enough pedigree it becomes something admirable: an aspect of aristocracy and tradition that the romances had not discussed. An American named Longmore comes to console Euphemia; the Baron has just enough of a conscience to hope that Longmore will take his wife on, but the lady is not for that kind of burning, and talks Longmore into renouncing her. Longmore himself doesn't want renunciation: he wants experience, even if respectable. However, he goes back to America; the Baron then suddenly has a change of heart and falls madly in love with his wife again, but as she will now have nothing more to do with him either he shoots himself. An exasperating story, but significant in many ways.

The generic affinities of the story are interesting. Euphemia is a kind of Courtly Love mistress, covering the entire spectrum of sexual frustration from the ideal of sublimation who demands total renunciation of sex from her lovers, to the frigid ice statue whose cruelty kills or otherwise destroys the essential life of her lover, in this case including her repentant husband as well. A similar figure appears in Aurora Coyne of *The Sense of the Past*, an American woman who has been to Europe, had some unknown bad experience there, and tries to extract a vow from the hero that he will never go to Europe, though she gives him no guarantees in return.

There are some remarkable episodes in this early story: Longmore has a dream in which he sees Euphemia across water, gets a boat to the other side, and finds she is back on the side he left. Boats and water are often associated with sexual experience in James, whether genuine, frustrated, or perverted: they appear prominently in *The Turn of the Screw* and *The Ambassadors*. Another episode features a pair of lovers, the woman socially a cut above the man, who is a fledgling artist, in a restaurant with the woman in charge of the restaurant making dire predictions. In later stories James would not feel the need of inserted episodes to show how the same archetypal situations recur in all ranks of society.

In *Portrait of a Lady*, already glanced at, we have an ironic parody of the type of magazine fiction that used to be addressed to a female reading public, and which usually featured a poor girl who eventually married a rich man, or else passed over the rich man and waited for Mr. Right. Isabel Archer, a rich girl, immediately passes over Mr. Right, Lord Warburton, and a group of American expatriates living in France pass her off on a Mr. All Wrong. In *Daisy Miller* there is no marriage, but Daisy is an attractive young woman who goes to Europe and is ostracized by the society around her for her free and unconventional American ways. She is not really "fast," much less loose: her trouble is that she refuses to think of herself, every moment of the day, as standing in a sexual trap as bait for some eligible young man, and posturing and displaying herself according to the rules of that game. Again the story is cut off by her death, but the essential point has been made. It was made again later by a reviewer who called the story an insult to American womanhood.

A minor and extremely unpleasant version of the same story-type is in a brief tale called "Four Meetings." Here an American woman who has always longed to see Europe finally gets to go there: as the ship docks at Havre a "cousin," a bum pretending to be an artist, descends on her and takes all her money; then she has to go back to America and the bum's whore, who calls herself a countess, settles in on her as a parasite. James says that every unpleasant story should have its beautiful counterpart: I know of no beautiful counterpart to this one, but perhaps the principle he is referring to is different in shape. The positive drive of a traditional comic story is toward a happy ending, which in James's international stories, we said, means an initiation leading to a greater and fuller intensity of experience. The story we read usually tells us of some failure to achieve this, whether a moral failure within an individual character or the result of a sinister or stupid social conspiracy. But we as readers can see something of what might have been achieved, and our wider vision is perhaps the beautiful counterpart James mentions.

Certainly there is a great deal of beauty in the three great novels at the end of James's career, *The Wings of the Dove, The Ambassadors,* and *The Golden Bowl,* and there are many suggestions of positive as well as ironic resolutions. In *The Wings of the Dove* Lilly Theale, with the hectic flush of death on her, nevertheless achieves a quality of life that carries her serenely over the heads of the lovers trying to get her money. In *The Ambassadors* four major characters all achieve something of the same quality, although their community disintegrates at the end. In *The Golden Bowl* Maggie Verver breaks out of her ironic dilemma by renouncing her emotional dependence on her father, whom she dispatches back to America, and her Italian husband discovers he has married a strong woman rather than a passive girl. Such positive achievements represent an escape from what I have called the narcosis of time, the simple drifting from birth to death. I spoke at the beginning of the ideal fusion of American and European contributions to a full human life as perhaps attainable only in a submerged Atlantis. In Blake Atlantis is the kingdom of the imagination, and the ocean that rests on top of it he calls the "Sea of Time and Space." At some point or other it seems to have occurred to James that the most concentrated possible treatment of his international theme would be one that cuts through our ordinary awareness of space and time.

It has been noted by James critics, Edgar among them, that in the traditional ghost story the dead haunt the living, whereas in James it is frequently the living who haunt the dead. One of the major reasons for well-to-do Americans going to Europe in the first place is to reinforce their sense of the past, to become more aware of their own cultural heritage. So Ralph Pendrell, the American hero of *The Sense of the Past,* having acquired a Regency house in London, becomes obsessed with the pastness of the house, and in particular with a curious portrait of a young man who has turned his back on the painter, evidently as a whim. We gradually learn that the subject of the portrait is another Ralph Pendrell of a century previous, who had come from an earlier America to marry the daughter of an English family and reconcile the two families. So the twentieth-century American vanishes into the Regency period, while his counterpart moves into the contemporary twentieth-century world.

The former finds himself in a dream world, where everything seems at first to go all right, as so often happens in dreams. Where certain things are not clear to him, he makes mistakes, and the mistakes produce some uneasiness in the people around him, as though they were subliminally aware of being haunted by a ghost from another age. Meanwhile he discovers that in addition to the daughter he is supposed to marry, there is another and considerably more attractive daughter, whom he is clearly going to fall in love with instead. His counterpart in the future, according to James's notes, is considerably displeased at this, and we realize that the arrangement is a rather unfair one: the hero of the story is imprisoned in the past, whereas his counterpart has all the freedom of the future.

However James would have worked the story out, it was a kind of abstract model of the type of story he had been telling all his life. The companion piece, "The Jolly Corner," is an even clearer example of the living haunting the dead, as the hero, an American named Spencer Brydon, who has spent his life in Europe, returns to New York to his ancestral house there, whence he proceeds to dig out a very reluctant ghost of the Spencer Brydon he would have been if he had stayed in America. Both stories leave it open to us to consider their central characters as simple lunatics, but somehow the willing suspension of disbelief does take hold; we accept the exchange of identities in time and space as imaginative realities, and can even see in them a structured form of some of the hidden entities that we get only fitful glimpses of in the more representational stories.

Another unfinished novel was *The Ivory Tower*. Here, for complex reasons we cannot here go into, a man named Graham Fielder is left a large sum of money by an American millionaire, has no idea of what to do with it, and gives it to a friend to look after it for him; the friend promptly embezzles it, and the hero thinks up various reasons for not doing anything about it. He got the money in the first place through the influence of one of the two heroines, Rosanna Spearman, who is a warm-hearted and generous girl, but his affections are clearly moving in the direction of a much more tight-mouthed female who would be more likely to go off with the embezzler. Three books and part of a fourth, out of a projected ten, about someone who seems clearly to be, in post-Jamesian language, a wimp and a nerd. Soon after James started on it the 1914 war broke out, and the book was abandoned. All around him was an outbreak of hysterical fury that made the evil of Peter Quint and Miss Jessel, to say nothing of the evil of people who embezzle money when they are practically asked to do so, look like children in Halloween masks. The well-dressed and articulate puppets were too wooden, too stiff and rattling, for James to have any more interest in maneuvering them. He turned once again to his ghost story just before he died, because in its fantasy he saw the reality he had sought as an artist, whereas the realism in the social manners of his time had left him with a sense of total illusion.

Approaching the Lyric

S ome people believe that literary terms can be defined: there was a purist in the Greek Anthology who maintained that an epigram is a poem two lines long, and that if you venture on a third line you're already into epic. But that seems a trifle inflexible. At the other extreme, there is a popular tendency to call anything in verse a lyric if it is not actually divided into twelve books. Perhaps a more practicable approach would be to say that a lyric is anything you can reasonably get uncut into an anthology. Or perhaps we can at least limit the subject by saying what the lyric is not.

The kind of formulaic, half-improvised poetry that, we are told, lies close behind the Homeric poems is poetry of pure continuity. Like motion in Newton, there is nothing to stop it except some external factor, such as the end of the story it tells or the beginning of the occasion it was composed for. If the poet does not read or write, the poem exists only in the one dimension of pure continuity in time, because such a poet is not thinking of lines on a page. If the poem is written, it appears in two spatial dimensions, across and down a page, as well as in time, and the crucial term *verse*, with its associations of turning around or turning back, becomes functional. The poem may still be continuous, but in "verse," where we keep coming to the end of a line and then starting another, there is a germ of discontinuity. The more this sense of the discontinuous increases, the more closely we approach the lyrical area.

In the lyric, then, we turn away from our ordinary continuous experience in space or time, or rather from a verbal mimesis of it. But we cannot simply identify the lyrical with the subjective. Continuous poetry may also be subjective, like *The Prelude* or *Childe Harold*, and lyrical poetry may be a communal enterprise, like the Old Testament psalms or the odes of Pindar. As these examples show, the discontinuous element in poetry is often linked to a specific, usually ritual, occasion, and the element of occasion means that the poem revolves around the occasion, instead of continuing indefinitely. If there is no public occasion, what corresponds to it may be a private occasion like drinking or love-making, to cite two standard themes. But even in this kind of "occasional" verse there is still an identity of subject and object. Many years ago, when logical positivism was in vogue among philosophers, I picked up one of their books and read the following: "Many linguistic utterances are analogous to laughing in that they have only an expressive function, no representative function. Examples of this are cries like 'Oh, Oh,' or, on a higher level, lyrical verses." This remark put me off reading philosophy for some years, at least until philosophers stopped chasing these red herrings of expressive and representative functions.

The private poem often takes off from something that blocks normal activity, something a poet has to write poetry about instead of carrying on with ordinary experience. This block has traditionally been frustrated love, as in the Petrarchan poetry of Elizabethan England, where the frustration is normally symbolized by the cruelty and disdain of a mistress. Such a block has much to do with creating the sense of an individualized speaker. Something similar occurred in ancient Greece: in fact, Bruno Snell, in his book on the evolution of what he considers a unique type of individual consciousness in the period between Homer and the age of Socrates, associates the decisive turning point with the early lyrical poets, Archilochus, Sappho, Anacreon, and their contemporaries.

Here the blocking point makes the lyrical poem part of what biologists call a displaced activity, as when a chimpanzee crossed in love starts digging holes in the ground instead. In another lyrical genre the block relates to the reader rather than the poet: this is what we find in the epitaph convention that we have had from Greek times on. Here the reader is assumed to be a traveler, pursuing his normal course through time and space, who is suddenly confronted with something he should stop and read. What he reads is the verbal essence of a life which has once had its own context in space and time but is now enclosed in a framework of words. He is often told, at the end, that he has been looking in a mirror: his own context is still in ordinary space and time, but it will eventually disappear, and the verbal essence of *his* life may make an equally short poem.

We notice in, for example, Mallarmé, a good many occasional pieces, as well as poems called *Toast Funèbre*, are thought of as inscribed on tombs. So we are not surprised that it is Mallarmé who gives us the best-known parable of the displacing operations of lyric in *L'après-midi d'un faune,* where a faun tries to pick up a nymph and finds that he has two nymphs stuck together, interested in each other but not in him. There is nothing for it but to retreat into the dream world where verbal creation begins, and where, as he says, he will see instead the shadows that they will turn into.

When the block ceases to be opaque and becomes transparent, the lyric of frustration expands into the lyric of mental focus. Gerard Manley Hopkins speaks of two kinds of poetic process: a transitional kind, which operates in narrative and story-telling, following the rhythm of the continuity of life in time, and a more meditative kind, which turns away from sequential experience and superimposes a different kind of experience on it. The superimposing provides an intense concentration of emotion and imagery, usually on some concrete image. It is on this level that we have Keats's contemplation of the Grecian urn, Hopkins's recognition of the presence of God in the windhover, Rossetti's remembering from a moment of anguish that "the woodspurge has a cup of three." In this kind of meditative intensity the mind is identified with what it contemplates.

In Oriental poetry the tradition of meditation is so well established that a poem can often simply give a few verbal clues and leave it to the reader to re-create the process. The meditative power of Japanese or Chinese lyric may have something to do with the nature of the written language, which seems to provide a visual supplement to the verbal intensity, so that the seventeen syllables of the haiku, for instance, can become a kind of exploding verbal atom. However much may be lost through ignorance of Japanese, no one can miss this exploding power that comes through a haiku of the poet Rippo, which must surely be one of the world's greatest death songs.

> *Three lovely things . . .*
> *Moonlight . . . cherry blossoms . . .*
> *And now . . .*
> *The untrodden snow.*

This hieroglyphic quality is mentioned by Hart Crane in one of his rare critical essays: "It is as though a poem gave the reader as he left it a single, new *word,* never before spoken and impossible to actually enunciate, but self-evident as an active principle in the reader's consciousness henceforward."

So far I have touched mainly on the visual side of the lyric, but of course traditionally the lyric is primarily addressed to the ear. A good deal has been said about the deferring of written language to the spoken word: much less has been said about the deferring of written poetry to music, especially in lyric poetry, where the very word *lyric* implies a musical instrument. For centuries poets refused to admit that their expression was verbal: they insisted that it was song, or even instrumental music. In pastoral poetry the instrument was often a flute or reed, like the "oat" of *Lycidas* or the pipe of Blake's *Songs of Innocence*, regardless of the fact that it is impossible to sing and play a wind instrument at the same time. The sixteenth century, more realistically, featured the lute: poets who do not think musically give us some curious musical images, such as Coleridge's damsel lugging a dulcimer across Abyssinia.

This association with music has two elements of importance. One is that the lyric turns away, not merely from ordinary space and time, but from the kind of language we use in coping with ordinary experience. Didactic or even descriptive language will hardly work in the lyric, which so often retreats from sense into sound, from reason into rhyme, from syntax into echo, assonance, refrain, even nonsense syllables. The strict forms of traditional lyric—villanelles, ballades, sonnets, and the like—form part of the same tendency. Many lyrics are written in stanzas, and the metaphor of "room" inherent in "stanza" suggests a small area complete in itself even though related to a larger context. So a stanza unit may impart a lyrical quality even to a long continuous poem: *The Faerie Queene* seems "lyrical" in a way that *Paradise Lost* does not. "We'll build in sonnets pretty rooms," as Donne says. If we start to read this poem of Wyatt:

> *Process of time worketh such wonder,*
>   *That water which is of kind so soft*
> *Doth pierce the marble stone asunder,*
>   *By little drops falling from aloft*

we can hear the imitative harmony in the rhythm that suggests a self-contained world where reality is verbal reality. Imitative harmony is sometimes called a trick of rhetoric, but in Wyatt, who is better at it than anyone else I know in English literature, it is certainly no trick. More important, we are circling around a defined theme instead of having our attention thrown forward to see what comes next. We hear, so to speak, the end in the beginning: we have stepped out of experience into something else, a world like the rose-garden in *Burnt Norton* from which we must soon return.

The second factor connecting lyric with music is that, for the most part, musical sounds are in a special area, different from the sounds we hear in ordinary life. The poet, however, has to use much the same words that everyone else uses. In lyric the turning away from ordinary experience means that the words do not resonate against the things they describe, but against other words and sounds.

Sometimes this verbal resonance comes from allusiveness, from deliberate echoes of classical and other myths, as in Swinburne:

> *And the brown bright nightingale amorous*
> *Is half assuaged for Itylus,*
> *For the Thracian ships and the foreign faces,*
> *The tongueless vigil, and all the pain.*

Here we are psychologically close to magic, an invoking of names of specific and trusted power. At other times the resonance is not allusive but, more vaguely, or at least more indefinably, an evoking of some kind of mysterious world that seems to be concealed within ordinary time and space. Verbal magic of this kind has a curious power of summoning, like the proverbial Siren's song. When Keats says that the nightingale's song has "Charmed magic casements, opening on the foam / Of perilous seas, in faery lands forlorn," half our brain closes down and says it doesn't know what Keats is talking about. The other half wakes up and recognizes a strange environment that still has something familiar in it. The poet, in the ancient phrase, unlocks the word-hoard, but a word-hoard is not a cupboard: it is something more like the world that our senses have filtered out, and that only poets can bring to awareness.

It is very common for a single line to possess this quality of resident and summoning magic. There is the line from Thomas Nashe's elegy, "Brightness falls from the air," which many people know who know nothing else of Nashe. One critic has suggested that the line may be too good for Nashe, who perhaps wrote the more commonplace "Brightness falls from the hair," the present version being a printing accident. I dislike the suggestion, but it is true that accident can play some part in verbal magic. There is a Newfoundland folksong with the original refrain: "I love my love but she'll love no more."

Through a lucky short circuit in oral transmission this turned into "I love my love and love is no more," a line that teases us out of thought like the Grecian urn.

So the frustrating or blocking point, the cruel mistress or whatever, becomes a focus for meditation rather than brooding, and thereby seems to be the entrance to another world of experience, "the fitful tracing of a portal," as Wallace Stevens calls it. This world is one of magic and mystery, one that we must soon leave if we are to retain our reputations as sober citizens of the ordinary one. But there is still a residual sense that something inexhaustible lies behind it, that it is good not merely to be there, but, as Ferdinand says at the masque in *The Tempest*, to remain there. Two highly cerebral poets, Mallarmé and Rilke, have said that the end and aim of lyrical poetry is praise. They did not say this in any sort of conventional religious context: they were not talking about a prefabricated heaven, but an earthly paradise we stumble on accidentally, like the castle of the Grail, a paradise we can bring to life for ourselves if we ask the right question, which is, according to Chrétien de Troyes: "Who is served by all this?"

For many centuries the lyric was content to be a relatively minor aspect of poetic experience, but Poe's essay "The Poetic Principle" reacted against this and identified the lyrical with the authentically poetic, dismissing all continuous poems as fragments of genuine lyric stuck together with versified prose. This essay had, as is well known, a tremendous influence on the French school that runs from Baudelaire to Valéry, and that influence made its way into English poetry in the generation of Eliot and Pound. I imagine that one reason for its influence was the belief that the standard meters of continuous verse had exhausted their possibilities, so that narrative shifted to prose, while long poems, even the poems of the master of the interminable, Victor Hugo, tended to become increasingly fragmented.

One of the by-products of this movement was the critical approach that developed two generations ago, which I suppose this volume would call "the old new criticism." This was a technique of explication that approached all literature, whatever the genre, in terms of its lyrical quality, and tended to place the great continuous poets, Milton, Goethe, Victor Hugo, below the poets of the greatest fragmented intensity, Hopkins, Hölderlin, Rimbaud. This movement in criticism seems to me essentially a practical one, excellent for classroom discussion but not well grounded in critical theory. Theoretical developments since then have tended to focus on continuous qualities and on narrative. I take it that the present book [*Lyric Poetry: Beyond New Criticism*] owes its existence to a feeling that it is high time for critical theory to come to firmer grips with the lyrical element in literature. I share this feeling, and have therefore an additional reason for being interested in it.

IV

Criticism and Environment

It seemed to me that I could contribute most usefully to this conference [Adjoining Cultures as Reflected in Literature and Language] by speaking out of my experience as a resident of Canada. An American hardly needs to concern himself much with problems of adjoining cultures in the ordinary sense, unless he has a special interest in them: if he does have such an interest, Mexico will provide him with far more dramatic examples than Canada will. But in Canada the cultural situation represented by the word *adjoining* is present and continuous, and there are many elements in the Canadian situation that are of great interest and relevance to the general questions of critical theory that arise from it. They are, in my view, of all the greater interest for being so muted and so camouflaged.

In 1950 I was asked to make an annual critical review of all the English poetry published in Canada during the previous year. I did this for ten years, when by a combination of good luck and instinctive cunning I retired just before it became humanly impossible to continue it because of the phenomenal increase in quantity. During this period I acquired my own sense of the context, in time and space, that Canadian culture inhabits. More important for me, these reviews formed a body of "field work" which entered into my more general critical attitudes, modifying some and strengthening others. In other words, the Canadian scene became a kind of cultural laboratory in which to study the relation of criticism to its environment. What I have to say, especially in the next few moments, I have often said before, if not to this audience, and I apologize to anyone who may be familiar with my other writings on Canada for the repetition.

We may begin with the geographical or spatial environment. In Canada there is nothing corresponding to the north-south frontier that has been so conspicuous in American culture. Entering Canada from Europe by ship—through the straits of Belle Isle into the Gulf of St. Lawrence and down the river to the Great Lakes—has no counterpart in the American Atlantic coastline. This movement is the center of the east-to-west thrust that Canadian economists and historians call (or used to call, there being fashions in such matters) the "Laurentian axis." The Laurentian axis suggests a mercantile economy, with sparse settlements along the waterway and long canoe and forest trails probing the hinterland for furs and other raw materials to be shipped to more populous markets.

Several features inherited from this economy may be traced in Canadian life down to our time. In the treatment of the indigenous peoples, the French record is considerably better than the English or Spanish records. The main reason for this was that the early Canadian economy depended on the cooperation of Indians for the long canoe and forest trails, and the close economic relation led to a good deal of intermarriage. In the opening up of the Canadian West, an embattled situation arose with the Métis, or French-Indian half-breeds, which was not an Indian war but a collision with another part of French Canada. The trauma left by the crushing of the Métis rebellion and the hanging of their leader, Louis Riel, still forms part of the tension between English- and French-speaking parts of the country.

Two aspects of the inheritance of mercantilism may be noted. First, there was a long period, a century at least, when there were extensive analyses of Canadian cultural production and critical articles with such titles as "Is There a Canadian Literature?", to which the answer, as a rule, was a highly qualified yes. That is, the answer was usually accompanied by a prophecy that a much greater literature was just about to begin. The rationalization given for the late arrival of major poetry and fiction was that Canada was a "young" country and had to establish a material basis for it culture first. The real reason that Canada had accepted the mercantilist conditions against which the United States revolted, of providing raw materials and resources to be consumed by wealthier centers, seldom emerged into the foreground. But the sense of cultural inferiority left from the conviction that the head office is always somewhere else is obvious enough to the least reflective of Canadians.

Second, we notice in early Canadian literature something that continues to our own time: the predominance of women among the more serious writers. The centrifugal rhythms of hunting, fishing, trapping, farming, and ranching were the "men's work": it was the centripetal rhythms presided over by the women and directed toward hearth and home, which in more elaborate societies expanded to parties and other social gatherings, that belonged to the embryonic culture. One of the first novels written in the New World, and certainly the first in Canada, is *The History of Emily Montague*, published in London in 1769, and written by Frances Brooke, the wife of a clergyman attached to the British military garrison in Quebec after its capture from the French. This is an epistolary novel of sensibility in the Richardson tradition, and is earlier than either Henry Mackenzie's *Man of Feeling* or Fanny Burney's *Evelina*. The world it describes is, in the words of one of the letter-writers, "like a third or fourth rate country town in England; much hospitality, little society; cards, scandal, dancing, and good cheer." It is not greatly different from many aspects of the world of Jane Austen, where there are also handsome officers to be flirted with, but certain tones betray a greater sense of desperation. The same correspondent, whose name, Arabella Fermor, evokes an echo from *The Rape of the Lock*, remarks: "Those who expect to see 'A new Athens rising near the pole' will find themselves extremely disappointed. Genius will never mount high, where the faculties of the mind are benumbed half the year. . . . I suppose Pygmalion's statue was some frozen Canadian gentlewoman, and a sudden warm day thawed her."

It is significant that Canada's first work of fiction is about life in a garrison, for the garrison encapsulates a great deal of imaginative feeling in Canada, even down to the twentieth century. What corresponded to the frontier in American life was never a border in Canada. It was a circumference: a frontier surrounded and enclosed all the tiny communities wherever they were. The sense of alienation from nature was nowhere distanced in space from the cultural centers. Canada is still divided by natural or political obstacles which even a world of instant communication does not wholly overcome psychologically. As the population increased with immigration, specific ethnic cultures appeared, like Icelandic in Manitoba, which were enclave cultures, totally surrounded by alien linguistic influences. It is clear that the culture of French Canada is, in the North American context, simply the largest of these enclave cultures. Still, an enclave culture with its own language has at least no problem of identity, and French writers in Canada, however limited their markets or audiences, have always had the advantage of knowing that they had a social function in carrying on the fight to preserve a threatened and beleaguered language. English Canada has lacked the advantage of an easily defined identity without much to compensate for it.

The particular problems of space in Canada, along with those of a terrifying climate, are naturally dissolving under modern technology. Problems of time and of cultural tradition are much more elusive. In its history, Canada has reversed the American sequence of a revolutionary war against Europe followed by a civil war to preserve its own federation. Canada had a civil war of European immigrants, English and French, on its own soil first, followed by the War of 1812 against its North American neighbor. This war, for all its grotesque muddle, was still from the point of view of the Canadian something of a war of independence; at any rate, it was an indication that the two halves of upper North America were to have different directions and destinies.

One consequence of this inverted history was that Canada missed the eighteenth century, with all its confidence in reason and progress. English and French in Canada spent the eighteenth century battering down each other's forts, and Canada went directly from the Baroque expansion of the seventeenth century to the Romantic expansion of the nineteenth. There are no culture-heroes corresponding to Washington, Jefferson, or Franklin, and no sense of a detachment from history and a fresh start such as the American Revolution provided. Much of English Canada was settled by disaffected Tories from America, and there was a strong reaction against that Whig spirit that won the American Revolution, with its liberal mercantile values, its confidence in laissez-faire, its equating of freedom with national independence. A good many English Canadian intellectuals, even yet, are some form of Tory radical, and when anti-American sentiments are expressed in nineteenth-century Canada, they tend to attack from the left and right at the same time. That is, they decry both the absence of distinctions in American democracy and the inequalities of wealth and privilege, especially in the slave-owning states, in American oligarchy. The Nova Scotian writer Thomas Haliburton has his Yankee peddler Sam Slick describe a Fourth of July celebration as "a splendid spectacle; fifteen millions of freemen and three millions of slaves a-celebratin' the birthday of liberty." But the positive side of this critical attitude is harder to find.

A cultural tradition founded, as the American one is, on a successful revolution tends to be deductive, drawing up a constitution based on "self-evident" principles, and continually revising and amending that constitution without discarding it. This deductive pattern has no counterpart in Canada, where nothing has ever been self-evident. Canadians usually try to resolve social tensions and conflicts by some form of compromise that keeps the interests of both parties in view, in the conservative spirit of Edmund Burke. The result is that the country seems to an outsider, and often to insiders as well, to be perpetually coming apart at the seams, with nothing to sustain it but a hope that some ad hoc settlement will keep it together until the next crisis. As a result there is a greater preoccupation with history in Canada, especially French Canada (the motto of Quebec, recently revived, is *je me souviens*), and much less with the sense of emerging from history that was so characteristic of American popular feeling down to about 1950, and was one of the central themes of Walt Whitman.

The fact that a revolution is based on the success of violence is doubtless connected with much of the lawlessness in American history: the lynching, the labor violence, the anarchy at the frontier as it proceeded through an increasingly wild West. Canada was controlled first by the British military occupation, after which a military police force moved into the northwest to keep order there. As a result violence in Canada has tended to be mainly repressive, or "law-and-order," violence. The effect on Canadian fiction has been very marked, because the obvious place for outbreaks of violence in such a society is the family.

II

We may distinguish three main phases in the development of Canadian literature, each phase having its distinctive interest for a student of the relation of criticism to environment. The first is the colonial or provincial stage, where culture is one of the things to be imported from more populous centers, and where the standards of culture are assumed to be established in those centers. It is characteristic of a provincial culture to think in terms of meeting an external standard. But as no mature standards can ever be met externally like an examination, but have to be established by the writer for himself, it is obvious that frustration and cultural lag are built into this kind of imitation.

In August 1606, a poet named Marc Lescarbot, one of the settlers in the tiny French outpost of Port Royal, or what is now Annapolis, Nova Scotia, wrote a nostalgic poem on seeing a shipload of his fellow countrymen returning to France. It was published in France the following year. There is some perfunctory rhetoric about expanding the glory of France in a new world and the like, but the pervading tone is one of almost unbearable desolation as he sees the ship go, taking so much of everything that makes life worth living along with it. There is nothing, he says, for those who remain stranded in Acadia except a rabble of savages who have no God, no laws, and no religion. We should be inclined to say only that the Micmac Indians did not have *his* God or laws or religion, but for a spokesman of Baroque Europe there is little difference between the two statements. Indians frequently appear for picturesque effect in Canadian literature down to our own time, but the notion of learning anything from their culture hardly appears before the middle of this century.

One does not obliterate a native culture with impunity, however, no matter how alien it may seem. In the United States this process was rationalized as a kind of crusade; in Canada it formed part of an excluding view of culture that I have often spoken of as a garrison mentality. The basis of this is a sense of the need for constant vigilance against attack that leaves one with no time to cultivate the kind of imaginative flexibility that is needed for culture. As a society, the garrison is under rigid discipline and class distinction; as a culture it forms a kind of mob rule that is alert to stamp out any expression or consciousness or opinion that might weaken the sense of social cohesion.

In a provincial situation one of the most illuminating forms of literature is the book written by a relatively sympathetic outsider who feels that the onlooker may see more of the game being played than the participants. Thus Mrs. Humphrey Ward, a British novelist of the turn of this century, has a story called *Canadian Born* (1908), in which the British heroine, impressed by the energy of the country and by an attractive young Canadian male she has met, remarks: "I am only a spectator. *We* see the drama—we feel it—much more than they who are in it." Similarly, perhaps the best known work of French Canadian fiction, *Maria Chapdelaine* (1913), was written by a European Frenchman, Louis Hémon, whose first novel, incidentally, was written in English and had an English setting.

The story is centered on a group of *habitant* farmers in Quebec whose instinct is to retreat from the more urbanized forms of life as they encroach. The heroine, brought up in a *habitant* household, has to choose between a suitor who will take her to Boston and a suitor who can offer her only the more grueling pioneer life she has known. Judging from the statistics of emigration from both English and

French parts of Canada to New England in this period, we can say with some confidence that any Canadian girl would have bought a one-way ticket to Boston before her deliverer had had time to reconsider. But Maria Chapdelaine is the exception: she stays with the tiller of the soil.

What Louis Hémon discovers in Quebec *habitant* life is in large part a literary convention. He is fascinated by a way of life that reminds him of certain aspects of French literature: he has a sharp ear for any *vieux parler* phrase he hears, and he encloses his action within a framework of assumptions about the mystique of the *terrior* and of the peasant's feeling for the soil. Nobody in Quebec could reasonably be called a peasant, even then, but the emotions of the Chapdelaine family are assimilated to literary conventions about peasantry. It is also significant that the book was attacked by French Canadian critics in its day for presenting *habitant* life in so primitive a form. There were many counterparts to such attacks in English Canada: they are part of the typical response of a provincial culture to an external view of it. Its insecurity takes the form of resentment at being thrust on a larger stage before it has had time to put on its best clothes. One is reminded of the Irish reaction to Synge's *Playboy*. It is not the genuineness of the heroine's decision to remain on Quebec soil that is in question: the same type of resolution recently appeared in the film *My Brilliant Career*, which was based on an Australian story. It is rather the ambiguity of a vision of a certain limited area of life that looks like the exposures of realism to those within it and like the concealments of literary convention to those outside it.

The second stage of cultural development in Canada revolves around the Confederation of 1867, the union of the two Canadas, now Ontario and Quebec, with two Maritime Provinces, and eventually British Columbia. This stage is characterized by a search for a distinctively "Canadian" identity, more particularly in English Canada, and attached to this search are a number of critical fallacies that are important to diagnose. The first and most elementary of these is the fallacy of the exclusive characteristic, or nonexistence essence, the attempt to distinguish something that is, in this case, "truly Canadian," and is not to be found in other literatures. There are no exclusive or even defining characteristics anywhere in literature: there are only degrees of emphasis, and anyone looking for such characteristics soon gets as confused as a racist looking for pure Aryans. It is not hard to ridicule the fallacy of the distinctive essence and to show that it is really a matter of looking for some trademark in the content. A satirical revue in Toronto some years ago known as *Spring Thaw* depicted a hero going in quest of a Canadian identity and emerging with a mounted policeman and a bottle of rye. If he had been Australian, one realizes, he would have emerged with a kangaroo and a boomerang. One needs to go deeper than ridicule, however, if one is to understand the subtlety of the deceptions involved.

The search for a distinctive Canadian identity was, naturally, a remote and minor development of Romanticism. Like other forms of Romanticism, it often fell into another critical fallacy that might be called the "harnessing of Niagara Falls" fallacy: the notion that literature derives its energy from nature or experience, and that a new literature is bound to arise in a new country simply because there are new things to look at and types of experience with no direct counterparts elsewhere. Getting really clear of this fallacy is a more difficult enterprise than it sounds. Man never lives directly in nature: he lives inside the construct of culture or civilization, of which the verbal aspect is a mythology. Literature is a constant re-creation of this mythology and derives its forms from it. The writer is not "inspired" by nature or even by experience: these things may supply incidental content, but the forms of literature develop out of litera-ture itself and are only projected on experience and nature. The shaping spirit of literature is literature, and a writer's quality is determined primarily by what he makes of what he has read, not by differentiating factors in his environment. Writers often tend to resist this conclusion because their imaginative attitudes seem to them to be directly shaping forces, and they are often unaware of the extent to which literary conventions are controlling those attitudes. Often too it is better for them as writers to be unaware of it, but it is part of the critic's business to see more clearly what is happening.

In English Canada, in the wake of Confederation, there was a certain amount of patriotic and rather phony poetry about a great emerging nation stretching from sea to sea, but the social reality corresponding to this was less a country than a means of transpor-tation, a waterway and a railway, which formed part of the network of communications within the British Empire. In proportion as Canadian writers began to realize their own environment on the North American continent, the effective contemporary influences became American rather than British. Haliburton, the author of *Sam Slick* referred to earlier, writing in pre-Confederation times, was fanatically loyal to the British connection, but he uses his Yankee mouthpiece to express a good deal of ambivalence about that loyalty. It seems clear, both from him and from other writers, that many Canadians felt that they would be treated with more respect elsewhere if they represented an independent country and that cultivated people in Great Britain had a strong tendency, only partly unconscious, to think of the colonies as essentially penal settlements. There is also the irony of the fact that no Canadian in this period could dream of living by his writing without a London or New York publisher, implying a mainly non-Canadian audience.

One very shrewd novel that reflects this change in perspective is Sara Jeanette Duncan's *The Imperialist* (1904). The author was born and brought up in the community she portrays in her book, but she had lived outside Canada a good deal and was a devotee of William Dean Howells and the earlier Henry James. Here one of the two central male characters develops a strong enthusiasm for Canada's role in the British Empire, which he sees as fulfilling both the destiny and the identity of Canada, but his somewhat incoherent expressions of this fail to impress the young woman he wishes to marry, and it is obvious that the cause to which he devotes himself will be short-lived. This story is all the more striking in that Sara Duncan herself was something of an "imperialist," but she was also a good enough writer to detect the false ring of a rhetoric that had no social reality behind it.

French Canada had at first an exceptional disadvantage in the severing of the political link with France. After the departure of the aristocracy, a very conservative form of Roman Catholicism came to be the dominant cultural influence, one that repudiated the ideology of the French Revolution and clung to the romantic blood-and-soil values reflected more obliquely in *Maria Chapdelaine*. (One may compare the later career of Haliburton, who retired to England in later life and entered the Conservative party there, only to find it far too radical for *his* conservatism.) There have also been cultural tensions connected with the spoken language, which for many French Canadians is a patois now called *joual* (the word is derived from its alleged pronunciation of *cheval*). Anyone at all familiar with English writing in Nigeria or Guyana or Pakistan will realize that English, like Latin a thousand years ago, is developing different dialect forms that are trying hard to become separate languages, and would do so practically overnight if it were not for the conservative grip of the written language and the news media. *Joual* represents an analogous development in French, and, like its English counter-parts, has been both condemned as substandard illiteracy and defended as a genuinely popular idiom. The defense has also taken the form of some lively literary productions, mainly in drama. I mention *joual* here because it is a particularly clear example of the change in environmental conditions in this century and has gone through the normal stages of resistance followed by gradual accep-tance. There are many other aspects of this change which have turned what seemed at first insuperable odds against French Canada's ever producing a literature of any significance into a major advantage. In my opinion, the maturing and intensifying of French Canadian imaginative life in midcentury, with the so-called "quiet revolution" and the turn to a more secularized culture, was the event that touched off a similar development in English Canada around 1960.

III

One of the difficulties in developing a Canadian literature is that Canada is too big and heterogeneous to be unified imaginatively. In other words, the assumption that cultural developments always follow political and economic ones does not work, at least in its more simplistic forms. Political and economic developments tend to centralize and to build up increasingly large entities, as national units combine into great continental powers. But there seems to be some-thing vegetable about the creative imagination, something that needs roots and a limited environment. This contradictory move-ment of centralizing economy and decentralizing culture makes the twentieth century a difficult but fascinating time for a critic. The emptiness of the "Canadian" rhetoric of the previous century, we can now see, was the result of trying to annex a cultural development to a political one, just as the separatist and neofascist movements of today represent the opposite fallacy of attaching a political move-ment to a cultural one.

In the first half of the century Canada was preoccupied with becoming a nation, but it had only just become one when the postnational developments of the modern world caught up with it. These developments have been, significantly, much more favorable to culture than to other aspects of Canadian life. Another possible critical principle appears dimly in the background: we do not know what social conditions produce good literature, except that we have no reason to suppose that they are good conditions. Canadian economic and political development today is that of a fully matured Western democracy, but its culture is that of an emergent nation. To put it another way, as Canadian economy becomes increasingly chaotic and its political leadership increasingly schizoid, its cultural life becomes more varied and lively.

Within the last twenty years a verbal explosion has taken place in English Canadian literature, a quantitative increase so dramatic as to amount to, or include, a qualitative change. The Canadian critic George Woodcock, reviewing English Canadian poetry for the decade 1960-1970, found himself confronted with a thousand volumes, exclusive of anthologies. This does not, of course, mean that they were all printed by solvent publishers: most of them were produced by what amounts to a resistance press. The implications of the word *resistance* will meet us again in a moment. Much of this increase is a by-product of a socially decentralizing movement, especially in fiction. As one previously inarticulate region after another has formed an orbit for the imagination, we discover that "Canada," culturally speaking, is really an aggregate of smaller areas stretching from Vancouver Island to the Avalon peninsula in Newfoundland. Here Canada has followed the rhythm of American literature, which has always been strongly regional. It seems to be a law of literature that the more strictly limited its environment is, the more universal its appeal. Faulkner writes of his unpronounceable county in Mississippi and gets the Nobel Prize in Sweden, while novelists writing of the dilemma of modern man would get nowhere.

However, American literature is no less American for being an aggregate of New England literature, Mississippi literature, and dozens of other areas. Similarly, English Canada now has a literature with an imaginative coherence that is recognized outside the country, so that some Canadian writers sell as well in Germany and Italy as they do at home. Within the country, Canadian literature, ignored in Canadian universities in my student days, is now an academic heavy industry. The main positive result of this has been to make contemporary Canadian writers aware of the tradition behind the work they are producing and thereby to give that work the rounded dimension of continuity without which no literature can be mature, whatever the merits of its earlier products.

So far we have been speaking of criticism in its traditional form as a servomechanism of literature. Poets and novelists, according to this view, produce literature, and then the critic comments on their work, explains it, and then retails it to the academic part of its audience. This conception of criticism has always reminded me of an early Chaplin film, in which Charlie Chaplin was portrayed as a street cleaner, in the days before automobiles, wearily trudging up one street after another in pursuit of the horses. It has been out of date for a century, but it lingers like other obsolete notions. I have known several academics who could have been fine scholars, but forced themselves to become indifferent poets or novelists because their egos demanded that they concern themselves only with the primary or "creative" process of literature. Nobody denies that commenting on preexisting literature is still a central function of criticism, but what with all the linguistic and semiotic developments of the last quarter-century a new perspective on it is overdue.

It was a Canadian economic historian, Harold Innis, who, in his studies on the fur trade and fishing industry in Canada, along with an earlier study (his thesis) of the Canadian Pacific Railway, laid the groundwork for the "Laurentian" view of Canadian development mentioned at the beginning of this paper, a view carried on and elaborated by the historian Donald Creighton, who also wrote a biography, or rather a personal sketch, of Innis. Innis then became interested in other contexts of communication, a word which enters the titles of two of his later books, *Empire and Communication* and *The Bias of Communication*. Here he is concerned mainly with verbal or written communication, the role of the printing press, the codex, the pamphlet, the newspaper, the periodical, and of paper itself and the other materials for writing, throughout history. In these books a vision of history emerges in which an ascendant class tries to monopolize the means of communication and in which every power struggle includes an effort to get control of it, to promote an ideology and censor or repress rival ones.

In our world the control of communications is concerned with what is called advertising in some contexts and propaganda in others, depending on the economic context involved. A somewhat unlikely disciple of Innis, Marshall McLuhan, published his first and I think best book, *The Mechanical Bride*, in 1951. This is a study of the psychological appeals and responses in advertising. As the title indicates, it seizes on that curious identification of the erotic and the mechanical that seems so central to the sensibility of our age: Eros and Thanatos locked together in a peculiarly twentieth-century embrace. My copy of this book classifies it as "sociology," but Mc-Luhan was a literary critic who remarks in his introduction that it is high time for the techniques of criticism, in literature and the other arts, to be applied to the analysis of society.

The Mechanical Bride has no specific reference to Canada, but it was, I think, written in Canada, and it reflects the perspective of a country committed to observing rather than participating actively in the international scene. The career of Innis indicates even more clearly that Canada affords some unusual perspectives for relating criticism to its social environment. As criticism expands in range and variety of subject, it will merge with communications theory, and the sprawling and disunited Canada, from its very beginning, has been preoccupied—obsessed would be a better word—with means of communication, whether animate or inanimate. As its literature has developed, it has formed an adjoining culture in time to the whole British tradition from *Beowulf* to Eliot and Joyce. From the point of view of a new culture using an old language, that tradition is not a moving belt in time but a kaleidoscope, all of it available for simultaneous study and imitation. One suggestion arising from this situation is that a major task facing criticism today is that of attaining a synoptic view of language.

I do not mean primarily the different languages spoken, with all of their untranslatable idioms pointing to many different habits of thought. I mean rather the different modes of language which have entered into our speech, many of which have become obsolete although they still contain great potential powers of utterance. There is a metaphorical language of immanence, of the kind we find in the poetry of so-called "primitive" societies, where subject and object are not clearly separated and where words are words of power that can affect the environment directly. There is a metonymic language of transcendence of a kind that we find in theology or metaphysics, where language points in the direction of something beyond itself. There is a language of objectivity and description and clear definition, such as we find in expository prose. There is a meditative language for which all physical objects become foci of converging forces, as in some of the later essays of Heidegger. There is the language of what is called ordinary speech, where meaning bursts through the words and is eked out by gesture and body language, of the kind studied in the later work of Wittgenstein. There is the disguised and hieratic language of the kind typical of the dream, which makes its way into the waking world in all sorts of disconcerting ways. And there are dozens of other kinds. The investigating of these different aspects of language forms probably what is the liveliest area of criticism today, but the subject is still in its scholastic period, undermining the postulates of other critics without arriving at an interconnected view. When that interconnected view begins to show some of its outlines, criticism will be a much more central subject than it is now.

The name of McLuhan also reminds us of the growth of electronic media. *The Mechanical Bride* appeared before the main impact of television, and in trying to grapple with that McLuhan lost the distinction between the positive and negative aspects of his global village. What is positive about the world opened up by the electronic media is the sense of all the time and space known to us as simultaneously present to us. What is negative about it is the control of it, along with so much of the press, by advertising, in our culture, with its ready access to our reflexes and its power of manipulating them.

Advertising is closely allied with what is called mass culture, which demands passivity of response and acceptance of unexamined clichés. Mass culture is a most misleading phrase for what it describes because it is something imposed on the so-called "masses" and not produced by them. To call it "popular culture" is clearly still more misleading. During the unrest of the sixties there was some confused understanding of this, and at that time the magic word that explained everything then going on was the word *subculture*, meaning something in revolt against the dominant or imposed culture. But there turned out to be no such thing as a subculture: what was called that was invariably a sucker of mass culture and was quickly absorbed into it. The situation was rather that what is called mass culture, supported as it is by advertising and working through advertising's control of television and the press, is really anticultural—not because it wishes or intends to be, but because its social context is anticreative. Hence all genuine products of the creative imagination in literature, in the other arts, and in film or television are forced by the dialectic of their social function into an adversary relationship to mass culture. In other words, in our day genuine culture has to take the form of a counterculture. It is one of the tasks of criticism now to help mobilize it in the direction of its ultimate goal, which is the creation of a counterenvironment, the opposite of the one being built by the architects of desolation.

Canada is sufficiently close to the United States to feel these mass-cultural influences as a threat to its identity, while being also sufficiently distinct from it to feel them as foreign influences. In any case, the phenomena are much the same everywhere. Culturally, we are glutted with possible influences: all the resources of human space and time are available to us. But we lack the hard core of knowing what we want to use them for. Every culture is an adjoining culture, in space or time: isolated or "buried" cultures may be common enough in romance, but history and archaeology, so far as I am aware, know nothing of them. Everything of value to us has grown out of conflicts and mutual influences among individual cultures. Some cultures have arisen as spatial frontier revolts, as the cultures of Periclean Athens and Elizabethan England were frontier revolts against worlds dominated by Persia and by the Papacy and Empire respectively. Some have tried to re-create a culture in time, as the Renaissance tried to re-create late classical culture. In our world, as we saw, most cultures grow up as decentralized enclaves in a technologically unified world, struggling for a voice of their own. All of them have had to fight against some threat to their existence, though in our day actual war only perverts the real issues. On the horizon appears a larger task of criticism for the future: to realize that our culture adjoins every other culture in time and space, to become aware of our particular cultural conditioning, and then to help in the fight against the passivity and paralysis of will that block up creative power.

Harold Innis: The Strategy of Culture

It seems only a short while ago that André Martin and Rodrigue Chiasson of the CRTC's [Canadian Radio-Television and Telecommunications Commission] Research Branch went, along with myself, to call on the late Mary Quayle Innis to obtain permission to edit the great block of unfinished manuscripts of Harold Innis's projected history of communications, which had been left in that state by his death. Our aim was eventual publication, so our next stop was the University of Toronto Press, which, of course, at that stage could do nothing but express general interest. On the way André remarked that he felt like a Renaissance humanist salvaging classical manuscripts out of monastic libraries.

We were aware that shortly after Innis's death a group of scholars chosen by Mrs. Innis had examined the manuscript and had recommended against trying to publish it in any form beyond microfilm. But, first, the CRTC was willing to make very considerable editorial efforts to put the manuscript in publishable condition, and it is doubtful whether anywhere else in Canada one could find people who either could or would make such efforts. Those who could were mostly academics who would have found the task an impossible addition to their working schedule. Although I am listed as editor of the book, there has been a great deal of detailed and painstaking editorial work done on the manuscript which I have not and could not have done. Second, after so many years Innis was no longer a contemporary thinker but a landmark in the cultural history of Canada, and for such a figure the conception of what was publishable was radically different. So the CRTC Research Branch went ahead, although a crushing administrative load made it impossible for years to direct enough organizational time and energy into completing the task. Mr. Chiasson has paid tribute to those who encouraged the project and to those who made it possible, and I can only endorse him on the point.

I can say with some confidence, however, from having seen various stages of the manuscript in progress, that the editorial work, extensive as it is, has gone in Innis's own direction, and its effort has consistently been to bring out his own theses from the materials he used. The original manuscript contained a great deal that was not Innis but his sources, as is inevitable with an unfinished work, and naturally this feature had to be essentially retained. One would not take advantage of his death to rewrite his book, and what is here offered, I think, comes as close as is humanly possible to indicating what Innis would have wanted to do himself.

There is at least one disadvantage inherent in the whole operation, however, and it is better to be frank about it. Even if Innis had lived to complete his own work, it would not now be a contemporary work of scholarship. The work of a scholar who died thirty years ago has to be based on sources even older than that, and the information explosion since then has made many of those sources questionable or obsolete. It is, perhaps, no more than amusing to find him quoting G. G. Coulton as saying that bilingualism "implies a lack of clearness of speech and therefore of thought." But there are certain areas, such as critical and cultural theory, where what was available to him can only be described as primitive. The manuscript must be read with a good deal of historical imagination in the 1980s, with the realization that whatever issues do not seem central now must have been central once, and if they were once they are still potentially so. The function of the historical imagination in reading is to change "potentially" into "actually" whenever possible.

In the preface to *The Bias of Communication* Innis remarks that he is starting with the methodological question: why do we attend to the things to which we do attend? He then says that changes in communication follow changes in the things to which we attend. I do not understand the word *follow*, as it clearly seems to be Innis's view that changes in communication are involved in, or accompany, or in many cases are even the causes of, historical changes of attention. The first question relevant to Innis's own work, in any case, is rather: why was it communication to which he was brought to attend? This is primarily a historical (and more incidentally a biographical) question relating to the period around 1950. He has answered the question himself, and all we need do here is summarize him. But next there is the problem of how to incorporate him into the background and tradition of our contemporary preoccupations. That will take a good deal of critical effort still, to which the present essay can be only a minor contribution. Yet I think it is essential for an introducer of the present volume, if he is to be genuinely useful, to exploit the hindsight of thirty years, so far as his knowledge permits. Everybody interested in the subject knows that Innis was a pioneer in his own day: we need not discuss that, only the relevance of his pioneering to "the things to which we attend" a generation later.

Innis was concerned primarily with verbal communication through the written word. For such communication to flow freely in society certain things are essential. One is a cheap, accessible, and practical material medium, which turned out to be paper. Another is an alphabetical system of writing. Third is a mechanical power of reduplication, such as we have in the printing press and its later technological developments. The Chinese invented paper but not the alphabet. The Hebrews had a consonantal syllabary that was practically an alphabet, and the Greeks had a true alphabet of both consonants and vowels. But they were still dependent on scribal transmission, and paper took a long time to establish itself in the West. We have paper, an alphabet, and a printing press, but that very fact has created a new set of difficulties.

Innis began as a Canadian economic historian, studying such areas as the fur trade and the fishing industry. He learned from this study that Canadian history, Canadian imagination, and the way of Canadian life had all been profoundly affected, in many respects determined, by the fact that the Canadian economy was based on the exporting of staples to foreign markets. The last major staple was that of pulp and paper, and at the opening of *Empire and Communications* (really the beginning of the total history of which the present volume is the continuation) he gives us a brief sardonic vision of the interminable churning out of written documents in British and American life through the last century, with Canadians obediently supplying the paper to write them on. But the ramifications of verbal communication were so vast that Innis found himself examining not merely the economy of exported staples but the larger question of the cultural use of the staple. Here he moved from economic history into a field where he was, in effect, taking all knowledge for his province.

Economic history demands immense assembling and patient sorting through of facts. Marshall McLuhan, in his preface to the reprinted edition of *The Bias of Communication* (1964), assimilates this technique to the "mosaic" type of discontinuous writing in which each detail is to be related to a total context as well as to the narrative sequence in which it is embedded. That is, each detail is separately symbolic of the whole argument, just as each story on a newspaper's front page is separately symbolic of the editor's notion of what should be front-page news for that day. Such a technique can be found in twentieth-century poetry, for example in the Ezra Pound *Cantos*, especially the more purely historical ones like the early Malatesta group.

Where one finds this "mosaic" writing in Innis, however, is not so much in his continuous books as in the collection of notes recently edited by William Christian as *The Idea File of Harold Adams Innis* (1980), which will be a constant and invaluable resource for the reader of this book as well. The omnivorous intellectual curiosity revealed in this work is something unique in Canadian culture, so far as I know. There cannot be many academics in any age who are so highly integrated that they can hardly have an idea on any subject whatever that is not, or may not be, or may not produce something relevant to their scholarly work. This is scholarship as not merely a total commitment but a total way of life, and few there be that find that way. Of course, such flexibility of reference is a quality of the subject as well as of the temperament of the scholar—anything may be relevant to communication. This is particularly true of the more plastic time when Innis became interested in it. In a very few years communications theory had become an academic discipline like other academic disciplines, congealing into a specialized jargon that prescribes the way one thinks about it. But for Innis communication was something more like the challenge to an author of science fiction: if there is too little left to discover in one world, explore another. Or, as e. e. cummings would say, "there's a hell / of a good universe next door; let's go." Not many scholars are attracted to such endlessly ramifying themes, however, or can sustain the Leacockian energy needed for riding madly off in all directions.

The disadvantages of exploration of this sort are, of course, equally obvious. It is not possible for any scholar to acquire scholarly expertise in unlimited areas. Hence while much of the present work is an amassing of factual details, as in the passages dealing with the spread of paper manufacturing in Renaissance Europe, there is much of it also in which generalizations, sometimes very simplistic generalizations, are being used as though they were facts. What this primarily means is that Innis is negatively as well as positively seminal. He will always be rewarding to study, but he will also be in constant need of modification, revision, and updating.

There is a general "bias" (a word Innis uses in several senses and contexts) predisposing the societies of the past either toward time or toward space. To emphasize time is also to emphasize tradition and continuity, and time-bound societies tend to use cumbersome or expensive materials for writing—clay and stone in the Near East, parchment in the Middle Ages—and to associate writing with secrecy and elitism, the ascendancy of a priesthood or other "oligopoly" that wants to keep knowledge in its own hands. Sometimes a special hieratic language, like Latin in the Middle Ages, is employed for the same purpose. When communications acquire one or more of the three attributes of free movement mentioned above (paper, an alphabet, a mechanical reproducer of copy), they become more accessible to a wider group. More people write and more people read, and the media of communication spread more widely in space. This spatial expansion has become worldwide since the Industrial Revolution. In the background of this "bias" thesis there seems to be a lurking analogy with military history, where the stonewalling defenses of a declining empire are usually destroyed by the rapid outflanking movements of the more mobile societies outside.

The general principle involved is that every ascendant class, in fact every pressure group within society, tries to establish a dominant or, if possible, a monopolized control over communications. Such monopolies are never permanently successful, because new techniques of communication, as well as new forms of knowledge and thought that require a different content for it, keep springing up even in the most stagnant societies. In ancient Egypt, at the very dawn of history, there was still a tension between the royal and the priestly power, of a kind that recurred in late Europe between the papacy, with its claims for both spiritual and temporal control of Christendom, and the secular princes. This latter struggle eventually became absorbed into the Reformation, with the Protestants demanding wide distribution of the Bible and its translation into the vernacular languages, and such resistance as that of Pope Gregory VII in the eleventh century, pronouncing that the Bible must on no account be put into the hands of ordinary people, as they would be certain to get its meaning wrong. Whatever the theological rights and wrongs of the issue, the central feature of it, from Innis's point of view, was a struggle within communications, between the classifying of information and the dissemination of it. The latter tendency grew spectacularly with the printing press, and now "freedom of the press" is so established that it has developed a monopoly in its turn.

One factor in Innis's time and space thesis is that time-bound societies, with their emphasis on continuity and tradition and elitism, are bound to the monumental as well, to erecting vast buildings and public works that express their devotion to the spiritual and temporal authorities of their times. The trouble is that, as Shelley's Ozymandias failed to discover, the monumental turns out to be surprisingly fragile. It is the verbal that has the real power of survival in time, and this power is inseparable from the spatial power of cheap and expendable material and devices for multiplication. In other words, it is only the temporary that attains a real control of time.

A famous passage in Victor Hugo's *Hunchback of Notre Dame* contrasts the David of print with the Goliath of the cathedral. *Ceci tuera cela*, Hugo says, "ceci" being the printing press and "cela" monuments like Notre Dame. Innis suggests in the *Idea File* that Hugo has exaggerated the power of print, but I think the facts support Hugo. Not only are medieval cathedrals very expensive to keep in repair, but the creative architectural impulse behind them is gone. Even if fifty new cathedrals were built this year, the cathedral would still be as dead as the step pyramid, at least as an imaginative power in our culture. Every city today exhibits churches dwarfed with high-rise buildings, but the latter are so prominent because it is relatively easy to knock them down again. An even more dramatic example of the *ceci tuera cela* situation is in the Book of Jeremiah, where the prophet's secretary reads the prophecy from a papyrus scroll to the infuriated king of Judah, who every so often cuts off a piece of the scroll with a knife and throws it into the fire. The Book of Jeremiah still exists, but the king's palace does not. One wonders what could be left to present a real challenge to the monopoly of the written word.

It is clear that the general attitude of Innis is rooted in what is called, in a somewhat foolish phrase, old-fashioned liberalism. He thinks of the Middle Ages as a rather sleepy period (despite the fact that he was working in the same university as Étienne Gilson), and of history since the Renaissance as revolving primarily around the relation of the individual to his society. The individual's opportunity comes when the power struggles over communication reach a deadlock.

In the sixteenth century the Reformed Church regarded itself as the fulfillment of the Catholic Church, as itself the Catholic Church purified of corruptions, so that the natural tendency of the Catholic Church, if unobstructed by selfish interests, would be to expand into the Reformed framework. That did not happen: Catholic societies seldom turned Protestant except when forced to do so by their princes, and Catholicism and Protestantism remained in a simply antithetical and adversary relationship. Renaissance humanism, Cinquecento painting, and Elizabethan drama came somewhere out of the middle. Later, Communism was conceived by Marx as the logical outcome of capitalism, after capitalism had reached a certain crucial point of contradiction in which a guided revolutionary act would permit of its transformation. Nothing like that happened: Communism got established only in preindustrial societies with a weak middle class, and the two systems have remained in a simply antithetical and adversary relationship. Twentieth-century science and literature have got what benefits they could from the absence of a final victory for either side. We may call this process of imaginative wriggling out of a power struggle by Innis's own phrase, "the strategy of culture."

One looks in every period of history for a *tertium quid*, for some cultural element in the middle that escapes from the competing pressure groups by having something of its own to communicate that neutralizes the conflicts of interest. For Innis there seem to be three aspects of this *tertium quid* of particular importance. One, as indicated above, is the creative and imaginative culture a society produces in the middle of all its power struggles: we shall return to this aspect in a moment. Another is law.

Law has always been an instrument of power for ascendant classes, and a great deal of law consists of various ways of rationalizing the existing power structure. It is interesting that one of the most incisive quotations in this book is from the sixteenth-century French jurist Jean Bodin. "It rarely happens, that any parties, even the best and purest, will, in the strife to retain or recover their ascendancy, weaken themselves by a scrupulous examination of the reasoning or the testimony which is to serve their purpose." Bodin should know, for he is said to have had one of the finest legal minds in history, and was also both a strong advocate of absolutism and a gullible and vicious witch-hunter.

At the same time, law, often against the will of the lawmakers, has evolved a technique of guaranteeing rights to both sides of a dispute.

This quality in law was expanded into a theory of social contract, in fact an entire social philosophy, by Edmund Burke. Nobody could have cared less about British freedom broadening slowly down from precedent to precedent than the barons who forced King John to sign the Magna Carta, but they started something that carried on with its own momentum. This tendency is much older than King John: Sir Henry Maine's *Ancient Law* is one of Innis's favorite and most frequently quoted books, and he makes a good deal of the interplay of "bookright" and "folkright": law as a written code and law as partly a matter of oral tradition. Keeping a balance between them has been a feature of the more empirical Anglo-Saxon tradition of law, in contrast to the revolutionary American and French procedures of starting with a written constitution and proceeding deductively from it.

It would be nonsense to think of any aspect of law as being in any way sacrosanct, autonomous, or detached from social influences or historical conditions. But to think of it as nothing but an instrument of social power would be equally wrong: it still contains an objective quality that lifts it clear of that. An island is certainly conditioned by the fact that it is surrounded by water, but still it is an island and not water, even when flooded by the storms of tyranny. There can hardly be a society that does not at least pretend to provide some legal rights for its citizens, and when a totalitarian state resorts to arbitrary violence it is still breaking its own laws.

The maintaining of the inner objectivity of law, therefore, is one of the ways by which the strategy of culture attempts to keep something going in society that is not simply a conflict of pressure groups, which are always and by nature anticultural. The language is stronger than the language Innis uses, but I think it reflects his view, that the alternative to the strategy of culture is simply systematized mob rule. What Innis says about law in the present book is supplemented by the third essay in *Changing Concepts of Time* (1952), on Roman law and the British Empire.

Another aspect of the cultural *tertium quid* is the objectivity of scholarly and scientific knowledge, which today is mainly institutionalized in the university. Once again, keeping the objectives of the university alive in society is part of the strategy of culture, part of the fight for human freedom. Again, it would be nonsense to regard the university simply as a secure bastion of such freedom in a hysterical world. But it does have some right to be called that, and it would be equally wrong to join the simple-minded chorus of those, many of them within the university, who maintain that objectivity in knowledge is a mere illusion.

Of course, the very structure of the university, with its hierarchies and protocols, revives the "time-bound" tendency to emphasize tradition and continuity and the confining of knowledge to an elite. Innis is deeply attached to the university in modern society, and he is not merely aware but sharply critical of its tendency to become a small-scale monopoly of communication in its turn, blocking new openings of knowledge by declaring that they are a distraction to the existing scholarly structure. But he has little use for political activism within the university, of the kind at least where liberalism and concerned citizenship cross the line into bourgeois masochism. Many intellectuals have a constant itch to try to help turn the wheel of history, to support social movements that are going in what they feel are the right directions, to show that in the power struggles of history ideas do after all count for something. They do, but for Innis not in that context: this kind of activism is what Julien Benda called, in a book Innis often refers to, the *trahison des clercs*, the betrayal, by the intellectuals, of their own standards in the interest of some form of mass movement. The university helps society by communicating with it on a solid two-way street in which, if the university is accountable to society, society is also accountable to the university. At least that seems to be the implication of such essays as the one on adult education which forms an appendix to *The Bias of Communication*.

The history of science gives us perhaps the clearest examples of how an element of culture, springing from the concerns of society and conditioned by them, nonetheless may acquire an authority of its own that rises above its conditioning. Thus the new astronomy of Galileo's time struggled through to a heliocentric view of the solar system although the religious and political concerns of society demanded a geocentric one, and the new biology of Darwin's time eventually established an evolutionary view of the order of nature in spite of the agonized protests of those who felt that without a divine creation there could be no real source of authority. Similarly in scholarship, where the accepted picture of a subject may be challenged by another that explains more facts, or facts previously inexplicable. The conflict of authority resulting is entirely within the area of that scholarship, or at least the effective part of it is.

It is more difficult to see that the painter, the writer, the creative artist in whatever field, also makes technical discoveries in that field, and that the serious writer or painter owes a loyalty to the authority of his art as well as to the concerns of his social patrons. When we look at the great works of art of the past, we know that they are products of a society as full of tyranny and folly as any other, and in fact may even reflect many of their contemporary social evils. But they have established their authority within their own area, while the tyranny and folly have vanished into nothingness. There are several reasons why it is more difficult to recognize such authority in the arts. The arts are weaker and less organized than the universities, hence more vulnerable to social bullying, and more directly dependent on patronage: "they that live to please must please to live," as Samuel Johnson said. Then again, critics of the arts, whose function it is in part to establish the authority of the arts they study, have tended to assume that the real authority belongs to them and the judgments they make about it.

Even allowing for Innis's vacuum-cleaner techniques of quotation, it is still startling to find in *The Bias of Communication* a remark of such stupefying imbecility as one ascribed to Sir James Mackintosh: "After art had been toiling in India, in Persia, and in Egypt to produce monsters, beauty and grace were discovered in Greece." One point here is that the statement is roughly contemporary with the introduction of the Elgin marbles into England (Mackintosh died in 1832), and hence in its day would have been considered a cultivated and perceptive thing to say. I find the remark very significant, however, because it points up the failure of the critical function so dramatically. The context is that of the nineteenth-century assumption, to which Innis recurs more than once, that great periods of art come very rarely and last only a very short time. There is some truth in this, from some points of view, but nine-tenths of the assumption is based not on the qualities of art but on the attention span of critics. Such provincialism in art criticism comes from the exaggeration of the importance of value judgments, which are always expressions of the dominant ideology of the time, and so tell us much more about the concerns and anxieties of that time than they do about the art. It is only when we begin to adopt more flexible standards of judgment, and realize that art is there to be studied and understood, not pronounced on, that its authority is recognized and it becomes another aspect of the *tertium quid* of culture.

As remarked above, Innis's earlier books were on specifically Canadian topics, and if he had moved to Chicago, as he could have done, his social vision would have had a different perspective, however similar in general outline. He realized the importance of the east-west Laurentian axis, the thrust down the river to the Great Lakes, fanning out from there into the far west and the north, that makes sense of the map of Canada and accounts for its having a political development distinct from that of the United States. The Laurentian axis has vanished into the past, but its cultural consequences have not. An economy founded on the export of staples leaves behind it a profoundly colonial mentality, proud of its natural resources but very diffident about its human ones, conditioned to accept somewhere else as the place where the main action is.

Several of Innis's essays about the growing cultural monopoly of print in Britain and the United States during the last two centuries allude to Canadian difficulties in taking part in this. (I am speaking now of English Canada: the French problem, though in some ways more difficult, is more clear-cut.) Without major publishers, except those controlled from outside the country, a Canadian, if he is to live as a writer, must write for a mainly non-Canadian audience, like Stephen Leacock or Mazo de la Roche. He must also conform to the conventions of these larger markets. Innis has a footnote on a Canadian writer who was told by a prospective British publisher to expand his manuscript and by a prospective American one to shorten it. Canadians, mutters Innis, ought to make good accordion-players. The essay of Innis that is specifically called "The Strategy of Culture" is largely a response to the Massey Report, which recommended setting up an agency to subsidize and encourage Canadian culture without trying to direct or control it. Such a procedure aligns itself very well with the strategy of culture by recognizing that the arts have an essential authority in society, that society has some responsibility for recognizing that authority, and that Canada faces exceptional difficulties in trying to find a place for its own culture.

We are now back to the question raised earlier. The technical achievements of the printed word today have made it an unchallenged medium of communications. This means a mass monopoly, the "propaganda" that we decry so much in totalitarian countries, without much noticing the effectiveness of a slightly different kind of propaganda in our own. Where are we to turn to find a liberating agency from this monopoly? At the beginning of *Empire and Communications* Innis refers, with a vagueness and imprecision unusual in him, to the "oral tradition" as something to set over against the monopoly of the printed word. His regard for the oral tradition is partly an appreciation of the metaphorical vividness of folk poetry and of Homer. He took an interest in the work of Millman Parry on the close relation of Homer to the half-improvised formulaic oral poetry still extant in Slavic countries, and he also refers to the parallel work of Eric Havelock, though Havelock's *Preface to Plato* (1963) is later than Innis. It is partly also, I think, an unconscious use of something in his religious background. The world's great religious teachers tend to avoid writing and keep to direct discourse, leaving the writing down of their teachings to secretaries. The claim of oral authority made by Jesus ("but I say unto you") seems especially to have impressed Innis. But how can oral communication be revived in a world like ours, except with the aid of mechanical reproduction? Innis knew very well how the devil had inspired Hitler to use the radio as a means of mass control, a fact Hitler recorded in *Mein Kampf* with all his usual contempt for the people he was bamboozling. So, not unnaturally, Innis adds a footnote on Hitler explaining that that is not at all the kind of thing he is talking about. But what is he talking about? Oral communication in its original form belongs to an ancient world that can never come back.

We are reminded here of Marshall McLuhan and of Innis's interest in McLuhan's *The Mechanical Bride* (1951). McLuhan in turn has described his own major books as a "footnote" to Innis's investigations: these books developed a large-scale revolutionary thesis about the displacing of linear and time-bound print by the simultaneous many-sided impact of the electronic media. For McLuhan this was primarily a psychological difference: still later he tried to suggest that it was a physiological one as well. What is disappointing about McLuhan's work, however, is the absence of any clear sense of the kind of social context in which electronic media function. Television in particular is geared to the rhythms of the social economy: however striking the psychological difference between its impact and that of print, the absence of any real social difference neutralizes nearly all of it. The usual television program, as the CRTC keeps rather irritably reminding Canadian broadcasters, is simply a talking journal, as the phrase "magazine format" indicates, a way of conveying the same words and images for the same social purposes. McLuhan felt, at least at first, that the electronic media would bring in a social revolution so pervasive that one could describe its social context only in terms of the future. But, as with other prophetic revolutionary theories, the existing power structures have refused to wither away on schedule.

I think "oral tradition" is being used by Innis as a symbol for something that he failed to identify, and if I venture a suggestion about it, it is because some aspects of the question have clarified a good deal since Innis's death, in Canada as elsewhere. Within the last twenty years a quantitative explosion has taken place in Canadian literature (and in other fields as well) which amounts to a qualitative change. In short, there is such a thing as Canadian literature now. But, on further examination, it seems to have developed a strongly regional quality, as though the creative imagination needed a smaller and more coherent unit than the vast sprawl of "Canada" affords. In this, Canada has followed the rhythm of American literature, which has always been strongly regional, so that we learn about American literature by adding together Mississippi writers, New England writers, Middle Western writers, and so on. It looks as though the "counter culture" we used to hear so much about is really the "strategy of culture" itself, decentralizing where politics centralizes, differentiating where technology makes everything uniform, giving articulateness and human meaning to the small community where economy turns it into a mere distributing center, constantly moving in a direction opposite to that of the political and economic tendencies of history.

If this countermovement of culture to political and economic developments is true of space, it is likely to be true of time as well. Innis's "time-bound" societies are obsessed with continuity, with handing down the authority of institutions to new generations with as little change as possible. The arts too often follow an established convention closely, even slavishly; but as time goes on, a greater variety of traditions appears. Nothing is more striking today than the expanded variety of influences available to the artist. In this situation culture tends to move backward in time, away from the merely continuous, and toward the constant recapturing and rediscovery of the imaginative life in neglected tradition. It continues to do so even when "time-bound" institutions are replaced or supplemented by "spatial" or marketplace monopolies. We have Mackintosh in one era asserting that everyone produced monsters in the ancient world except the Greeks, and fifty years later we have Gauguin speaking of the Greek tradition as "the great error." The second statement is quite as silly as the first one, but indicates the variety of responses involved.

In the present book there is a good deal of data about the way in which the printing press established a market, with Renaissance humanists using it to provide scholarly editions of the classics, despite what one would think would be the economic impossibility of doing so. They were fighting according to the directives of the strategy of culture, in the opposite direction from the tendencies of the market. Today, apart from our writers and painters and other artists, there are many profoundly creative people in film, radio, and television who are continuing the same fight. The evocation of the phrase "oral tradition" thus begins to make sense as indicating the headwaters of tradition, the end of the re-creating backward movement in time that, in all forms of creation, brings the past to life as a new and enlarged form of present experience. I hope this introduction has done something at least to show that the present book, for all its often bewildering masses of detail and its many outmoded sources, is still an integral part of a social vision of a scope and comprehensiveness unparalleled in Canadian culture. Such a *Nachlass* would be, I think, well worth publishing if for no other reason than to indicate the proportions of the whole conception. Innis was always a difficult and sometimes a dull writer, and he was not interested in exploring the resources of rhetoric. He often seems to feel that where the facts do not speak for themselves, one should be silent. But, of course, facts do not speak: it is only the ordering and arranging of them that speaks, and the editorial effort that has gone into this book has been directed towards giving it its author's real voice. There are limits, as explained, to what can be done in this way. But in looking through the present volume, along with its successors and the books completed in the author's lifetime, one is often impelled to echo Goethe, when examining the interpolated and corrupt text that is all we have left to us of Marlowe's *Faustus*: "How greatly it was all planned."

Levels of Cultural Identity

I suppose that nowhere in the world is there a relationship between two countries even remotely like that of Canada and the United States. The full awareness of this relationship is largely confined to Canada, where it has churned up a good deal of speculation about "the Canadian identity," the extent to which Canadians may be said to be different from non-Canadians, meaning, ninety percent of the time, Americans. I am not concerned with this approach to the question, which seems to me futile and unreal. A nation's identity is (not "is in") its culture, and culture is a structure with several distinct levels. On an elementary level there is culture in the sense of custom or life-style: the distinctive way that people eat, dress, talk, marry, play games, produce goods, and the like. On this level culture in Canada, including both English and French Canada, has been practically identical with the northern part of American culture for a long time. This fact is not, in my view, one of any great significance. The time is past when we could speak of the "Americanizing" of this aspect of Canadian life. What faces us now is the homogenizing of the entire world, including the United States, through twentieth-century technology. Today Canadians, like other people, are hardly more Americanized in their lifestyle than they are Japanned or common-marketed.

Then there is the middle level of cultural identity, which is the product of tradition and history, and consists of the distinctive political, economic, religious, and other institutions that shape a nation's life and give direction to the main currents of its ideology. This is an area where Canadians have always felt beleaguered and threatened by American influences, and where, by an inevitable irony, that influence keeps increasing through divisions among Canadians themselves. In every part of Canada there are strong separatist feelings, and separatism can lead only to increased American penetration, especially economic and ideological. This is not to say that such penetration must be sinister, merely that it is the opposite of what separatism aims at.

Finally, there is an upper level of culture as the product of a nation's specialized creative powers. In Canada it seems to be particularly literature, painting, film, and radio drama that have attracted most attention, both within the country and outside it, and we should now add architecture, as this building [the new Canadian Embassy in Washington, D.C.] is one of the three at least to achieve such recognition in the present year. In theory, culture in this more specific sense is the product of the people as a whole and the shared heritage of all the people. In practice, it is the product of an often neglected minority, and in its appreciation there is a strongly elitist element. To bridge this gap between theory and practice is largely what the process of education is all about.

The middle level, the specific nation formed by a historical process, is the place where the conception "Canada" is to be found, but it is not the place to look for cultural symbols. Those come from either the lifestyle level or the creative level. On the lifestyle level, Canada has shown an extraordinary ability to absorb ethnic groups without essentially violating their folkways. The treatment of the indigenous peoples is an exception to this that I shall return to later. But the Icelandic and Ukrainian immigrants in the nineteenth century, the Italians and Portuguese and Jamaicans of the twentieth, have been able to preserve much of their lifestyle cultures. The extent to which they have been eroded, as just said, is due to worldwide rather than national pressures. The same thing was true of the original British and French groups. In fact, John Kenneth Galbraith, with no sense of incongruity, wrote a book called *The Scotch*, which was concerned entirely with a community of Scottish origin in southern Ontario.

In lifestyle culture there is little that is typical of Canada as a whole. Canada is the Switzerland of the twentieth century, surrounded by the great powers of the world and preserving its identity by having many identities. Its distinctive identity is represented by its creative culture, in its literature and painting and the other arts just mentioned.

As for the American awareness of Canada, one may say that Americans are conscious of Canada first of all as insulation. And perhaps one should not ignore the importance of Canada as a geographical object, apart from its inhabitants, in sealing in the United States on one point of the compass much as the oceans seal it in on two others. The physical existence of Canada has helped to confirm the American sense of separateness from the world up through the earlier decades of this century, and perhaps later had something to do with the fact that the Cold War remained relatively cold. But, of course, there are people in Canada, and it has been of immense benefit to the United States, whether it knows it or not, to have across its northern border not merely a friendly ally but another nation with a different history and tradition, closely related to yet contrasting with its own.

The contrasts relate to what I have called the middle level of culture, the distinctive paths formed by history. The American Revolution was a Whig revolution, and one of the things it revolted against was the mercantilist theory that the function of colonies was merely to produce raw materials. English Canada was settled, in upper Canada and much of the Maritimes, largely by disaffected Tories. These made common cause to some degree with their former enemies in French Canada, who felt doubly betrayed, first by the lack of interest in Canada shown by the government of prerevolutionary France, and secondly by an atheistic French Revolution. It is perhaps fair to say that France has never shown any real concern for Canada since, except when promoting its own interests. And English-speaking Canadians, even those who remained uncritically loyal to Britain, had to put up with massive ineptitude, indifference, and an attitude that showed much more respect for the independent United States than the dependent colonies. The feeling of not being wanted except as a place for exploitation forms a ground bass under Canadian themes and, among other things, has forced Canada to retain the dependence on commodity exports which makes its economy so different from the American one.

One always has to oversimplify situations like this, unless one is writing scholarly history, but in the forming of Canada there *was* something like this Tory-Whig division of ideology, and one that went much deeper than the Republican-Democrat or Conservative-Liberal divisions arising later in the separate countries. The revolution produced a written constitution and a deductive attitude to social problems, whereas the Canadians, in rejecting the revolution, adopted something more like an Edmund Burke theory of a continuous contract, including the dead, the living, and the unborn, an unwritten constitution based on precedent, and a tendency to look for solutions to crises by safeguarding the rights on both sides. Canadian history is a series of ad hoc compromises, in contrast to the

American practice of reinterpreting and amending an eighteenth-century document. Each crisis brings with it a settled belief in the minds of many Canadians that this is really the end, that the country is irremediably torn apart by its own inner contradictions. So far such feelings have proved to be mistaken, but if a sculptor were making a statue symbolizing Canadian loyalty to Canada he might well portray someone holding his breath and crossing his fingers.

The entrenched Tory oligarchy in nineteenth-century Ontario, known as the Family Compact, provoked a rebellion of sorts in 1837, though the history of that rebellion, at least in Ontario, makes very curious reading. Canadians have always refused to believe in any kind of political logic, whether the logic of revolution or the logic of repression. The liberal opposition that began to take shape was continentalist in tendency, and some of the more myopic liberals, such as the English Goldwin Smith, who resided for some time in Toronto before going to Cornell, assumed that the union of the British colonies was a chimerical fantasy and that annexation to the United States was only a matter of time. But even Toryism in Canada has always had a radical element in it that opposed American tendencies from the left as well as the right. This element emphasized the gross inequalities of wealth and privilege building up in the United States, and it was more aware than the liberals of the aggressive and imperialistic side of American development. The Monroe Doctrine, through much of the nineteenth century, seemed to imply that Americans were claiming the right to exploit the New World for themselves. The effects in Canada included the War of 1812, the Fenian raids, the "Fifty-four forty or fight" crisis, and various other incidents. But as regards Canada the United States seems to have realized very early that, to paraphrase Clauswitz, economic penetration is the continuing of war by other means, and with a far greater chance of success.

There was also the Canadian opposition to slavery. During the Civil War the liberal John Stuart Mill in England attacked the Tories of his time for supporting the South and rejoicing over the apparent disintegration of the great republican experiment. One might have expected Canadians to take a similar view, and some did, but Canadian volunteers produced a sizable contingent for the Union army. Much earlier, the Nova Scotian writer Haliburton, who was about as Tory as one could get, made his stage American Sam Slick refer to the Fourth of July as "fifteen millions of free men and three millions of slaves a-celebratin' the birthday of liberty."

The point all this is leading up to is that the continuity of certain British elements in Canadian life is not simply vestigial relics of Canada's colonial past or reactionary nostalgia. One very obvious example is the retaining of the monarchy, along with a Governor-General as, so to speak, the resident Canadian crown. When there is no question of British rule any more, keeping this memento of the fact that we were once a British colony is one way of qualifying the extent to which we are now an American colony. In any case, the monarchy in both Britain and Canada seems to be genuinely popular, its connection with an aristocratic class having largely disappeared.

The monarchy is a symbol of a national unity transcending the conflicts of all political and religious pressure groups. The corresponding symbol of such a unity in the United States is the flag, something Canada did not even have until it acquired one along with the new Third World nations about a quarter-century ago. The real point about a monarchy is that it puts the cult of personality where it belongs, in the area of ceremonial symbolism. A flag, however useful for covering the mental nakedness of political speeches, lacks the accessibility of a personal symbol, like a royal family; it is pointless to complain about it, and impossible to gossip about it. A parliamentary system, where a leader stands or falls with his party, reduces the personality cult in other ways, although there is a growing emphasis on leadership conventions and the like in Canada, which reflects American influence.

Then again, Canada has had for the last fifty years a Socialist (or more accurately Social Democrat) party, which is normally supported by twenty-five to thirty percent of the electorate and has been widely respected through most of its history for its devotion to principle. Nothing of proportional size or influence has emerged among socialists in the United States. When the CCF [Cooperative Commonwealth Federation], the first form of this party, was founded in the 1930s, its most obvious feature went largely unnoticed. That feature was that it was following a British rather than an American tendency, trying to assimilate the Canadian political structure to the British Conservative-Labor pattern. The present New Democratic Party, however, never seems to get beyond a certain percentage of support, not enough to come to federal power. Principles make voters nervous, and yet any departure from them for expedience makes them suspicious.

The American ideology of assimilation, expressed in such phrases as "hundred percent American," "un-American activities," and the like, can hardly operate in Canada, with its roots in a coalition of two founding groups. Recently Canadians have become aware that a large proportion of the population, including, of course, the indigenous peoples, comes from an ethnic and linguistic background which is neither English nor French. Hence the policy of bilingualism, so sharply intensified in the Trudeau era, has been qualified by the newer buzzword of "multiculturalism." In Toronto, for example, where the teaching of French in elementary schools is heavily stressed, the Italian-speaking population is much greater than the French-speaking one. The result, or so an irritated educator once remarked to me, is to send an Italian child to school to destroy his native language and to make him illiterate in two others. Not that it is all that easy to destroy a native language.

I am entering an area here which is thickly sown with emotional minefields, and any advance into it has to be cautious. I have first to return to my three levels of culture, a level of lifestyle, a level of ideology and historical process, and a level of creativity and of education in the arts and sciences. On the level of lifestyle there are immense pressures towards uniformity, including uniformity of language. Economic forces in particular make for increasing centralization. One frequently sees the statement that such trends are changing and becoming more decentralized, but applied to Canada the statement is nonsense.

The creative arts, on the other hand, have to be planted in a very limited environment. Literature, in particular, is intensely regional in Canada, as it is in the United States, and even in the much smaller Great Britain. Canadian critics have realized for a century that the more Canadian a writer tries to be, the less chance he has of becoming a really distinguished writer. The reason is that the conception "Canadian" belongs to a different aspect of culture and can have little direct or positive influence on the creative one. At the same time, the *aggregate* of writers in Canada will produce a Canadian body of literature, which is felt by both Canadian and non-Canadian readers to be distinctive of the country.

Regional literature grows out of provincial literature. The provincial writer assumes that literary standards have been established for him outside his environment. English and French writers in nineteenth-century Canada both tended to follow models in their ancestral countries. But the notion of meeting established external standards is a fallacy: literature changes too rapidly, and standards are no longer mainstream influences by the time the provinces get around to imitating them.

As a provincial culture matures, it becomes more aware of the variety of new ideas and ideologies, new techniques of narrative, and new forms of imagery that are sweeping across the world, and it begins to respond to them and become part of an international idiom. Such an idiom does not, like lifestyle fashions in food or clothing, make for uniformity or mass production: it works in quite the opposite direction, though in ways too complex to go into here. What it does not do either, or does very seldom, is uproot the writer in his localized place in his own community. There is a curious law in culture, at least literary culture, which says that the most specific settings have the best chance of becoming universal in their appeal. It is clear that a multiplicity of ethnic backgrounds is highly favorable to culture, and any writer or artist will exploit everything he has that is distinctive in his regional, ethnic, or religious background. But as he matures as a writer and his horizon expands, he wants to be read on his own merits and not as an ethnic specimen, however unusual. Similarly with the consumer. A reader interested in Canadian literature may feel in the position of one who has bought a box of candy and discovered from the fine print on the box that he has acquired a melange of twenty-three food, chemical, and additive substances. But he still expects some unity of taste in the final product, not a mere recognition of the subtle contributions made by invertase or lecithin. As for minority languages, they seem to be one area where privatization does seem to work. I think that among the Celtic languages in the British Isles, Welsh has fared better than Irish, because Welsh has been spoken and studied by the people who wanted to speak and study it, whereas Irish was made compulsory in schools and given the rank of an official language, to the great detriment of its popularity.

There remains, however, the unique historical development which has made Canada a bilingual country with two recognized Canadian languages. I suppose no reasonable Canadian denies the extraordinary advantages of a bilingual culture, despite all the complaints one may hear in English Canada about "shoving all that French down our throats," though those who use such phrases are unlikely to have much French in their throats. Corresponding complaints can be heard in French Canada. But one should keep in mind the different aspects of cultural life already referred to, as well as the fact that a creative benefit may be a political burden. The conception "Quebecois," for example, belongs culturally to the area of political leverage, not to anything genuinely creative.

Many languages, including earlier English, have no word for space but only for place, or space-*there*. For the imagination of, say, Shakespeare's original audience, the entire cosmos was filled up by objects or beings with assigned places. Nature abhors a vacuum, the philosophers said, at a time when vacuum and empty space meant much the same thing. But as the influence of Copernicus and Galileo began to make itself felt, the imaginative responses changed. The French who settled Quebec and Acadia belonged to the seventeenth-century world of Descartes and Pascal. Descartes was, I think, the first to make the conception of space as pure extension, apart from whatever it contained, functional in philosophy. Pascal, certainly no Cartesian, expressed his terror of "these empty spaces" and their silence, in one of the most famous epigrams ever uttered. By "these empty spaces" he meant much more than what is now called "outer space" beyond the sky, but the phrase reflects a time when, to adapt a remark of Blake, the human imagination was beginning to be more impressed by the amount of space between the stars than by the stars themselves.

It was a sense of space without place, descended to earth to become a natural environment, that confronted the Canadian imagination in its formative years. A universe of places means a hierarchical universe: earlier human imagination was dominated by the sense of a natural hierarchy, with everything occupying the place that God had assigned to it. As the sense of natural hierarchy waned, distinction of ranks in human life seemed increasingly to be imposed by human will expressed in violence. Some time ago I used the phrase "garrison mentality" to describe the psychological effects in Canada of the Anglo-French wars, fear of Indian attacks, and protection against an implacably indifferent nature, with its cycle of intense heat, intense cold, and the coming of spring along with the black flies. I grew up in a town in the Maritimes about thirty miles from where, in the eighteenth century, a French fort and a British fort scowled at each other across the isthmus that separates New Brunswick from Nova Scotia. It was an eloquent if primitive symbol of the "two solitudes" that Hugh MacLennan later described in his novel of that name about the Anglo-French relations in Montreal. Similar survivals of this "two solitudes" construct were still around me in my early years. My phrase, however, has been rather overexposed since, and like other overexposed images has got blurred and fuzzy, its specific historical context being usually ignored.

As I understood it, a garrison brings social activity into an intense if constricted focus, but its military and other priorities tend to obliterate the creative impulse. In one brief interval of relaxation, after the peace of 1763, a novel called *Emily Montague* was written by a woman named Frances Brooke in the garrison town of Quebec. It is not only the first novel written in Canada; it is one of the earliest novels to be written anywhere. But a more typical garrison attitude survived psychologically in the rural and small-town phase of Canadian life, with its heavy pressures of moral and conventional anxieties. Canadians are now, however, one of the most highly urbanized people in the world, and the garrison mentality, which was social but not creative, has been replaced by the condominium mentality, which is neither social nor creative and which forces the cultural energies of the country into forming a kind of counterenvironment.

The same paradox of space without place confronted American life too, but the Americans lived in a two-dimensional country, and were able to fill up their empty space more systematically, with the aid of a frontier. Canadians were compelled by geography to live in much more scattered communities, the main divisions of the country being widely separated from one another. The writers or speakers who eventually emerged from this environment were confronted first of all by the physical problems of being able to communicate at all. De Tocqueville, in his magisterial survey of democracy in America, says only one thing about Canada, but what he says bears on our present point. "In Canada," he says, "the most enlightened, patriotic and humane inhabitants make extraordinary efforts to render the people dissatisfied. . . . More exertions are made to excite the passions of the citizens there than to calm them elsewhere." He is speaking mainly of French Canada, but the remark applies to the whole country. One reads between the lines the desperate frustrations of the earlier communicators, and the massive indifference of those they attempted to address. The silence of the eternal spaces remained at the bottom of the Canadian psyche for a long time, and in many respects is still there. Communication is, of course, a major preoccupation, almost an obsession, with Canadians, but in the nineteenth century the impressive part of it was a matter of building railways and bridges and canals. Articulate communication has now taken its normal place in Canadian life, but with rare exceptions

Canada has avoided the movements of mass hysteria that have swept over the United States so frequently during the last century.

Some time ago, in looking through an anthology of American poetry, I came across Theodore Roethke's poem "Journey to the Interior." The "interior" in this poem is both a landscape and a psyche, but the journey is out of the self and not into it. We begin with the image of driving a car or jeep over rough and dangerous roads. Then the car goes faster and we are traveling at breakneck speed past a place where "some idiot plunger" has previously met his death. The car disappears and the poet's spirit expands to become merged with the nature around him, as all the dormant powers within him break into renewed life. I had read the poem before, but had not realized how superbly it caught the dominant mood in American imaginative experience: the conquering of nature through the sheer force of technology, the exhilaration of danger and high speed that comes as technology develops, and the arrival through the speed at an ecstasy of an expanding consciousness.

I remembered too that there was a Canadian poem called "Journey to the Interior" in Margaret Atwood's first volume, *The Circle Game*, so I turned to it. Here the "interior" is again both psychic and physical, but the journeying narrator is apparently walking through woods, moving very cautiously, as much aware of the rough going and the tangles of branches as her counterpart but with a total uncertainty about her direction. The Atwood narrator wonders if she is going in circles; Roethke speaks only of the "detours" in a straightforward quest. But if the Atwood traveler has no trust in direction, she is intensely aware of presences, which may be menacing presences. It is important, she says, to keep one's head but useless, perhaps dangerous, to call out or utter words in such a wilderness. Roethke, in contrast, is aware of no presence except his expanding self. I am not, of course, comparing the poems in merit, merely looking at them as documents illustrating two kinds of sensibility. Both poems come from the sixties, Roethke's being a late poem, composed near his death, and Atwood's being early and experimental. I know how easy it is to deceive oneself in such matters, but I feel sure that one sensibility represents something centrally American and the other something centrally Canadian. One is preoccupied with speed, machinery, progress, the intensity of consciousness, the other with loneliness, diffidence, uncertainty of direction, and a divided consciousness. In the twenty years since then great changes have come over the imaginations of both countries to the point almost of a merging of attitudes.

According to the Canadian economist Harold Innis, the development of techniques of communication tends to create a "bias" in culture. There are two main biases, according to Innis, a bias toward time and a bias toward space. Innis felt that the Canadian sensibility has a time bias and the American a spatial one. This is not as a rule the type of observation I find very cogent, but let us follow it up for a moment. It may seem to contradict what I said earlier about the impact of space on the Canadian imagination, but the contexts are very different.

Countries that have a long record of oppressive foreign rule are intensely aware of their history: Ireland and Poland are obvious examples. Nations expanding into empires think in terms of acquiring space, and English Canada felt something of this by proxy when it was a part of a British empire on which the sun was alleged never to set. French Canada, on the other hand, has been very conscious of its history and traditions: Quebec automobile license plates still bear the motto *je me souviens*, "I remember." But in fact all Canada, with its sense of precedent and continuous contract, seems oriented to history in a way that the United States, until quite recently, never has been. The sense of irreversible progress that has been so central in American imagination seems to carry with it a sense of an escape from history itself.

The bias toward time may become neurotic, preoccupied with Don Quixote's vision of some imaginary historical idea that ought to exist now. Ideological terrorism in particular is usually inspired by an obsession with reshaping the past. But the same bias may go in a genuinely creative direction, recognizing that it is tradition more than anything else that creates identity. From about 1960 on English Canada began to achieve something of the sense of self-definition that French Canada had had for much longer, and a renewed historical sense began to realize how much Canadian historical traditions had been mutilated by the two European peoples who refused to continue, in fact did their best to extinguish, the culture of the Indian and Inuit peoples already there.

Of course, appreciation for the arts and culture of native peoples has not been lacking. The Haida mask from the early documentary *The Moon's Necklace* has been practically a Canadian logo for some time, and the outpouring of Inuit (Eskimo) sculpture and painting has been one of the most remarkable cultural developments in modern history. A great deal of scholarship has been devoted to collecting the oral literary culture of the indigenous peoples, who, of course, still produce it. What is more recent is the sense of the absurdity of regarding native peoples as foreigners and their culture as an exotic curiosity. Clearly it forms a tradition which should be at the headwaters of our own and should be absorbed into our traditions in the same way that English and French traditions are. In Canadian literature one could point to many examples of such absorption in the work of Susan Musgrave, John Newlove, Robert Kroetsch, M. T. Kelly, Yves Thériault, and others. Even careless popularizers are more hesitant about writing such sentences as "Jacques Cartier was the first man to set foot on Canadian soil," which were fairly frequent usage not long ago. Even when the word "white" was inserted, the implication "first genuine human being" was often there.

But the new sense of cultural kinship with the indigenous people was not really an expanded historical or temporal awareness: it was part of a new attitude to space, specifically the space within Canada. The closer relationship of the indigenous peoples to their natural environment was what gave them a new significance to the Canadian imagination. The nineteenth-century sense of a hostile and amoral nature, the early twentieth-century sense of a land of mystery with its huge and so seldom visited lakes, rivers, and islands, have been almost reversed in a world where anything that is natural may be precious. Rupert Brooke spoke seventy years ago of the "unseizable virginity" of the Canadian landscape, but this will hardly apply to a situation in which even uninhabited land may still be polluted.

Of course, a concern for the environment is a worldwide movement, politically as well as culturally, but the Canadian economy has been marked by a peculiarly reckless exploiting of natural resources, in which trees, fish, and fur-bearing animals were sacrificed on a scale that has left a cultural residue of intense guilt feelings in the Canadian consciousness. There has hardly ever been a time when Canadian writing has not expressed some resentment or apprehension at the treatment of the environment. But it is fairly recently that large numbers of people have come to feel that the exploiting of nature is just as wrong and immoral as the exploiting of other human beings. There is an essay by Heidegger, "The Origin of a Work of Art," which has been a strong influence on two very distinguished works of Canadian criticism, Dennis Lee's *Savage Fields* and Bruce

Elder's *Image and Identity*, the latter concerned mainly with film. Heidegger's argument turns largely on a distinction between "World" and "Earth." "World" means the universe of human consciousness, "Earth" the universe of animals, plants, and inanimate nature. "World" tries to dominate and enslave "Earth," but "Earth" has its own modes of survival, and it is dangerous to violate it beyond a certain point. In a poet of an older generation, E. J. Pratt, the main themes are still "World" themes. He wrote narrative poems about whaling expeditions, shipwrecks, the building of the Canadian Pacific railway, the martyrdoms of Jesuit missionaries in which the Iroquois are assimilated to a mindless and ferocious nature. But even he has a late poem called "The Good Earth" in which he warns:

> Hold that synthetic seed, for underneath
> Deep down she'll answer to our horticulture:
> She has a way of germinating teeth
> And yielding crops of carrion for the vulture.

In the last two or three decades there has been a remarkable growth of the feeling that "nobody owns the earth," as bill bissett says (a poet who chooses lowercase and unconventional spellings). There have been startling works of fiction, such as Marion Engel's *Bear*, where an erotic relation between a woman and a pet bear has clearly an allegorical implication that Canadians have to love their environment instead of exploiting or ignoring it. Some poets, again, have internalized the nineteenth-century landscape, with all its fears and loneliness, realizing that the real fears are there and not outdoors. The development in painting has run closely parallel. When I spoke in Washington some years ago, there were two exhibitions of Canadian painting on view, representing two phases of "World" culture in Canada. One was concerned with the early twentieth-century painters, the Group of Seven and their contemporaries, who were the pictorial successors of the explorers and the missionaries of earlier centuries. The other and more highly publicized exhibit gave us the Clement Greenberg version of painting in Canada, the trend to abstraction which was at once the climax of the "World" view and the beginning of something else, although the something else was even then much more present in Canada than the exhibit suggested. Techniques in painting and film of directly confronting natural imagery, such as the one often called "magical realism," are part of the evidence that a new kind of spatial consciousness has come into the

Canadian imagination, in all its arts, and has given it a new confidence and stability.

I spoke earlier of the Tory ideology in early English Canada: it was never associated with an aristocracy, though some of the Family Compact may have regarded themselves in that light. But, of course, their Tory counterparts in England did include a good many of the aristocracy, who devoted a large part of their energy to preserving their game, working up anxieties about poachers and the like. Consciously, there was nothing to this but the selfishness and arrogance of privilege, a subculture of what Matthew Arnold accurately called "Barbarians." But in unconscious symbolism there was some preservation of "Earth" from the encroachments of "World." Canadian consciousness may be slowly moving toward a conception of Canada as something like a gigantic national park, with a string of cities along or near its southern border. Some years ago Buckminster Fuller used the metaphor of "spaceship earth," but this suggested an overcrowded ship with all its space outside. The writers, painters, and filmmakers whose function it ought to be, in part, to tell us what the rest of the public will be thinking fifty years later, are providing us with a different metaphor, an internal reservoir of space, an "Earth" that can live with "World."

Great changes have come over the American consciousness too in the last few decades, and I suspect that the more strident and readily politicized issues, such as feminism or racial prejudice, are not the really underlying ones. I spoke earlier of a certain sense, in American imagination up to about 1950, of outrunning history, of a linear progress that would still move in a straight line even if it were headed for disaster. It seems to me that the Vietnam War has brought about the beginning of a profound shift in perspective. In the days when I taught for brief periods in American universities, many students would ask me if I noticed any difference between American and Canadian students. I said that students conditioned from infancy to be a part of a world empire must necessarily be very different from students conditioned to be part of a secondary power, observing history from the sidelines rather than playing a major role in it. But I think American consciousness since then has acquired a new sensitivity to history, including its own history, and sees its recent ascendancy as part of a parabola that goes up and down. History has no record of any empire that did not, *qua* empire, decline and fall, and the process is still inevitable, even though the decline and fall of the Russian and Chinese empires has still to come. There is nothing to regret in this, because the phrase "decline and fall," in this context, means only the straightening out of priorities, throwing away phony ones and, with luck, acquiring more genuine ones.

Of course, it takes some effort to become more self-observant, to acquire historical sense and perspective, to understand the limitations that have been placed on human power by God, nature, fate, or whatever. It was part of President Reagan's appeal that he was entirely unaware of any change in consciousness, and talked in the old reassuring terms of unlimited progress. But the new response to the patterns of history seems to have made itself felt, along with the growing sense that we can no longer afford leaders who think that acid rain is something we get by eating grapefruit. I wish that I could document this change from recent developments in American culture, but I am running out of both time and knowledge. It seems clear to me, however, that American and Canadian imaginations are much closer together than they have been in the past.

I make no apology for having talked mainly in terms of the creative aspect of culture. In the first place, you can get better informed political commentary by turning on a television set. In the second place, imaginative developments give one the real clues to political and economic ones. Third, and most important to me, fifty years of teaching have only confirmed my conviction that only the arts and sciences are stable social realities: everything else simply dissolves and re-forms. The world of 1989 is no more like the world I was born into in 1912 than it is like the Stone Age, but nothing has improved since then except scientific and scholarly knowledge, and nothing has remained steady except human creative power. The students crushed under tanks in Tienanmin Square may have been, in a way, as much in the grip of illusion as the thugs who crushed them. But they showed very clearly that all human beings want the same things, freedom and dignity and decent living conditions, that those are very simple and reasonable things to want, and that nothing but the release of the power to apply our knowledge and creative energies can get them. If the process I have tried to trace in the cultural history of Canada and the United States has any validity, that is what it has for its moral.

Index